The Changing Transition to Adulthood

Understanding Families

Series Editors: *Bert N. Adams, University of Wisconsin*
David M. Klein, University of Notre Dame

This book series examines a wide range of subjects relevant to studying families. Topics include, but are not limited to, theory and conceptual design, research methods on the family, racial/ethnic families, mate selection, marriage, family power dynamics, parenthood, divorce and remarriage, custody issues, and aging families.

The series is aimed primarily at scholars working in family studies, sociology, psychology, social work, ethnic studies, gender studies, cultural studies, and related fields as they focus on the family. Volumes will also be useful for graduate and undergraduate courses in sociology of the family, family relations, family and consumer sciences, social work and the family, family psychology, family history, cultural perspectives on the family, and others.

Books appearing in **Understanding Families** are either single- or multiple-authored volumes or concisely edited books of original chapters on focused topics within the broad interdisciplinary field of marriage and family.

The books are reports of significant research, innovations in methodology, treatises on family theory, syntheses of current knowledge in a family subfield, or advanced textbooks. Each volume meets the highest academic standards and makes a substantial contribution to our understanding of marriages and families.

Frances Goldscheider
Calvin Goldscheider

The Changing Transition to Adulthood

Leaving and Returning Home

UNDERSTANDING FAMILIES

SAGE Publications
International Educational and Professional Publisher
Thousand Oaks London New Delhi

For information:

SAGE Publications, Inc.
2455 Teller Road
Thousand Oaks, California 91320
E-mail: order@sagepub.com

SAGE Publications Ltd.
6 Bonhill Street
London EC2A 4PU
United Kingdom

SAGE Publications India Pvt. Ltd.
M-32 Market
Greater Kailash I
New Delhi 110 048 India

Printed in the United States of America

Library of Congress Cataloging-in-Publication Data

Goldscheider, Frances K.
    The changing transition to adulthood: Leaving and returning
home / by Frances Goldscheider and Calvin Goldscheider.
       p. cm.—(Understanding families; v. 17)
    Includes bibliographical references (p.) and index.
    ISBN 0-7619-0991-5 (cloth: acid-free paper)
    ISBN 0-7619-0992-3 (pbk.: acid-free paper)
    1. Young adults—United States—Psychology. 2. Adult children—
United States—Psychology. 3. Family—United States. 4. Home—
United States. I. Goldscheider, Calvin. II. Title. III. Series.
HQ799.9.P75 G65 1999
305.242'0973—dc21   99-6321

This book is printed on acid-free paper.

99 00 01 02 03 04 05 7 6 5 4 3 2 1

Acquiring Editor: Jim Nageotte
Editorial Assistant: Heidi Van Middlesworth

To

Ben and Franny

Contents

List of Tables

List of Figures

PREFACE

This book places changes in leaving and returning home in the context of the major events of 20th century-America. The timing of the departure of young adults from the parental home, the routes taken out of the home, and the patterns of returning home are major elements of the transition to adulthood and are key links to changes in our society and changes in family relationships. The United States has moved between peace and war and between depression and affluence, and each has made its mark on the family and the nest-leaving process. By examining the historical patterns of moving out of, and returning to, the parental home, we observe and assess changes in relationships not only between parents and children but also between men and women, given the importance of marriage as a route out of the home.

The transition to adulthood via residential independence is a complex phenomenon, negotiated between parents and maturing children. In part, it is about whether marriage should be the primary criterion for adulthood and residential independence or whether young people should leave home even when they have not achieved adult economic and family statuses. Leaving the parental home to establish an independent residence also reflects more than the location of educational institutions, the demands of military service, and the importance of distant job opportunities. It reveals core values about the centrality of new family formation in the lives of young adults and about whether unmarried adults have a place in their parental families. No matter the route, the decision to leave the parental home to a home of one's own requires a realignment of intergenerational relationships and a reassessment of family priorities.

Patterns of leaving home have been changing over the 20th century. The age at which young adults leave home declined substantially between the 1920s and the 1970s before beginning a partial recovery. The routes taken have shifted even more, with a major decline in the proportions leaving home at marriage or to take a job, a dramatic rise in the importance of military service that made this route critical for young men for 30 years before falling to insignificance, and a long-term increase in leaving home just for "independence" as well as the recent rise in nontraditional family formation— cohabitation and unmarried parenthood. The likelihood of returning home has almost doubled over the same period. Historical changes in leaving and returning home therefore point to important changes in the relationships between the generations. We link these changes in the transition out of the nest to the critical periods of change in American society, focusing on the periods in which young people reached adulthood (age 18).

Using data from the National Survey of Families and Households (NSFH), we have retrospectively constructed patterns of leaving and returning home. We have been able for the first time to study the nestleaving process in historical context. We systematically trace changes in leaving and returning home from the 1920s to the 1990s, examining (1) the Roaring Twenties and the movement from rural to urban areas in search of jobs, (2) the economic depression of the 1930s and the struggles with unemployment and financial hardship, (3) World War II and the mobilization of young adults for military service, (4) the post-World War II period of prosperity and baby boom, and (5) the Vietnam war years and the period of the "baby bust." We conclude the analyses of cohort changes with a portrait of the emerging patterns of the 1980s and 1990s, when the "20-somethings" and "Generation X" are experiencing diverse transitions to adulthood, increasingly returning to the nest after a period of independent living.

We examine the timing of leaving home and identify the routes out of the home for each of these periods over the 20th century. We are therefore able to document the distinctiveness of the most recent period when young adults have become more likely to leave home for "independence" than for any specific reason. We are able to create detailed connections between returning home and both to the routes taken out of the nest and to the ages when young adults leave. These links are examined for each of the periods that we have identified to provide a full portrait of leaving and returning home in 20th-century America as a prism through which we are able to assess changes in the transition to adulthood.

Our historical perspective allows us to link changes in this aspect of the transition to adulthood to sweeping external changes in the economy, education, religion, race, and ethnicity. However, processes of leaving and returning home are also responsive to internal changes within the family and to the complex transitions involved in the twin agendas of adulthood—the achievement of stable and satisfying work and family roles. In our unfolding analysis, we demonstrate the importance of family values and the financial and noneconomic dimensions of the lives of men and women. One master theme that we explore in depth connects changes in the transition to adulthood to powerful family changes now ongoing in American society. In particular, we examine how changes over time in young people's experience of their parents' divorces, remarriages, and the arrival of new siblings have affected the processes of leaving home—accelerating its timing, refocusing toward the less productive routes taken out of the parental home, and decreasing returning home.

While investigating these general patterns for the nation as a whole, we also recognize that America is a diverse society. We systematically document how the transition to adulthood differs between young men and women; among Blacks, Hispanics, and Whites; between religious groups; and among those with different social class backgrounds and living in different regions of the country. We are thus able to connect the transition to adulthood to the major revolutions in gender patterns, changes in American race relations and ethnic assimilation, secularization, regional redistribution patterns, economic and educational changes, and the emergence of the middle classes. The critical question we address is how the broader changes in American society in the 20th century have differentially characterized the diverse family patterns in America as reflected in the transition to adulthood. Our historical perspective allow us to investigate the characteristics of innovators and followers in the leaving-home process and the general tendencies toward convergence in these patterns among diverse groups over time.

We began this project shortly before the NSFH data became available, making plans while on sabbatical in Jerusalem in 1988-89. Pieces began to emerge as we traveled to Santa Monica, California; Stockholm, Sweden; and even Lake George, New York, yet always returned home to Providence, Rhode Island. Some of the threads that are the bases of the specific analysis that we present here appeared in outline form in the Population Reference Bureau Bulletin titled "Leaving and Returning Home in 20th Century America" (Goldscheider and Goldscheider 1994b). Over the last several years, we have used the opportunities of the annual meetings of the American Sociological Association and the Population Association of America to present some of our findings to fellow researchers and colleagues. A paper prepared jointly with James Hodges and Patricia St. Clair on "Living Arrangements Changes in Young Adulthood: Evidence for the Twentieth Century" was first presented in 1994 at the RAND Conference on the Family and Public Policy in Santa Monica, California (Goldscheider, Goldscheider, Hodges, and St. Clair 1994).

Several of our analyses were published for limited circulation in professional journals. Some of the materials in Chapter 9 are drawn from an article on "The Trajectory of the Black Family: Ethnic Differences in Leaving Home over the Twentieth Century" that appeared in the *Journal of the History of the Family* (Goldscheider and Goldscheider, 1997b). A portion of the comparative review in Chapter 11 was first presented in "Recent Changes in US Young Adult Living Arrangements in Comparative Perspective," in a special issue of the *Journal of Family Issues*, edited by Cherlin, Scabini, and Rossi (Goldscheider 1997). Other materials in that paper appear in Chapter 1. The technical comparisons of the data from the National Survey of Families and Households and the Census appeared in a study with Ann Biddlecom and Patricia St. Clair, "A Comparison of Living Arrangements Data in the National Survey of Families and Households and the U.S. Censuses, 1940-1980" (Goldscheider, Biddlecom, and St. Clair 1994). Aspects of our analysis of the role of family structure in nest-leaving were published in French as "Family Structure, Leaving Home, and Investments in Young Adulthood," in *Cahiers Quebecois de Demographie* (Special Issue on Childhood) (Goldscheider and Goldscheider 1994a) and other aspects in an article in the *Journal of Marriage and the Family* (Goldscheider and Goldscheider 1998). An early version of the section in Chapter 10 on the Jews was published as "Generational Relationships and the Jews: Patterns of Leaving Home, 1930-1985," in *Papers in Jewish Demography, 1993*, Proceedings of the Eleventh World Congress of Jewish Studies, Jerusalem (Goldscheider and Goldscheider 1997a).

The volume as an integrated whole, however, is entirely new, as are the specific analyses in most chapters. The richness of the empirical details on historical family changes and the analysis of changing rates of returning home are unique features. These themes are presented as part of an integrated, theoretical argument that structures the details. Our analyses of runaways and those who stay at home, changes over time in the regional variation in leaving and returning home, and of the changing role of education and resources, gender, religion, race and ethnicity make this volume a comprehensive treatment of these dimensions of the transition to adulthood.

The analysis of the data was supported by the National Center for Child Health and Human Development, particularly Grant P50HD12639 to the Labor and Population unit of RAND and to Brown University and Grant P30HD28251 to Brown University. The final editing of the manuscript was facilitated by the continuous and generous research support provided by Brown University and our appointments in the Department of Sociology and the Population Studies and Training Center. We are particularly grateful to our colleagues at Brown who have been supportive of us and our research. We acknowledge the contributions of Patricia St. Clair of RAND for superb data organization and processing; to James Hodges formerly at RAND and currently of the University of Minnesota for statistical advice. At the Population Reference Bureau we want to acknowledge the helpful contributions of Carol De Vito and Mary Kent. At RAND where we first started the analyses for this project and at Brown when we completed them we want to thank our colleagues Julie DaVanzo, Jacob Klerman and Michael White. We acknowledge the contributions of our colleagues, as well as those of the editors of this series at Sage of which this volume is a part, David Klein and Burt Adams. David and

Burt read over our manuscript with care and with attention to detail. They made valuable suggestions, which resulted in revisions of our draft and in a better book. We are grateful to them. The final formatting and preparation of the text, figures, and tables for publication was carried out by Joan Picard of the Department of Sociology at Brown University with her customary skill, patience and superb talent. We are most grateful to Miss Rhode Island's mom.

We dedicate this volume to our children and their growing families, particularly to Benjamin and Franny, who have entered the nest while we were working on this volume and who, along with their parents, aunts, and uncles, have contributed to the joy of our lives. We look forward to sharing their nest-leavings and returnings in the 21st century.

CHAPTER 1

Leaving and Returning Home in 20th Century America

Much to the great surprise of scholars who study young adulthood, recent cohorts of young adults have been increasingly appearing in parental homes across the industrialized world. In some countries, young adults are remaining at home until they are older, a pattern closely connected with delays in the ages that they marry. In others, the increase appears to be linked with the instability of the nest-leaving transition—that is, with an increase in returning home (Cherlin, Scabini, and Rossi 1997; Cordon 1997; Goldscheider and Goldscheider 1994b; Young 1987).

Both the increase in remaining in the parental home until later ages and the increase in returning home after spending time away have been puzzling because these trends appear to run counter to a central "idea of progress" underlying many family trends. This theme emphasizes the growth of individualism (Bellah et al. 1985; Lesthaeghe 1995), which in the last portion of the 20th century is understood to have led to delays in the age at which young people marry and when they become parents as well as the rise in divorce and the increased residential independence of the unmarried across the life course.

Signaling the sense that the increase in young adults (still) living at home is new and unusual, terms to describe this phenomenon have begun to appear across Europe, all of which express to some degree a sense that young adults are dependent on their mothers—tied to her apron strings or addicted to her cooking. Belgians speak of "hotel families," with young adults essentially provided a room with laundry and hot meals (Boulanger, et al. 1997). The Swedes have gone a step further and, based on their term for cohabiting partner *samboende*, which they have colloquially shortened to *sambo*, have added a maternal echo, to create *mambo*, or children remaining or returning home after age 18. What is going on, and how should we understand these changes in the nest-leaving process in young adulthood?

1

Leaving the parental home to establish some independent residence is considered by many a critical step that young adults take in their transition to adulthood. Young adults are eager, if not always ready, for their own space and freedom. Their parents often have more mixed feelings, with some trying to postpone the inevitable and others counting the days until their children leave so they can enter their own new life course phase associated with the freedom of the empty nest. Both children and parents often view leaving home as a major statement about that vague and ambiguous time when children are no longer "children" and are redefining their roles as adults, even though the relationship between the generations clearly does not end with the act of leaving home. Children normally continue to love and honor their parents, visiting and often helping out in a range of ways as their parents age and become frail. Parents often continue to subsidize their children after they leave home, investing money, resources, and emotional support.

Sometimes, and increasingly, leaving home is less permanent than children or their parents expect. Returning home may be the cushion that children need when they no longer can be as independent as they had wanted. The terms of the return home are negotiated between parents who have experienced an emptier nest and children who have been living autonomously so that the return home is usually not a return to "childhood" in the same way that leaving home was a new phase in the transition to adulthood.

Nevertheless, no matter at what age it occurs and whether a return follows, the process of leaving the parental home marks a shift from some forms of dependence to new types of autonomy, restructuring important relationships and beginning others. The cycle itself is as old as the human family, but this means that the new pattern of leaving home, which no longer requires marriage, is a major break from the past. A modern translation of Chapter 2, Verse 24 of Genesis might read: "Thus a young adult should leave the parental household to find a partner and share a life together."[1] It does not read: "Thus young adults should leave the parental household, to live as independent adults, creating privacy for themselves and their parents." Nevertheless, for many young adults in the late 20th century, like John in our first vignette (see vignette #1), the transition to adulthood is about individualism and independence, not about finishing their education, getting married, entering the labor force or becoming a parent (Arnett 1997).

When new household formation is not tied to marriage, the key questions become these: When should the new cycle begin? Does it depend on money, and if so, whose; that is, should parents subsidize their children's residential independence? Does it also depend on "family values"? If so, might not the preferences of parents matter, as Janet discovered (see vignette #2)?

The processes associated with leaving home, and the possibilities of returning, are family matters involving joint household decisions by parents and children. These decisions, however, are not simply internal to the family;

the society as a whole is intimately involved in shaping and facilitating them. How have the series of revolutionary changes that have occurred over the last century affected the transition to adulthood? Changes in the structure of families may have been critical in the relationship between parents and their children, as new forms of family life have emerged. New definitions of gender relationships have altered the ways parents relate to each other and to their sons and daughters and may also affect how everyone relates to the institution of marriage, the central route out of the home. The decline in the centrality of religion in the decisions that parents and children make about their lives, often referred to as secularization, may have reduced the value placed on marriage and family formation, altering the relative importance of independence and shaping the ways that resources are allocated within the family.

Significant changes in the economy, the opportunity structure, and the labor market have had an impact on the resources available to families and, as a result, may have speeded residential independence. Increases in educational opportunities may have changed how family resources are allocated to the next generation and the investments that children make in their futures.

Vignette #1

RETURN HOME? NEVER!

John couldn't wait to go to college. He was a good student in high school and wanted to go to school away from home. California seemed to be the best bet—exciting things happening on campus and freedom from the pressures at home. John's mom had remarried after the divorce from his dad, and there was now his three-year-old baby sister at home. She was cute and fun, but his mom had less time to spend with him, and George, his stepdad, wasn't very interested or supportive of him. It was a rough several years when John was finishing high school with George around, but at college John was independent.

John is in his senior year, majoring in psychology. He wants to eventually go to graduate school or law school but is not sure. He is planning on taking a year or two off from school to travel, see the world, and have fun with his friends. "I don't know when I will have a chance to travel again, and I am stressed out with schoolwork." He adds, "When I finish school, I will get a real job and start on the career track." When pressed, he said, "Return home? To visit, yes. To live? Never! They have their life to lead and I have mine. I need my privacy and they need theirs. I have been away from home too long to easily return to the suburban lifestyle they lead." For now, he is just finishing up his courses and planning—to be independent and on his own.

Not everyone, however, has had equal access to the resources needed to afford independence. Some minority groups have experienced discrimination, which may have shaped the relationships between the generations. As these forces have shifted over the 20th century, they may have reshaped the critical life course decisions linked with the nest-leaving process.

In short, the transition to adulthood and the processes of leaving and returning home are likely to have responded to internal changes within the family as well as to the sweeping external changes in the economy, education, religion, race, and ethnicity. Living independently is an increasingly important component in the constellation of the American definition of adulthood of work, family, and living arrangements. Changes in the transition to adulthood are linked to historical processes of 20th century America, altering (1) when young adults leave home, (2) the paths they take out of the parental home, and (3) their likelihood of returning home.

Hence, the importance of leaving home for understanding the transition to adulthood and the connections between leaving home and broader social changes raise fundamental questions: What have been the changes over time in leaving and returning home? How have the timing and the reasons for leaving home changed over the last century? And how are these transitions linked to the broader family and social changes that have characterized American society?

Vignette #2

WHEN KIDS DON'T LEAVE

Janet was surprised when her mom invited her to lunch at the local restaurant. After all, Janet was an employed but somewhat underpaid 24-year-old and was still living at home. She and her mother saw each other all the time. But now Mom had something important to discuss: Within the next three months, Janet was to find an apartment she could afford and move out. Her parents had discussed this for a while, and they had decided to help Janet make the move and provide the security deposit, but beyond that, she was on her own.

Janet was dumbfounded. As much as she had complained to her friends about living at home, and as much as they had sometimes teased her about it, she never thought she would be asked by her parents to leave. She left the lunch upset and in tears.

Hours later, she phoned her mother and asked, "Are you kicking me out because you love me or hate me?"

"Love you," replied Mom.

"Okay," said Janet. "Then I'm ready to go."

SOURCE: Adapted from Estess, 1994.

Analyzing these trends and their causes over time will help to illuminate changes in American families and the likely future of intergenerational relationships in the 21st century.

Understanding the processes related to leaving home is critical because the home is the major site of the socialization of children, where many of the transfers of the resources needed by the next generation are made. It is the safety net young adults often need as they embark on the complex set of transitions involved in the twin agendas of adulthood—work and family. The home is also the source of experiences and values that will shape their work and family lives and how they balance the complex and often contradictory demands of these two agendas. As such, the access young people have to their parental home—when they leave and whether they can return—is of central importance in the complexities of young adulthood.

We know very little, however, about the factors shaping young people's access to the resources in their parental home. Even the trends in leaving and returning home are only vaguely known, and for only a small fraction of the next generation of the world's adults. Our goal in this book is to provide a thorough exposition of recent and historical trends in leaving and returning home in the United States. At the same time, we will link these trends to broader changes in the family and the social world that parents and children inhabit. In the process, we shall identify some of the critical factors that are influencing these trends and shaping the lives of young adults and their parents. Throughout we argue that a careful and systematic analysis of the processes at work in nest leaving and returning will enhance our understanding of some of the basic family processes unfolding over the last century.

CHANGES IN THE LIVING ARRANGEMENTS OF YOUNG ADULTS

Our understanding of trends in the living arrangements of young adults in the 20th century is extremely recent. Some data on the decline in age at leaving home for the period of 1940 to 1970 for the United States as a whole and also for the state of Rhode Island did appear earlier (Kobrin 1976; Goldscheider and LeBourdais 1986). Nevertheless, researchers focusing on the two decades to 1989 concluded that there had been no historical decline in age at leaving home, since there was an increase in the period they studied (Buck and Scott 1993). Another research report also found only the recent increase in the age at leaving home, despite using data covering most of the 20th century, because it used a continuous cohort specification and the result was weighted by the much larger number of cases of younger than older respondents (Aquilino 1991:1007).

Studies showing both the decline in age at leaving home and some part of its more recent increase became available only in the mid-1990s. These studies have been based on two types of sources. A recent survey allowed us to retrospectively reconstruct the past (Goldscheider and Goldscheider 1994b), and also allows for a rich analyses of young adults (e.g., Aquilino 1990, 1991; Jayakody 1996; White 1992). The analyses in the rest of this book build on these strengths. The other source for the study of change in young adults' living arrangements is contemporaneous data from the Bureau of the Census (White 1994), which we update and extend below. The majority of studies before this time followed a single or narrow range of cohorts (e.g., Buck and Scott 1993; Goldscheider and DaVanzo 1989; Goldscheider and Goldscheider 1993; Thornton, Young-De Marco, and Goldscheider 1993).

This lack of clarity about the trend in young adults' living arrangements was partly the result of a lack of interest in the subject in the early years of the development of family sociology and demography. There also was an inherent difficulty of conceptualizing the complexities of living arrangements. When Paul Glick and his colleagues defined the "family life cycle" and outlined how its contours had been changing in the United States (Glick 1947; Glick and Parke 1965), he assumed that young people leave home (and so shape their parents' entry into the empty nest) when they marry. This was a more nearly tenable assumption during the period in which he wrote—the baby boom—than either before or after. The average age at marriage at that time was so early that few young adults had the time to leave home in other ways.

This formulation of the family life cycle diverted attention, however, from the simple fact that young people in their late teens and 20s have been found in three different kinds of living arrangements during most historical periods: (1) with their family of orientation, i.e., in the parental home; (2) with a new family of procreation—that is, with a partner and/or children; and (3) in some variably independent and usually nonfamily situation (boarding houses, dormitories and barracks, and separate homes). Given the rapid velocity of change at this life course stage (Rindfuss 1991), young adults often move so rapidly among them that it is difficult for them or those reporting about them to provide consistent answers about their living arrangements.

With three major types of living arrangements to be tracked and analyzed, it is not surprising that those studying one of them often neglected to think about what was happening between the other two. In the 1960s and 1970s, most family demographers were concerned with the dramatic fluctuations in marriage age under way (Cherlin 1992). Few thought much about what young people who were not getting married were doing. Some of those studying women interpreted their results as if the contrast was only between getting married and remaining with parents (e.g., Michael and Tuma 1985). Others assumed that the nonmarried women were enjoying new opportunities of independent adulthood (e.g., Becker 1991). Those studying men normally did not comment at all on their alternatives to marriage (e.g., Hogan 1981; Modell 1989).

As a result, few studies noticed the increases in nonfamily living under way in young adulthood, since they were obscured by the fluctuations in new family formation. When the increase in living with parents among young adults first came under scrutiny after the "marriage bust" of the 1970s and 1980s, many studies did not take into account the marital status of young adults. Hence, they did not focus on the fact that the proportion of unmarried young adults living with their parents continued to decrease during the period.

Furthermore, early research on the "return to the nest" was confused by the very different treatment of the population living in group quarters (particularly dormitories and barracks) in the censuses of the United States and the Current Population Surveys (CPS). The CPS is designed to track monthly trends in unemployment, but it also produces annual estimates of the marital status and living arrangements of the U.S. population. A comparison of 1980 census data and 1983 CPS data appeared to show a substantial increase in the proportion of young adults living with parents (e.g., Saluter 1984). Nearly all of the increase could have been the result of the fact that the CPS places many college students who are living in dormitories back in the parental home, whereas the census is able to count them where they are living at the time of the census.

Nevertheless, it is possible and appropriate to put together a series of data on young adult living arrangements drawn from both the decennial censuses and the CPS. This analysis will allow us to extend previous work and to provide an anchor against which to compare the analyses of trends and continuities we present in subsequent chapters.

Examining official data over time from the Bureau of the Census is important because they refer to the time period immediately before the census (or survey) and little memory bias is likely. The major limitation of the survey that we use for the rest of our analyses, the National Survey of Families and Households (NSFH), is that it was carried out in the late 1980s (Bumpass and Call 1988). Information it collected is refracted through the memories of those who survived to be interviewed, often many years after the events they were asked to describe. The NSFH provides a rich body of information unmatched by the census, including (1) precisely when leaving and returning home occurred (all one can tell from the census is whether young adults are living with their parents) and, in particular, (2) why those who left home early or by a given route did so, based on the characteristics of young adults' families when they were growing up (characteristics that cannot be observed at all in the census for those who have already left home). An analysis of census data can both update our NSFH analyses and indicate how well memories of distant events fit with trends based on information collected at the time. What trends do these data show?

We first examine the proportions of young adults living with their parents some of whom may have returned home while others had never left (see Figure 1.1). At the time of the 1940 census,[2] 63 percent of young adults aged 18 to 24 were living at home; this share had decreased to 42 percent by 1960, a drop of 21 percentage points. This was the "low point" in the proportions living with parents or the "high point" in the speed with which young adults left the parental home. This level was essentially maintained for the next decade, with little change between 1960 and 1970.

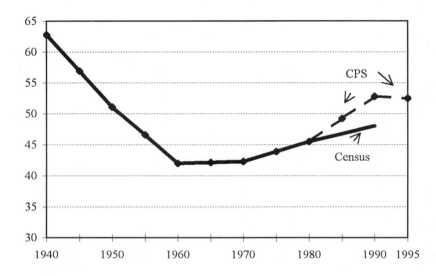

Figure 1.1. Proportions of Young Adults Aged 18 to 24, Living with Parents, 1940 to 1994
SOURCE: Calculated by the authors from U.S. Bureau of the Census tabulations.

There is a clear increase between 1970 and 1980 in the proportions of young adults of this age living with their parents, although the level is still far below that of 1950. For 1990, we present two points, one based on the 1990 census, the lower point in Figure 1.1, and one based on the 1990 CPS, which we can continue to 1994. We do this because it is important that the switch between data sets (necessary because the results of the year 2000 census will not be available for several years) should not dominate our understanding of recent trends.

This strategy makes it clear that although there was some further increase in the proportion of young adults living with parents between 1980 and 1990 (based on the comparison of the two census points), there was little between 1990 and 1994 (based on the two CPS points). Most previous accounts of the increase in young adults living with parents had used the census-CPS switch for their last comparison so that the differences in definition would reinforce a story of recent great increases in the proportions of young adults living at home. There has indeed been an increase in the proportions of young adults living with their parents, both in this age group and among those in their later

20s (Goldscheider 1997), but much of the increase occurred between 1970 and 1980.

This, however, is only part of the story that can be told with these data. Much of the 21 percentage point decline between 1940 and 1960 was the result of the rapid decline in age at marriage during those decades. The proportion living in new families (almost all of whom were married during this period, when young single parents were extremely rare) increased 16 percentage points, from 24 percent to 40 percent, reflecting the growth in early marriage that accompanied the post-World War II baby boom in the United States.

Some of the decline among those aged 18 to 24 classified as living as a "child," however, resulted not from leaving home for early marriage but from the increase in nonfamily living, providing an increasing alternative to remaining in the parental home among the unmarried even during the baby boom. We capture this dimension of the changes in living arrangements of young adults by calculating the proportion living as children among those who are not household heads or spouses in a new family. This measure closely approximates the extent of nonfamily living among unmarried young adults (Figure 1.2).

These trends show that living at home among the unmarried declined from 82 percent in 1940 to fewer than 70 percent by 1960. Furthermore, the transition to adulthood grew much more complicated in the post-1960 period, because the marriage boom ended abruptly. As a result, the share of young adults aged 18 to 24 living as heads or spouses of families dropped from 40 percent to 28 percent between 1960 and 1980. However, not all of those who would have left home to get married remained at home. The nonfamily group continued to grow so that the proportion living as children among the unmarried fell from its 1960 level of about 70 percent to just over 63 percent in 1980.

This trend has continued, although again, we have to contend with the differences in definition between the censuses and the CPS. For this analysis, we switched from the censuses to the CPS after 1980, but we provide more detail for the post-1980 period from the CPS (1983, 1986, 1990, and 1994). There is a clear increase between 1980 and 1983, as a result of the differences in the definition of those away at college, but thereafter, the CPS data continue to show the decline in the proportions living with parents among the unmarried, which reached a low of 59 percent in 1994. This new route out of the home to nonfamily living is likely to be a very different experience than leaving home in conjunction with marriage, because it does not entail the stabilizing commitments of a family. Hence, it is not surprising that this route is also more likely to result in returning home than is the case among those who leave home for marriage (DaVanzo and Goldscheider 1990; Young 1987). This growth in nonfamily living may have contributed to the increase over time in returning home that has been observed in the United States and

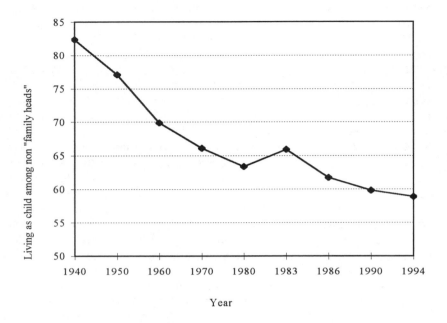

Figure 1.2. Long-Term Change in the Proportions of Young Adults (aged 20-24) Living as Children Among Those Who Have Not Established New Families of Their Own
SOURCE: Calculated by the authors from U.S. Bureau of the Census tabulations.

Australia (Goldscheider and Goldscheider 1994b; Young 1987).

The overall trends linked with nest-leaving have become clear: The age when young adults leave home has fluctuated, declining with the fall in age at marriage in the 1940s and 1950s (the major route out of the home at that time) and then rising in response to the reversal in marriage behavior. At the same time, however, the likelihood of remaining home among the unmarried has dropped continuously for more than half a century. Perhaps as a consequence, the likelihood of returning home has also increased continuously.

Hence, trends in leaving home are becoming increasingly less sensitive to the timing of marriage, because nonfamily living arrangements have steadily increased their importance in early adulthood. By the 1990s, nearly all of the decline in marriage showed up in increased nonfamily living outside the parental home. The growth in nonfamily living has not reversed, but the leaving-home transition itself has become steadily more "reversible" as young adults increase their likelihood of returning home once they have left.

These overall trends point to the need to examine the diverse routes that young adults have taken out of the home and the patterns of returning home for each of the various routes taken. In subsequent analysis (Chapters 2 and 3), we focus on the types of routes taken out of the parental home and specify how to understand returning home for each of these routes. We build on these analyses in later chapters, linking trends in nest-leaving to other factors likely to be influencing them. What are they? What do we know about changes in broader family patterns, and how do they help us understand these emergent changes in leaving home?

RESOURCES AND VALUES IN FAMILY RELATIONSHIPS

Trends in leaving home and in nonfamily living are likely to be tied to changes in the two fundamental axes of the nuclear family system: the parent-child dimension and the male-female dimension. Changes in the relationship between parents and children shape the launch out of the home. Changes in the relationship between men and women help to shape the destinations, or the routes taken.

Both of these relationships have economic and value (or preference) components. Each is based on a set of expectations and obligations that requires resources to be met, and in each case, values have been changing about these expectations and obligations. The emerging research literature has begun to make important contributions to understanding the importance of these different components. They particularly help to clarify those forces likely to be changing young adult living arrangements that have involved changes in the parent-child relationship and other changes in the resources available to (and costs faced by) young adults, at least late in the 20th century. The puzzle of changes in the relationships between young men and women, however, remains just that.

On the parent-child axis, the economic dimension clearly matters, because holding values constant, increases in the ability of young men and women to support themselves relative to their parents' level of living should increase intergenerational household fission. In a nuclear family system, young adults are expected to leave home sooner or later. And research has shown that the age group of 15 to 25 is most responsive to economic factors in their decision to form households (Short and Garner 1990). This was certainly Claire's experience (see vignette #3).

Other economic dimensions include housing costs (Christian 1989; Haurin, Hendershott, and Kim 1993; Whittington and Peters 1996) and job opportunities (Whittington and Peters 1996). The extent of government-provided cash assistance to low-income parents and their children is particularly important for the residential independence of women (Ellwood and Bane 1985). Growth in such government programs may have had as much impact on the increase from 1961 to 1979 in the proportion of those aged 15 to 24 in the United States who head their own households as the growth in wages (Kent 1992).

Values matter, as well. Overall, both generations normally have an obligation to support, and parents also have the responsibility to "rear" their children, with all that that involves on the noneconomic side, from teaching to disciplining (which, by young adulthood, appears as "control"). Even in the 1980s, parents seem to take the rearing responsibility seriously, using their income to retard very early departure but to facilitate leaving home at older ages (Avery, Goldscheider, and Speare 1992; Whittington and Peters 1996). More directly, the children of parents who expect them to leave home before marriage are more likely to do so (Goldscheider and Goldscheider 1993), highlighting the importance of the parent-child relationship for the living arrangements of young adults.

Values, however, have not remained constant over the 20th century. Parental control over major domains of young adulthood—who and when to marry, what career to choose— has clearly eroded, and the extent of obligations between aging parents and their adult children has changed dramatically. At the beginning of the 20th century, responsibilities for the financial and residential support of impoverished aging parents belonged solely to their children (Qiang 1993). The extent of this responsibility had been greatly reduced by century's end as a

---

Vignette #3

RETURNING TO ROOST IN THE EMPTY NEST

Baltimore resident Claire was a 1992 graduate of the University of Maryland who never imagined living with her parents at age 25. "After living at school for four years, you don't want to move back with your parents," she says.

But sharing a Washington, D.C. apartment with three friends quickly lost its allure. The rent was expensive and the bathrooms too few. She was a travel agent assistant and decided to move back to her parent's home after three years so she could save money to travel and perhaps rent her own place. Her younger brother Paul was already living at home, having returned a year before. He was 23 and had finished Georgetown with a major in English. He had a part-time job writing, but he wasn't sure how long it would last.

Their parents never figured on this. "Two years ago, nobody was at home," says their father. "It was like a second honeymoon."

Adds their mother, "I was one of those parents who said, 'Graduate from college and don't come back except to visit'. But it's more complicated than that. We never thought they would return home. We didn't; when we left it was for good. But then again, I was married when I was their age, and I never left home to go to college."

SOURCE: Adapted from Perin (1995).

result of the growth of publicly and privately funded income and residential support systems. The effects of this growth can be clearly tracked in changes in the living arrangements of the elderly (Ruggles 1996). The increased economic independence of the elderly from their children may have freed younger children to leave home who in the past, like Gregory (see vignette #4) might have had to remain to provide support, perhaps to a widowed mother.

The changes we have described in living arrangements of young adults may also reflect the reduced commitment of parents to support their children (reflecting, perhaps, their reduced "control"). Whether discussed in terms of actual returning to the parental home or in terms of delayed nest-leaving, recent studies have projected an image of adulthood that requires residential independence from an early age, in most cases long before marriage (Riche 1990; Schnaiberg and Goldenberg 1989). The rhetoric in the popular press is even more extreme, referring to the emergence of "Peter Pan syndromes" (i.e., young adults who refuse to grow up) and implying that young adults are not deserving of their parents' residential support (e.g., Gross 1991), even in the difficult economic climate young adults have experienced since the mid-1970s. This image, and the pressure it may put on young adults to leave home early, is problematic, given the negative effects of early nest-leaving on educational attainment

---

Vignette #4

GREGORY'S WOMEN

Gregory is surrounded by poverty. His mom lives in a small but clean apartment with Gregory and his two sisters. She works long hours, but work is not steady and there are no health benefits. She doesn't make enough to pay most of her own medical bills and also to take care of her aging mother. She also needs her monthly welfare check to pay for food and clothing for the girls. She has lived in public housing over the last 10 years. It has its own problems, noise, dirt, safety, but it is home and that's all there is. Gregory helps out at home by giving his mother part of his weekly salary from working at the supermarket 40 to 50 hours a week for minimum wages.

Gregory is 27 and lives at home in south Philadelphia. He had lived off and on with his girlfriend and their two-year old child, but that didn't work out. He provides some money for her as well but there is not much to go around.

Gregory responds to his living at home with a shrug. "This is home until I can find a better job and make more money. My friends and I hang out in the neighborhood, and I go to my mom's place to sleep. My mom needs me and so do my sisters. The neighborhood is tough, so is life." He reflects on his own daughter, "For now, home is with my mom. Maybe I will move back in with Tawanda and her mom. But not right now. It is not working out. The last time we fought and I moved out." He adds with a smile, "I seem to have too many women to take care of."

(White and Lacy 1997; see also our discussion in Chapter 4). It appears that some parents are actually pushing their children to leave the nest before they are ready.

Parents clearly have something to say about who will live in their households and often have the resources to back up their views. One piece of evidence emerges from research that included measures of both parental and young adult attitudes. The results showed that parents' attitudes and decisions mattered as much or more than did their children's (Goldscheider and Goldscheider 1993). The increase in parental divorce and remarriage also appears to be changing the structure of parental obligation to children, in most cases reducing it, when absent fathers do not provide and the new fathers in the household do not make up the difference. One of the most consistent findings in the nest-leaving literature is that young people leave home faster from nontraditional families than from two-biological-parent families (Aquilino 1991; Goldscheider and Goldscheider 1993; Mitchell, Wister, and Burch 1989; White and Booth 1985; Young 1987). The differences are particularly large when leaving home to attend college is separated from other routes, because this is the one route that young adults from traditional family structures are significantly more likely to take (Goldscheider and Goldscheider 1998).

Another study found that values about various dimensions of familism had far more impact than measures of financial resources on whether young adults expected and experienced living in a nonfamily setting in early adulthood. Direct measures of values, such as attitudes about traditional gender roles and about parent-child relationships, as well as indirect measures, in which familism was inferred from ethnicity and religiosity, had powerful effects on the routes young people took to residential independence (Goldscheider and Goldscheider 1993).

Supporting this view is the finding in the same study that young Hispanic Americans and Asian Americans were much more likely than non-Hispanic Whites[3] to remain home until marriage. For Carmella, family counts the most (see vignette #5). This pattern of ethnic difference appeared even within socioeconomic levels, again suggesting that cultural values associated with ethnic communities may be as important as economic resources in influencing the pathways out of the home. Direct measurement of attitudes among young adults during the 1980s also influenced the route taken.

The more traditional their views of the centrality of family relative to work for women, the more young people, and particularly young women, expected to and remained home until they married. Young adults were particularly responsive to religious influences. Fundamentalist Protestants are more likely than any other Christian group to remain at home until they marry, as are those who have attended Catholic schools. In contrast, the vast majority of young Jews leave home before they marry and they have parents who are the most likely to support this move. But values do not separate the lives of young

African Americans from the White majority: They are very likely to leave home when they are still single, but largely because they marry at a much later age than White Americans.

These differences in nest-leaving patterns by religion, ethnicity, and values during the 1980s suggest that nonfamily living has simply not been as well accepted in more familistic ethnic groups and religious denominations as it has been in the dominant, largely secular culture. This new life course stage is virtually taken for granted among highly educated Protestants and Jews, both parents and young adults, but it is much less clear among other communities.

On the male-female dimension, both the financial and noneconomic dimensions of the contract between men and women are in flux, which is likely one reason for the recent avoidance of marriage. In turn, the decline in marriage is clearly involved in the changes in the living arrangements of young adults, contributing to the growth in nonfamily living. To those who view cohabitation as a close substitute for marriage, some of the growth in nonfamily living is clearly artifactual—many of those living with roommates are actually living in a sexual union, and cohabitation is often a prelude to marriage. However, these relationships are nearly as fragile as other living arrangements based on roommates (on cohabitation, see

---

Vignette #5

FAMILY COUNTS THE MOST

Carmella is the first in her family to go to college. It takes about an hour by subway to commute from her parents' home in Washington Heights to school. She takes a full load of courses and works part-time as a cashier in the bookstore on campus to help pay for her expenses. She doesn't mind living at home, although some of the responsibilities of taking care of her younger sister and brother often interfere with her schoolwork. She has a steady boyfriend who works as a mechanic and makes good money. They have talked about finding an apartment and moving in together before they marry, but Carmella has said no. "I have always been taught about the importance of family, and I will probably live in my parents' home until I have a family of my own. My father has not always had steady work, and my Mom works full-time. I want to help out at home as much as I can and get married when I have saved enough and completed my education."

She talks about her older cousin, who quit her last year of high school and moved in with her boyfriend after she got pregnant. "They haven't married in the church yet, and they fight all the time over money. She doesn't have much of a chance of getting a good job without an education. I want my children to have a better chance than that," she says. "I don't think that it's right when girls and boys live together before they are married, even if they are going out with other." She adds, "The family counts the most and my family would not be happy if I was living together with my boyfriend before we married."

Bumpass, Sweet, and Cherlin 1991; on roommates, see Speare and Goldscheider 1983). Of particular relevance to the differences between cohabitation and marriage is their impact on the parental home. Ending a cohabitation is much more often followed by a return home than is ending a marriage (Goldscheider and Goldscheider 1994b). On this dimension, as on many others, those who are in cohabiting relationships in the United States more closely resemble the single than the married (Rindfuss and VandenHeuvel 1990).

Many other puzzles remain. One is the racial cross-over in age at leaving home that brought African Americans from a situation in which they left home earlier than whites prior to 1960 to one of leaving later (Glick and Lin 1985; Goldscheider and Goldscheider 1997b). This cross-over parallels a similar racial cross-over in the extent and timing of marriage between African Americans and Whites (Koball 1995) and may provide clues to the link between leaving home and changes in male-female relationships. We shall analyze in detail the family structure, gender, economic, and racial/ethnic puzzles in subsequent chapters.

THE NEED FOR HISTORICAL PERSPECTIVE

These findings on nest-leaving late in the 20th century, although suggestive of change, provide us few clues about our central question: How have patterns of leaving and returning home changed over the 20th century? Are the unmarried of the 20-something generation really staying home longer than previous generations? Does their increased coresidence reflect more than their later marriage? Or does it only seem as if they are staying longer, both to them (who had not anticipated the economic reverses of the 1980s job market for entering workers) and to their parents (many of whom had themselves left home early to marry young)? What are the changes over time in the age at leaving home?

Furthermore, what changes have occurred in how the timing of marriage has affected leaving home? Studies in the 1980s seem to suggest that a revolution has occurred in the transition to adulthood, in which most young people once remained in the parental home until they married, whereas in the last few decades leaving home before marriage has become normative. If this is the case, when did these new patterns begin to emerge? Did they emerge at different times for young women and young men? What are the trends in leaving home to get a job, to be "independent" or to cohabit, to get married, to join the military, or to go to college? Have these routes out of the parental home changed over time? When young adults leave home before they marry, are they searching for "independence" from their parents or looking for a job or for educational opportunities located in another city? In short, we need to know more about how the routes and reasons for leaving home have changed over time.

Detailed information and analysis about many cohorts has been lacking until recently. Most of the details about changes over time have been inferred from static correlations. For example, research has documented that as income increases, the rate of leaving home before marriage increases. Some have inferred from this cross-sectional, positive relationship between income and leaving home that as affluence increased over time, leaving home before marriage increased. Similarly, some infer from the negative relationship between religious (and family) values and leaving home that secularization over time (and individualism) reduce the chances that young adults will remain home until they marry. If leaving home before marriage is higher among the college educated or among those who marry late, one can argue by inference that as college education increases and as young adults postpone their marriage, leaving home before marriage should increase. But are these inferences correct?

We now turn to a new body of information that will allow us to examine these contemporary patterns in historical perspective. New data have become available that allow us to systematically reconstruct patterns of leaving home (and returning) covering much of the 20th century for the United States. For the first time, we are able to adequately address these and related questions. In 1987-88, a representative sample of adults in the United States were asked a series of questions on nest-leaving. We shall be referring in this book to these data as the National Survey of Families and Households or the NSFH. Respondents were asked the age when they first "left home for four months or more." They were also asked to provide the reason they left home and whether they returned home to live for the same length of time, and the age and reason they returned. With these data, we shall be able to test these inferences directly and to identify which of the contemporary patterns are distinctive and which are continuous with the past. Our analysis will provide a firmer foundation for understanding the connections between changes in leaving and returning home and the broader transformations that have characterized American society over the 20th century.

We first examine leaving home in detail, placing changes in the timing of leaving and in the routes taken in the context of the major events of the twentieth century. We consider patterns during the Great Depression of the 1930s, World War II, the baby boom, Vietnam era, the baby bust, and the 1980s (Chapter 2). We then turn to examining changes in the likelihood of returning home and link them with changes in leaving home (Chapter 3). We investigate the sources of variation over time in these patterns, first studying nest-leaving at very young and older ages (Chapter 4) and examining variation by the regions where young adults grew up (Chapter 5). In the second part of the book, we explore five revolutionary changes to identify the contexts of these historical patterns. These include the revolution in family patterns, the transformation in gender roles, economic and educational changes, race and ethnic patterns, and the changing nature of religion.

These analyses allow us to answer questions such as these: How did economic affluence and the increase in educational attainment alter the timing of the routes taken out of the home? How did the divorce revolution change the timing of leaving home and the paths taken and the families that were there for them when they needed to return home? Was the impact of family patterns on the paths out of the home similar in the 1950s when divorce rates were low and stepparenthood rare as in the 1980s when divorce rates were high and reconstituted families more common?

In the decline in the age when young adults were leaving home, who were the innovators and who were the followers? Did the more educated and those with more resources lead the way? Was it young men or women, the secular or the religious, the native-born or the immigrant, who were in the forefront of the transformation of the nest-leaving experience? Has there been a general convergence over time in nest-leaving and nest-returning among groups?

Finally, we explore how changes in the ethnic and religious mosaic of American society has influenced the values that shaped the pathways out of the home. We investigate the historical basis for the distinctive features of leaving home among the African American and Hispanic populations to determine when these emerged in American society.

The answers to these questions rest with a detailed and systematic analysis of newly organized data. Uncovering the historical dimension of nest-leaving and nest-returning patterns will clarify the distinctiveness and continuities of the contemporary patterns. They will also clarify the emergent features of the transition to adulthood as the 20th century draws to a close.

NOTES

1. The King James version more familiarly reads; "Therefore shall a man leave his father and mother, and shall cleave unto his wife, and they shall be one flesh."

2. Such calculations are not yet possible for the 1930 census.

3. When we refer to White non-Hispanics, Blacks (or Black Americans), and Hispanics we use capital first letters to signify that these are formal racial and ethnic constructions, not categories based on biology or nationality.

CHAPTER 2

Out of the Nest

A complex series of changes has transformed the lives of Americans as they make the transition from being a child in their parental home to having adult work and family roles. These go beyond the long-term decline and recent increase in age at leaving home, coupled with the continued increase in nonfamily living in young adulthood, that we documented in Chapter 1. Much more dramatically, the 20th century has seen early marriage and parenthood emerge as *the* central transitions to adulthood and then move abruptly off center. During the baby boom after World War II, ages at family formation dropped into the low 20s for both men and women; age at parenthood hit a historic low. Following the baby boom, fertility rates halved and marriage ages hit a historic high, as the median age at marriage increased by nearly five years after the late 1950s. Marriage also has become less committed, with the rise in divorce and cohabitation. Whatever has happened in the relationships between adult men and women, it has reverberated throughout the life course. It makes its first major mark on the lives of men and women during the nest-leaving process, however, by shaping the routes young people take out of the home.

The transformations in marriage and family formation, together with the decoupling of leaving home from marriage, have confused many dimensions of early adulthood. As recently as the 1970s, historians could describe changes between the late 19th and mid-20th centuries in the young adult life course as creating "a situation of far greater age-congruity" as a result of the compression of transitions between school and work and between the parental home and a new family. Transitions that had spanned more than a decade in the last century had been compressed into a few short years around age 20 at the mid-point of the current century (Modell, Furstenberg, and Hershberg 1976:29). The rapid reversals that have occurred since then in leaving home, as in other family realms, have confused the entire leaving-home process, straining the relationships between parents and their maturing children as it has between men and women.

It is no longer clear what young adults *should* do. Many still expect that they should wait until they marry to be residentially independent, but even more seem to expect that they should leave home after high school and never return home except to visit, even when the reason for leaving was to attend college or serve in the military, and these temporary roles have ended (Goldscheider and Goldscheider 1993). Further confusion has arisen because many take independent living as the most important indicator of being an "adult." Young people who live with parents, even if they are working and saving for a home or attending school to increase future earnings, often feel that their friends view them as somehow not truly grown up, and their parents may feel that they have failed to raise them properly (Schnaiberg and Goldenberg 1989).

Although recent research has begun to provide information to clarify what factors influence nest-leaving at the end of the 20th century, we are on shaky grounds when we examine the past. We do not know the extent to which contemporary patterns are distinctive or whether there are important continuities in patterns of leaving and returning home. The obvious continuity, of course, is that nearly all young people eventually leave the homes they were raised in to establish new households. The 20th century, however, has not only witnessed massive changes in family formation but also great social and economic shifts associated with the Great Depression of the 1930s, World War II, the baby boom and bust, and Vietnam, as well as the revolutions in family structure, gender and race relations, immigration, affluence, and secularization. As the century nears its end, diversity seems to be the word of the day. One painful result is that the family experiences of parents have been radically different from those of their own children, making the negotiation between the generations much more problematic. Given this, how are the generations handling the emerging patterns of leaving and returning home?

To understand changes in nest-leaving patterns, we need to describe them precisely. Many of our explanations and inferences about the past have been drawn from the analysis of contemporary patterns and the theories and explanations that have been developed from them. We have tended to read history backward, by inferring from the present snapshot, murky as it is, to the dynamics of changes over time. These inferences may have distorted both our understanding of the unique features of the present as well as the comparative changes over time. Differing family values might have more impact now, amid flux and diversity, than they did in the past, when there seemed to be a national consensus on leaving home to marriage. Previously, perhaps the major issue had been acquiring the resources for a family, which had been very difficult in the early decades of the century but which became easy in the early years of post-World War II affluence.

Until recently, however, the quality of our historical picture has been limited by the absence of systematic evidence. We now have a comprehensive body of data to revisit the historical past and to systematically reconstruct the patterns of leaving home and its correlates. We can build on the descriptions of change that have been recently identified (Goldscheider 1997; Goldscheider and Goldscheider 1994b; Ravanera, Rajulton, and Burch 1995; White 1994) to examine contemporary family themes in the context of the transformations of the past. More completely than ever before, we can explore whether the economic and value components of leaving home have always worked the same way to encourage nest-leaving, or if they have emerged as new factors in leaving and returning home in the last two decades of the 20th century. This will enable us to take our understanding of leaving home in early adulthood to a new level, integrating it with the larger changes in the relationships between parents and children and men and women underway as we enter the 21st century.

As we consider the historical context, we can begin to address specific themes associated with leaving home. Some of the detailed questions that we shall be addressing in this chapter include the following:

- What were the effects on leaving home of the economic depression of the 1930s, when economic conditions were not conducive to early residential independence of young adults?
- How did the military mobilization of the World War II years affect the timing and the pathways out of the home? Did these effects persist through the Korean and the Vietnam wars?
- What were the influences of the marriage and baby booms of the post-World War II era on the timing and routes out of the home?
- When did the desire for independence spread as a major route out of the home? Are young adults moving to early independence relative to their parents' or their grandparents' generation? How closely do the changes in the routes out of the home parallel the changes in marriage timing, the expansion of educational opportunities, and the changes in the labor market?

Finding the answers to these questions requires a systematic historical perspective and a body of evidence that can delineate nest-leaving and related changes over time in American society.

THE HISTORICAL DIMENSIONS OF LEAVING HOME

The National Survey of Families and Households (NSFH) data provide information that allows us to reconstruct the nest-leaving process for most of the 20th century. Because the sample included many people who were quite elderly, we have detailed information that can illuminate the nest-leaving process in the period for which little had been known before—the critical years before the 1970s, about which previous studies of leaving home have provided almost no information. This allows us to connect the timing of leaving home to the major events of the 20th century, all the way from before the economic depression of the 1930s to the emerging "20-something" generation, who came of age in the 1980s.[1]

Although these data describe nest-leaving patterns from the distant past, stretching back up to three-quarters of a century ago, they are based on the memories of people living in the late 1980s. To reduce our concerns about the accuracy of these remembered activities, we estimated the proportion of young adults living with their parents and the proportions married from the official U.S. censuses taken in those decades. We compared the information on residential histories in the NSFH with trends shown in the U.S. censuses of 1940 to 1980 (such as those presented in Chapter 1).

We found that although the respondents' marital status matched census data quite well (the proportion married at a given age in each census year reconstructed from these histories is similar to the proportions recorded in the relevant census year), respondents in the NSFH may have considerably understated their age at leaving home. The censuses recorded many more living with their parents than would be deduced from NSFH information, particularly for the earliest time periods (Goldscheider, Biddlecom, and St. Clair 1994). Some of this difference may reflect errors in the census (in ambiguous situations, parents might report on census forms that a child is living at home even though the child in question feels that he or she has left home and would report this way many years later).

By the time the survey was taken in the late 1980s, however, young adults had been leaving home at quite young ages for several decades. This could have lead to changed expectations about when young adults *should* leave home and to defining young adults living with their parents as a "problem" (Chapter 4). In this context, it seems more likely that older adults may have slanted their memories of events in the past, perhaps misreporting their age of leaving home or magnifying very brief, earlier departures, describing them as their "first" departure from home. As a result of this bias, the trend in leaving home shown in the data we present is flatter than the trend we observed based on the census data in Chapter 1, which showed a greater decline in the early period than appears in these survey data. This bias thus leads to an underestimate in the extent of decline in leaving home and likely also in the decline of leaving home for marriage.

Another problem with data in which people report on events in the distant past is differential survivorship. If those who did not survive to be interviewed are different in their nest-leaving or returning behavior from those in the survey, it would affect our historical results. Certainly, those who left for the armed services, and fought and died in World War II, Korea, or Vietnam, are not included in a survey conducted in the 1980s. Neither are many immigrants to the United States, since some return to their home countries (if not to their parental homes) and, of course, the nest-leaving experiences of emigrants from the United States are not included in the survey. Analyses that examine nest-leaving need to take into account that those interviewed do not fully represent those who died or left the country. However, there is no particular reason to assume that had those who died in war-related service survived, they would have been different from others who left home to serve in the military during those years; the bias due to immigration, if any, is also not known.

These concerns, however, are relatively minor, given the unique spotlight these data shine on a little studied but important phenomenon shaping young people's transition to adulthood in the 20th century. These reconstructed data place into sociohistoric context the current changes in nest-leaving patterns in contemporary America. Using this new evidence, we can understand more clearly the historical patterns shaping the plans young people and their parents are making about their living arrangements and determine whether they represent a radical shift or are more continuous with the past. We will reconstruct the historical changes in the timing of leaving home—that is, changes in the ages when young adults set up an independent residence. We use the information on the reasons they provided about why they left home, particularly "reasons" that indicate leaving home to get married, to obtain a job, for military service, and just to be independent in their living arrangements, to identify where they go, the routes they have taken out of the home.

NEST-LEAVING COHORTS

The timing of leaving home and the routes taken out of the home will be examined for groups of young adults, defined by the era during which they reached their 18th birthday. For most people, this is when the decision to leave home begins to be seriously considered. We call these groups *nest-leaving cohorts*. Nest-leaving cohorts have been constructed from information on the ages of the respondents of the 1987/88 NSFH, which asked each person his or her date of birth. We added 18 years to this birth date to define entry into the life course transitions associated with adulthood.

Cohort is a demographic concept indicating a group of people who shared some common experience at the same time. Usually, cohorts are defined by year of birth: The baby boomers are normally defined as those *born* during the baby boom. But there are other ways to use the cohort concept: Demographers analyze *marriage cohorts*, which consist of people whose marriages began in the same years. Marriage cohorts share the experience of a particular historical period, including expectations about marital relationships and commitments, expectations about who does what in the household, and whether conflict might be resolved through divorce. College "classes" may also be viewed as cohorts—

for example, the class of 2003 is defined by the year their members are expected to graduate, given college entrance in 1999.

We have constructed the nest-leaving cohorts according to the historical circumstances they encountered when they entered adulthood. Hence, what we call the baby boom nest-leaving cohorts are those reaching age 18 during the baby boom years. They should not be confused with those born during the baby boom. It was the baby boom nest-leaving cohort who *created* the baby boom by marrying young and having children early in their marriages.

We experimented with a number of different groupings to identify which periods differed from others as historical gateways to adulthood. We started with five-year nest-leaving cohorts (e.g., 1920-24, 1925-29, . . . 1980-84). From there, it was a process of "fine-tuning" to combine adjacent periods that were similar in terms of their ages and routes out of the home. There were too few cases among the oldest cohorts to make such fine distinctions, leaving us with the pre-1930s as our oldest cohort. Many who reached age 18 prior to 1940 were still living at home at the beginning of World War II, so we expanded the World War II cohort to include those reaching age 18 in the waning years of the depression. The first baby boom cohort extends from 1945 to 1958 because there were few differences among young people reaching age 18 throughout this period. The baby boom has become such an important demographic-historical phenomenon not only because so many were born then but because its placidity lasted such a long time, especially relative to the turbulent periods that both preceded it and followed it.

These nest-leaving cohorts have been defined to focus attention on the key conditions of the 20th century that have shaped young adulthood, either by depressing their economic options (the major depression of the 1930s and the near depression young adults have faced since the late 1970s), by wresting them from their homes and delaying investments in schooling and family (World War II and Vietnam), or by impelling them rapidly into marriage (the baby boom periods) or putting on the brakes to marriage hard (the baby bust). This allows us to compare the experiences of those becoming 18 years of age during the eight time periods identified in Figure 2.1, all but the first two of whom had parents in one of the earlier time periods.

The last group, the 20-somethings, have sometimes been called "the X generation," because they are the most difficult to characterize. In part, this is because there is no way to know how their lives will turn out until we have new data that takes them past their early 20s. But even based on what we know, they have given very mixed signals, which we will connect to their nest-leaving patterns. Our goal in the remainder of this chapter is to outline the major changes in the timing of leaving home and the routes out of the home and to link them with the historical conditions that have likely shaped these changes.

Figure 2.1

NEST-LEAVING COHORTS

• The Roaring Twenties: All who reached age 18 before the depression (1929 or earlier, most of whom did so during the 1920s).

• The Great Depression: The economic depression of the 1930s (1930-1937).

• World War II: The mobilization of young adults for World War II (1938-1944). The parents of this cohort were the older members of the first nest-leaving cohort, many of whom experienced World War I firsthand.

• Baby Boom I: The post-World War II period of the rising baby boom (1945-1958). Most of their parents came of age either in the years just prior to or during the depression.

• Baby Boom II: The waning baby boom years (1959-1965). The parents of this cohort were almost all young adults during the great depression.

• The Vietnam years (1966-1972): Like the young adults of the World War II cohort, the parents of this cohort lived many of their young adult years in wartime; hence, many of them were a third wartime generation.

• The "baby-bust" (1973-1979): This post-Vietnam cohort came of age during the depths of the baby bust. They are the children of the baby boom and of parents who reached adulthood during the late 1940s and early 1950s.

• The "20-somethings" (1980-85) are also the children of the baby boom, whose parents came of age in the full flush of the 1950s.

THE CHANGING TIMING OF LEAVING HOME

What do these new data show about the changing timing of leaving home among young adults? We first examine changes in leaving home for these nest-leaving cohorts by constructing quartiles segmenting the nest-leaving process: The age by which the first quarter left, the first half (also called the median age), and the third quarter (Figure 2.2). This allows a broader view of the timing of nest-leaving, because it shows not just the central or average age at leaving home (the median) but also the ages by which a substantial fraction has already begun the process (the first quartile, whom we will call the "early leavers") and the age after which a substantial fraction still remain in the parental home (the "late leavers"). These trends will indicate how long it was common or usual for members of a cohort of young adults to remain home. These data document a substantial decline in the timing of leaving home that

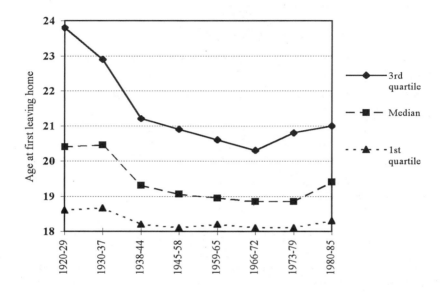

Nest-leaving cohort (year reached age 18)

Figure 2.2. Age at Leaving Home, by Nest-Leaving Cohort (Quartiles)
SOURCE: Calculated by the authors from the NSFH.

continued throughout most of the 20th century. This pattern is consistent with the census data that we presented earlier and the review of studies that indicated a decline. However, the decline has ended, and even reversed, for the last two nest-leaving cohorts. For a long time, each subsequent cohort of young people reaching age 18 was leaving faster than the cohorts that preceded them. The brakes went on sometime during the 1970s, and young adults have been increasingly delaying their leaving into the 1980s.

The first quartile has changed the least. There is a substantial basis for the perception that nest-leaving soon after reaching age 18 is very common: The first 25 percent of each cohort had left by sometime in the year after they turned 18. Among the oldest two cohorts, who were all leaving more slowly than nest-leaving cohorts at mid-century, the first quartile left closer to age 19. The age at which the first quartile left declined slightly after that, so that it was closer to age 18 during the baby boom, and has since increased slightly. But looking at the early leavers shows that the transition from the parental home seems to have been seriously launched at about the same age for all these cohorts.

In contrast, the late leavers have been much more volatile. Prior to the Great Depression, it was common to find a substantial group of young adults aged 24 or older who had never left the parental home. Even during the

Depression, however, nest-leaving was beginning to accelerate, since the third quartile of the Depression cohort had left by age 23. Likely, young people living in depressed areas (and most were) had to leave home to look for work.

World War II produced the sharpest drop, so that three-quarters had left by soon after their 21st birthdays. This was a critical period in the transformation of young adulthood of the 20th century, which paved the way to a "return" to a "normalcy" of rapid entry into adult roles and a rapid exit from adolescence that had never really existed before. Later cohorts continued the decline, if more slowly, so that by the Vietnam cohort, three-quarters had left home by shortly after age 20. The reversal that took place after the Vietnam cohort indicates that it became slightly more common to see young adults older than age 21 living with parents, but not much older.

Change in the median age of nest-leaving has been intermediate between these two extremes. The median age at leaving home was about 20.5 years for the two earliest cohorts. It then dropped a full year for those reaching adulthood in the period before and during World War II. Since the end of World War II, the decline was slower, dipping below age 19 for the Vietnam and baby bust cohorts. The 20-somethings have clearly experienced an increase in the age at leaving home, although it is not dramatic. The new generation has reached the age levels of nest-leaving of the World War II cohort, but they leave much faster than the two earliest cohorts.

These data are consistent with popular reports that regularly appear in the daily press or in magazines suggesting that there has been some delay in the timing of leaving home. Yet it is clear that the historical memories of the popular press are very short. The overall story of the timing of leaving home in the 20th century has been one of decline.

Taken together, the intergenerational changes in the timing of leaving home mean that for most of the 20th century, young adults were leaving home faster than their own parents had left home. This was probably most dramatic for the two baby boom cohorts, whose parents came of age during the Great Depression. The Vietnam cohort was much more similar to their parents in the timing of leaving home, since their parents were making decisions about leaving home during World War II. As we will show below, the routes taken were so different that it would be hard to argue that the generation gap was any smaller for this group than for older cohorts, and it might even have felt larger. The youngest cohorts are having the opposite experience, leaving more slowly than the baby boom nest-leaving cohorts of their parents. This may contribute to the expectations of their parents that their children would leave earlier than they actually did.

CHANGING ROUTES OUT OF THE HOME

The pattern of change in the timing of leaving home seems to reflect the well-documented changes in the timing of marriage—late marriage prior to World War II, a major decline in age at marriage during the baby boom years, and the more recent increase in delaying the timing of marriage. The swing in median ages at marriage has actually been much more dramatic than these changes in the timing of leaving home. Does the 20th-century decline and later increase in the age at nest-leaving simply reflect the changes in marriage timing? Or has marriage become less important as a route out of the parental home, which would account for the smaller swings in nest-leaving timing than in marriage timing?

Change in the timing of leaving the nest is the first important dimension of our historical analysis, focusing our attention on relationships between parents and children and their sharing a home and its resources. The context, or the reasons young adults gave for leaving home, sharpens our understanding of these timing trends and focuses our attention on the changes in the structure of adult lives they go to. Do they move directly to a new family, based perhaps on marriage and parenthood, with no family "role hiatus" (Presser 1972)? Do they first experience some sort of semiautonomy, away at school or in military service, separate from parents but not yet responsible for the residential dimensions of adulthood? Or do they begin their adult lives fully responsible for themselves, but not for others?

We approximate these possibilities based on the retrospective reconstruction of the reasons given for leaving home. We distinguish several key routes: Marriage (the formation of a conventional new family); school and the military, the two major forms of residential semi-autonomy in the 20th century; and leaving for a job[2] or just to be "independent" as routes leading to nonfamily residential independence. Furthermore, because the complexities of young adulthood have increased even more at the end of the 20th century, we distinguish as well those who leave for nontraditional family reasons (cohabitation and single parenthood).

Respondents could give only one reason for leaving home, although in many cases, no doubt, many factors were involved, not all of which they even were aware of. When there was more than one possibility, the one chosen no doubt also varied. When someone left home to get married and also to begin a first full-time job at the same time, it is not clear which would appear more salient or whether this might differ by gender. Hence, we will normally call their replies to the question on "reason for leaving" nest-leaving routes or pathways. Nevertheless, the reasons they gave were largely congruent with those that could be constructed by observing their actual marital, parental, and educational transitions (Goldscheider and Goldscheider 1998).

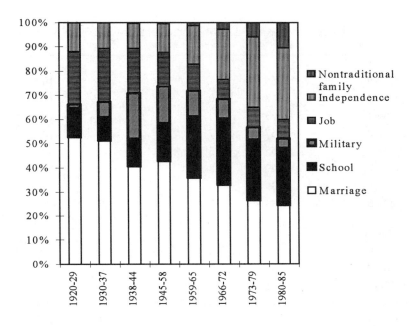

Year reached age 18

Figure 2.3. Changing Distribution of Routes Out of the Parental Home
SOURCE: Calculated by the authors from the NSFH.

LEAVING HOME FOR MARRIAGE

Throughout the early part of the 20th century, over half of young adults remained in their parental home, never living away for even four months, until they got married (Figure 2.3). Even during the two decades that included World War II and the major baby boom cohorts (1938-1958), this route was still the most common, taken by more than 40 percent of young adults. Among the last three nest-leaving cohorts, however, the importance of marriage as a route out of the home declined fairly rapidly.

It is not possible to tell the story of changing routes out of the home in the 20th century, however, without considering the differences between men and women. We defer our major examination of changing gender differences in the nest-leaving process to Chapter 7. Nevertheless, they underlie our discussion of changing routes, because it is important to examine the ways they have differed. Hence, we also show part of the percentage distribution that appears in Figure 2.3 separately by sex, focusing on the marriage and the military routes that differ the most between men and women (Table 2.1).

Table 2.1. Reasons for Leaving Home by Sex and Nest-Leaving Cohorts

Leave Cohort	Marriage	School	Military	Other	Total
Females					
1920-29	66	11	0	23	100
1930-37	68	10	0	22	100
1938-44	63	12	2	23	100
1945-58	67	17	0	16	100
1959-65	55	23	1	21	100
1966-72	49	28	1	22	100
1973-79	39	27	1	33	100
1980-85	33	28	0	39	100
Males					
1920-29	40	13	5	42	100
1930-37	37	7	17	39	100
1938-44	21	11	47	21	100
1945-58	26	16	39	19	100
1959-65	25	27	27	21	100
1966-72	23	31	18	28	100
1973-79	24	25	11	40	100
1980-85	10	36	9	45	100

SOURCE: Calculated by the authors from the NSFH.

These data show, for example, that although leaving home for marriage was always more important among the women's routes out of the home than among the men's, the differences were not always great, particularly early in the century (even about 40 percent of men in the first two decades remained home until marriage).

Marriage was at a late age for members of these early cohorts, and those young men leaving home for marriage during these years remained home until around age 24. They were likely working, probably saving for a family when they could, and contributing to the support of their parents and siblings when the Great Depression made survival difficult for everyone. However, World War II ended this life course option for most men, and little more than 20 percent of young men have remained home until marriage in any of the more recent cohorts.

The increase in nest-leaving pathways that did not involve marriage for both men and women, and especially for women, must have seemed quite shocking to their parents and other older relatives, most of whom never lived on their own between living with their parents and marrying and having children. However, it is clear that it was not just among those who married late that remaining home until marriage was becoming less attractive. Despite the increase in overall age at marriage, the ages at leaving home of those remaining home until marriage continued to drop, declining below age 19 for the most recent cohort (Figure 2.4). Thus, even those expecting to marry early (at age 20 or 21) were leaving home via some other route—to attend college or perhaps to achieve residential independence some other way.

LEAVING HOME TO SEMI-AUTONOMY

The two routes out of the home that lead to semiautonomous living arrangements—away to school and into the military (the dotted portions of Figure 2.4)—both changed substantially over the century. The proportions leaving home to attend college, which hovered at around 10 to 15 percent among the oldest three nest-leaving cohorts, expanded rapidly in the post-World War II era. This route attracted more than 25 percent by the baby boom and Vietnam cohorts (1959-1972), and then stabilized at that level, with similar patterns and trends for both men and women. It also shows the greatest stability in the ages left among those choosing this route. Unlike in the 18th and 19th centuries, when colleges often enrolled children as young as 14 and adults as old as 25 (Modell, Furstenberg, and Hershberg 1976), students going away to school in the 20th century were centered on age 18. We see no sign of returning GIs in this trend, although it is clear that the Depression often forced young people to work for a year before beginning college.

The military route, however, has shown a very different pattern, both in terms of the ages of those enlisting and in changes in incidence over the 20th century. And of course, it is a route dominated by men during most of the period. This route was an important one from World War II through Vietnam, before fading away after the end of the draft. Its impact, however, was felt even in the nest-leaving cohorts of 1930 to 1937, because many of the younger members of that cohort were still at home when the war started, with the result that their average age of leaving home (at enlistment) was between 22 and 23.

The dominance of the military in the early lives of men during the middle of the century should not be underestimated. Nearly half (47 percent) of the young men in the nest-leaving cohort of 1938 to 1944 first left home to go to war. It was their "family role hiatus."

Even after World War II, the importance of military service in the early adult years of young men continued. Despite the rapid postwar demobilization, nearly 40 percent of the cohort of young men reaching age 18 in the early baby boom cohort (1945-1958) left home to the armed services, and only a few could have enlisted prior to the end of the war. Sharp declines characterized each younger cohort, but still more than a quarter of young men in the later years of the baby boom first moved out of the parental home in the military.

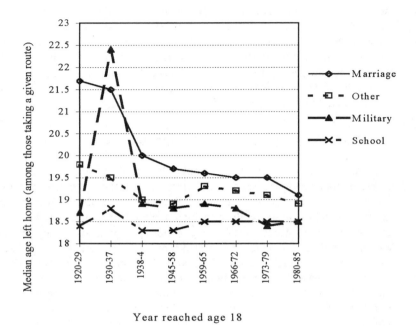

Figure 2.4. Changes in Age at Leaving Home, by Route Left
SOURCE: Calculated by the authors from the NSFH.

The Vietnam years showed a further drop, with about one-sixth of young men serving in the military without prior independent residential experience. Military service as a first residential experience after living with parents stopped being important for young men beginning with the cohorts who came of age after the end of the draft—the baby bust cohort of 1973 to 1979 and the 20-somethings of the 1980s, dropping to a level below 10 percent.

With the decline in the military route and the end of the expansion of the proportions leaving home to attend school, semiautonomous living arrangements, which were so important between the 1950s and early 1970s, have become relatively unimportant as an intermediate pathway out of the parental home. Full residential independence becomes necessary. With the decline in marriage, this means either nonfamily independence or some sort of nontraditional family arrangement (cohabitation or parenthood). Together, these choices have come to dominate the routes young people are taking out of the parental home at the end of the 20th century. We divide the two truly nonfamily routes into those associated with leaving home to take a job and those for which independence, having one's "own place," is reason enough for leaving home.

NON-MARITAL RESIDENTIAL INDEPENDENCE

Of these three "new" routes, only one is truly new—nontraditional family formation. It really should not be considered "nonfamily living," although we tend to treat it that way, because it is part of the package of changes that have decreased the importance of marriage as a route out of the home. In this sense, leaving home as part of a cohabitation or a one-parent family, like leaving home for school or the military, to take a job, or to be independent, is nontraditional family living. Hence, when we describe the decline in marriage as a route out of the home as part of the growth in nonfamily living, we are not totally correct. Viewing the data in Figure 2.3, with its divisions of marriage, the two semiautonomous routes, and the three full independence routes, obscures the changes in family living.

Many argue that the growth of cohabitation in young adulthood is simply a substitute for marriage, not really different, or at least, not really nonfamily. We understand these new forms of family living as very different from marriage (with very different rates of returning home compared with those who leave home in conjunction with marriage, as we will document in Chapter 3). In response to this concern, however, we have reorganized the data in Figure 2.3 to highlight changes in "true" nonfamily living (Figure 2.5). This makes it clear that even including these forms of nontraditional family formation with marriage, there has been a growth of leaving home via nonfamily pathways.

Leaving home to truly nonfamily living arrangements, of course, is not new. Some people of all ages reported "independence" as the reason they left home, but it has moved from being an extremely marginal route (10 percent or less) to a dominant position. Leaving home just to be independent or to start a nontraditional family accounted for over 30 percent of the nest-leaving cohorts of the 1970s and almost 40 percent of the nest-leaving cohorts of the 1980s. The growth of these two routes—independence and nontraditional family formation—has revolutionized the leaving-home process for those neither getting married nor taking an intermediate route. Until the late 1930s, the most important route out of the home when not in conjunction with getting married was to find a job, and this was true for men and women (data not presented).

When young people left home before marriage in the 1920s and 1930s, it was probably because their parents did not live in an area where they could find jobs. The 1920s saw a major move from rural and farm areas (as well as from places outside of the United States) to the expanding cities of America. These industrializing cities were characterized by new developing employment opportunities. In some cases, undoubtedly, whole families made this move. But

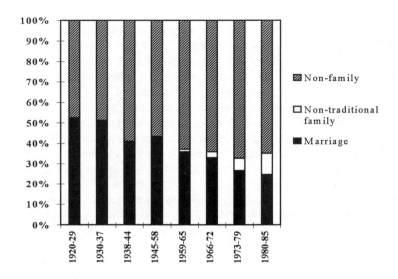

Nestleaving cohort (year reached age 18)

Figure 2.5. Family Versus Nonfamily Routes Out of the Home
SOURCE: Calculated by the authors from the NSFH.

most of the time, young people left the farms and small towns of rural America on their own, often by leaving home for the first time.

The Great Depression of the 1930s also meant that most people found no jobs in their local areas, and many left to go elsewhere, simply because they did not yet know that there were few jobs anywhere else. Hence, the story of these two nest-leaving cohorts is one of economic change forcing or pushing young people to leave home, because the best jobs required migration away from parents. Like leaving home for marriage, however, this pathway has faded continuously over the century.

The need to find a job is simply not the way young adults in the post-World War II world construct their first move away from home, if it is not in conjunction with such obvious reasons as marriage, school, or the military. They define their leaving the parental home as an expression of adulthood; independence has become an end in itself. Most of them now live in the major metropolitan areas of the United States and can find jobs within commuting distance of home, as their parents do. Even if there is no "good reason" (such as getting married, going to school, joining the military, or finding a job), leaving the parental home to set up an independent residence has become an important transition in young adulthood in the 20th century.

HOW DID WE GET WHERE WE ARE AND WHAT'S NEXT?

So far, we have sketched in broad outline the trends over time in the timing and routes out of the home. A major decline in age at leaving home was underway throughout most of the 20th century, which has reversed in the 1970s and 1980s, driven in part by shifts in the role of marriage in the leaving-home process.

This historical account of changes in the timing of leaving home and in the routes taken out of the home leaves open the question, Why has the age at leaving home been increasing for recent cohorts when young people had been leaving home at progressively younger ages for most of the 20th century? How did we get to such a strange place in the transition to adulthood and where do we go from here? How does the story of the changing routes out of the home influence changes in timing? To pull together the pieces of the leaving home story, we did an analysis that relates timing and routes to provide a set of "risks" or probabilities of leaving home by various routes. The risk associated with a given route out of the parental home is increased both by how young those taking that route actually were when they left home as well as the proportion who took the route. The results appear in Figure 2.6, in which the likelihood of leaving home via a given route, for a given nest-leaving cohort, is compared with the situation for the Vietnam nest-leaving cohort (1966-1972), adjusted to reflect the overall importance of the given route in the constellation of routes out of the home.

The lowest odds of leaving home by any route appear for the earlier cohorts, those of the pre-1930s and the 1930s economic depression. Although dominated by marriage, even this route does not have the prominence it attained for the baby boom cohorts. Presumably, conditions during the 1930s were exacerbated by the economic depression, with jobs difficult to obtain and, hence, marriage difficult to plan. The slight increase in the military for the Depression cohort are the very late nest-leavers who were still at home at the beginning of World War II.

World War II represented a major break, with a spike in the odds of leaving home for the military that is one of the most dramatic in the figure. But things did not return to "normal," however much those returning home from war wanted them to, at least, not to the normalcy of late nest-leaving. Instead, the next several nest-leaving cohorts reaching adulthood produced echoing spikes, each based on a different route.

The baby boom cohorts, increasingly freed of the pressure to join the armed forces, generated a spike in leaving home to marriage (which remained high through the Vietnam cohort). They thereby continued the early nest-leaving of the war and in so doing changed the process of leaving home through their early marriages and childbearing. Their early nest-leaving contrasted with that of their parents, most of whom entered adulthood during the Depression.

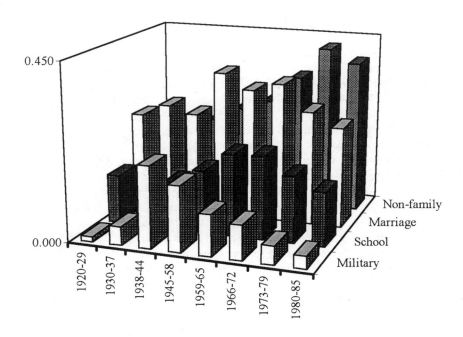

Figure 2.6. Odds of Leaving Home Via Given Route Relative to the Vietnam Cohort, Adjusted for its Share of Leaving Home
SOURCE: Calculated from Table A.2 in the appendix.

The Vietnam cohort experienced a spike in leaving home to attend school. Some of this may have reflected the need to avoid the military, which maximally affronted many of their parents and grandparents, who had served in the world wars, but it likely served as an important contribution to their eventual success as adults. It was also a time when the increasing momentum of the gender revolution increased the emphasis on individualism, magnifying their rejection of the parental generation (although the probability of leaving home to marriage remained high).

The baby bust generation of the 1970s experienced reduced risks of leaving home both to school and to marriage (and had dramatically reduced risks of leaving home to join the armed services with the ending of the draft). However, they managed to emulate the very early nest-leaving ages of their early baby boom parents by finding a new route—nonfamily living. In part, they were able to take advantage of the still relatively low housing costs of the 1970s and a willingness of their now affluent parents to provide subsidies for them to do so.

However, no new route out of the parental home emerged for the 20-somethings of the 1980s. The likelihood of leaving home to marriage, school, and the military continued to decline. For the first time, the odds of leaving home to nonfamily living also began to decline. Even more than the baby bust nest-leaving cohort, those entering adulthood in the mid-1980s are characterized by marriage delays and poor economic prospects. Furthermore, despite the increased need for higher education to succeed in the labor market, the costs of college attendance and decreased federal subsidies have depressed this route to a financially more secure adulthood. It may also be that their parents are less willing to subsidize their leaving to college. This generation of parents became the leading edge of the divorce revolution in the late 1960s and 1970s, which greatly reduces the access young people have to their parents' educational subsidies.

As a result, this generation has no "call" to leave home, not to the armed services via the draft, certainly not to marriage, and increasingly not to go to college away from home, at least, not right away. At the same time, there may be a strong economic "push" to remain home, given the difficulties young adults of the late 1970s and 1980s have experienced in a difficult job market, together with the enormous increase in the costs of housing. In many ways, they have experienced a return to conditions during the economic depression, although this cohort has much more affluent parents than did the cohort that confronted young adulthood in the economic depression of the 1930s.

This emerging pattern provides contemporary young adults with a stronger family "safety net," because their parents usually do not share their levels of poverty and unemployment (and have housing costs based on interest rates of a distant time). It also places the age at leaving home in a more consistent position in the transition to adulthood. The declining age at leaving home had always seemed anomalous, given the large number of other changes that have been serving to delay young people's readiness for full adult roles, most notably the increased importance of education. Economic changes in the last decades of the 20th century have intensified the long-term importance of higher education, making college attendance increasingly necessary. As a result, full economic "adulthood" has been delayed well beyond its legal attainment.

It is not always clear, however, that parents fully appreciate the importance of delaying when their children leave home. Instead, many parents (and the popular press) expect them to leave home very young, as they themselves did during the baby boom. These parents also bore their children in the 1960s, just before the baby bust of the 1970s, too late to join their friends by having fewer children. They may be anxious to reduce their "fertility," their burden of parenthood, at the other end of childhood, having missed the chance to delay or even prevent their birth. Amid these conflicting pressures, young adults of the 20-something cohort have often had to choose between remaining home (and finding themselves in generational conflict) and taking a step into unknown and fragile situations of independence based on dead-end and temporary jobs and insecure relationships. And not surprisingly, as we will document in the next chapter, this evidently means that they are increasing likely to return to their parents' home, when money runs out or relationships falter.

NOTES

1. For details on these data see our discussion in the appendix.

2. This category also included immigrants whose reason for leaving home was to move to the United States, as well as a small group who joined the Civilian Conservation Corps during the Depression.

CHAPTER 3

Back to the Nest

Leaving home is a fundamental life course transition, but it is nevertheless highly volatile. It is unlike men's work-related transition, which is typically portrayed as a transformation from student to full-time worker that lasts until retirement or death, and unlike women's transition to motherhood, which lasts at least until the children are grown. The dimension of the transition to adulthood that involves moving out of the parental home rarely has this durable character. Many who leave come back to live in their parental home.

PREVIOUS RESEARCH ON RETURNING TO THE NEST

Although "How many return?" is frequently asked by journalists (and parents), the answers have been few and far between. Only a small number of studies have assessed rates of returning home, and their results are not very satisfying. The nest-leaving process is highly variable as well as volatile so that studies are affected strongly by the ages of those considered, the time and place, who answers the questions (because parents will often not define the living arrangements situation the same way their children do), and even the definition of leaving home itself. If "leaving home" requires only going away to live for as little as one month, the vast majority return (more than 70 percent), because such a definition will capture not only major residential moves but also extended sojourns traveling or even being away at camp (Goldscheider, Thornton, and Young-DeMarco 1993). Taking an extreme position and counting only the "last" time young adults leave their parents' home as "true" nest-leaving, as some studies do (Ravanera, Rajulton, and Burch 1995), means that no one would return.

Unfortunately, the few studies available have varied so much in how these fundamental issues are defined that a wide variety of answers have been offered. In the United States, about 12 percent of the members of the high school class of 1972 who left home during the 1970s were living at home two years after they were observed to be living away (DaVanzo and Goldscheider 1990), compared with 28 percent returning for a cohort that reached age 18 in 1979 (Goldscheider, Thornton, and Young-DeMarco 1993). The level of returning was even higher in a study of Australia (41 percent), which examined nest-leaving from the late 1960s to the early 1980s (Young 1987).

It is difficult to give an overall answer to the question How many return? from studies like these. There is no way to piece their results together to compare either countries (is the United States different from Australia?) or time period to answer the question, Has returning home increased? The two American studies noted above could be interpreted as showing a dramatic increase in returning home between the 1970s and the 1980s, but the differences are likely to result from fundamental differences in research design. The earlier study covered a wider range of ages (through age 27), whereas the later one ended at age 23. As we will document, rates of returning home normally decline with age. Furthermore, the earlier study could not observe intermediate, short returns; it could only measure whether, two years later, those living away from home were again living at home. The latter study was based on a life history calendar that captured every intermediate transition. The high levels measured for Australia also resulted from allowing the inclusion of every leave and return and extended the possibility of returning home as late as age 34.

Two studies have attempted to measure changing rates of return with (nearly) comparable data, and each has reached the same conclusion: There has been at least some increase in the rate of returning home. In a preliminary analysis of the National Survey of Families and Households (NSFH) data, the primary source of the evidence we present in this book, we found an overall increase from 22 percent to 40 percent in returning home between those reaching adulthood before World War II and those who did so in the 1980s (Goldscheider and Goldscheider 1994b). Young has estimated an increase in returning home for Australia from 34 percent to 56 percent between the cohorts who reached age 18 between 1965 and 1969 and those who did so 10 years later. The public perception that young adults have recently become more likely to return home appears to be correct.

It is difficult to interpret increasing rates of returning home because there is considerable confusion about why young adults return home at all. Some point to the economy. Young people often have difficulty establishing a secure economic niche as the "last hired, first fired." This view of returning home views it as an indicator of "failure" in the transition to economic independence. This explanation is reinforced when we consider the increase in returning home. Since the labor market has been changing with the growth of high turnover "lousy jobs" (Burtless 1990), the transition out of the parental home appears to have become financially more precarious. Others suggest that marital dissolution is a major contributor to the rates of returning home and that the rise in divorce among young couples is the major link to increases in returning home (e.g., Jayakody 1996). It follows that young people who left home to take a job or to get married may have become more likely to return home over time as their jobs and marriages have become more unstable.

There is also considerable speculation that the behavior of the "boomerang age" (Riche 1990) may reflect a general refusal on the part of many young people to "grow up," increasing the tendency either to remain in the parental home for a longer period of time or to exhibit a "returning young-adult syndrome" (Schnaiberg and Goldenberg 1989). This would imply that there should have been a decrease in young adults' interest in independence as a reason for leaving home. We have already documented that this is not the case; "independence" has become a much more important route out of the home (Chapter 2). Such independence, however, may have become less highly valued as it became less rare so that those who did leave for this reason might have been increasingly likely to return when the going got rough.

Many other factors could affect the likelihood of returning home, and many of these have also been changing over the 20th century. For example, there have been great increases in affluence. Increases in affluence might affect the likelihood that young adults return home in two very different ways. On the one hand, increased affluence might have increased returning home, because it has made the parental home more attractive for young people to return to. Returning home among those raised in the affluence of the 1950s and 1960s should therefore be higher than for those whose parents were struggling with the rigors of the Great Depression of the 1930s. On the other hand, increased affluence could have made it easier for parents to subsidize their children's independence, decreasing the odds of returning home.

The other great changes of the 20th century reshaping the relationships between parents and children in the home and between men and women in the homes young adults might form—family structure, secularization, and gender, as well as the great transformations associated with race and ethnicity—may also have had strong effects. In subsequent chapters, we will examine these in detail. Our approach in this chapter is to investigate changes over time in returning home, focusing on the nest-leaving process itself (controlling for changes in these other factors).

The links between changes in leaving home and in returning home should be strong because research has shown that returning home is more likely among those who left home at a young age or who left home for reasons other than marriage (DaVanzo and Goldscheider 1990; Young 1987). We have documented both processes for the United States over the 20th century: (1) a reduction in the age that young people leave home that has only partially been reversed and (2) an increase in leaving home for reasons other than marriage (Chapter 2).

These considerations point to the need to investigate trends in returning home in the context of changes in the timing of leaving home and in the paths out of the parental home. In particular, we shall consider the extent to which returning home reflects the increase in leaving home for reasons other than marriage and how much can be attributed to the changed ages at which young people leave home. With these issues clarified, we will then be better able to estimate how much variation in rates of return result from other changes in the home and in family patterns, in the relationships between parents and in the relationships between parents and children, and in the general importance of leaving home in the transition to adulthood.

The information obtained by the NSFH allows us to address all of these issues. We will first examine the determinants of returning home, to establish who is likely to return home and to what kinds of homes they are returning. We will then turn to an analysis of change, and ask, How new is the increase in returning home? Specifically, how is returning home connected to changes in the timing of leaving home and the changing routes out of the home, particularly the increase in leaving home for reasons other than getting married? Examining these issues brings us closer to systematically documenting changes in returning home and understanding its changing contexts.

UNDERSTANDING RETURNING HOME

We begin our analysis by investigating which factors do—and which do not—influence whether young adults who have already left home for more than four months return, once other factors are controlled in our multivariate models. These models include measures of the respondents' gender, ethnicity, and U.S. birth; their parental social class (education) and family structure, and the circumstances (age and reason) under which they left home. Our analysis is based on the questions included in the NSFH of adults of all ages about when adults left home, the reasons they gave for leaving home, and if they had ever returned to the parental home after living away for more than four months.

Although information was also collected on reasons for returning home, we use those linked with leaving for two reasons. First, the reasons given for returning were more ambiguous than those for leaving, including "wanted to come home" (142 cases), "my parents wanted me to" (31 cases), "had no choice (25 cases), or just "moved home" (14 cases). Second, our theoretical interest is in the link between the increase in returning home and the changing routes out of the home.

Nevertheless, using reasons for leaving approximates closely the results that would be obtained if we had used reasons for returning. Of those who reported divorce or separation as their reason for returning home, 82 percent had left for marriage. Of those who gave school-related reasons for returning home, 88 percent were coded as having left for school (compared with 28 percent of all returnees who left for school), and of those who gave military reasons for returning home, 91 percent had left home to join the military. The connection was still quite high among those who gave job-related reasons for returning home. For this group, only 44 percent had actually left home for job, but another 34 percent had left for marriage, and most of this group reported that they came home because their spouse's job required a separation, most of which was military related.

Although the data collected allowed up to three returns home after leaving, only 6 percent of those who ever left home returned home a second time (24 percent of those who had returned once and then left). We therefore focus only on the information on first returns and the departures that preceded them. Our classification of the routes young people took out of the parental home differs slightly from that used earlier (Chapter 2), because we combined routes out of the home sharing similar characteristics. They are school, military, job, independence, and new family (combining marriage and single parenthood). We also included those who left home because of nonmarital cohabitation in the independence category rather than with those forming new families, because their likelihood of returning home was much closer to those who gave independence-related reasons. Although both cohabitation and independence show very similar trends of rapid increase, cohabitation is always a relatively small fraction of the total (less than 20 percent of each cohort, except for those reaching age 18 after 1980, for whom it was 29 percent).

Nest-leaving context has a strong affect on the likelihood of young adults returning home, but the effects of the other factors are much less consistently strong, and some of the results are quite surprising. Three factors emerge as important predictors. Each factor reduces young adults' likelihood of returning home relative to the appropriate reference groups of U.S. born non-Hispanic White males, with parents who had a high school education and maintained a stable two-parent family (Figure 3.1). It is equally important to note, however, that several factors that we assumed would be important were not large enough to attain statistical significance. The strongest factor affecting whether young adults return home is having their home in another country. Those who were born outside the United States were less than three-fifths as likely to return home as those born in the United States. We do not know whether their parents came with them, but presumably, many did not, making a return much more difficult. (It is also likely that many who did return to parents living in another country did not subsequently come back to the United States to be included in the survey, leading to an underestimate of returning in this group.)

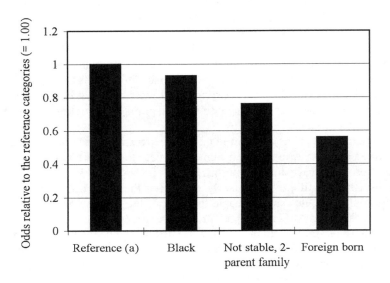

(a)   Reference group: Non-Hispanic whites for "black"; stable, 2-parent families for
"not-stable, 2-parent family"; and U.S. born for "foreign born."

Figure 3.1. Major Factors Affecting Returning Home
SOURCE: Calculated from Table A.3 in the appendix.

Those who did not grow up in a stable two-parent family seem to have found their parental homes nearly as inaccessible as did the foreign-born. Most of this group experienced one or more family changes, primarily parental separation and remarriage. We will examine this effect in more detail (Chapter 6) to investigate which types of childhood experiences affect the nest-leaving process and how, examining the timing of leaving home and the routes taken and whether changes in family structure occur in adolescence or younger in childhood.

Even at the basic level we examine here, the data show that not having a stable, two-parent family has a powerful effect on returning home, reducing the odds to barely three-quarters of those who did not have this experience. Remarried couples often have difficulties over their unequal relationship with their children that are resolved either by divorce or the early nest-leaving of the children (White and Booth 1985). These results suggest that reconstituted families may continue to create problems for those children later on, when conditions arise that would be improved by a return home. The effect of family structure on returning home should be contrasted with the noneffect of parental social class. The social class of parents appears to have no effect on returning home, despite the widespread theorizing about the powerful lure of the comforts of home (e.g., Schnaiberg and Goldenberg 1989; Bianchi 1987). Evidently, what "attracts" young adults to return home is not the material resources their parents might provide but the social and emotional atmosphere; for young adults as for others, these are the real comforts of coming home.

Like parental resources and family structure, there are some differences by ethnicity. Blacks are somewhat less likely to return home than non-Hispanic Whites, but Hispanics do not differ significantly from non-Hispanic Whites. The Black-White difference is not great, however: Blacks are about 92 percent as likely to return as those in the other two groups. Although there are some greater ethnic differences in returning home from various pathways, even this overall difference becomes statistically not significant under more detailed specifications (Chapter 9).

This is also the case for gender (Chapter 7). Young men and women do not differ in their overall likelihood of returning home, once other factors, particularly age and reason for leaving home, are controlled. There are, however, greater gender differences in leaving home and in returning home from different routes. Women are much less likely to return home than men overall, primarily because women have been much more likely than men to leave home for marriage over the 20th century. As we shall document, rates of return are lowest for this route out of the home.

THE LEAVING HOME-RETURNING HOME CONNECTION

Consistent with other studies, our research shows a close connection between patterns of leaving home and returning home (DaVanzo and Goldscheider 1990; Goldscheider and Goldscheider 1994b; Goldscheider, Thornton, and Young-DeMarco 1993; Jayakody 1996; Young 1987). Because leaving home usually takes place during late adolescence, before many young adults have finished their education or had much experience in adult economic or social roles, it is not surprising that those who leave home at a younger age are considerably more likely to return. The route taken also implies different futures and different degrees of planning for those futures. When leaving home occurs in the context of getting married and any return home is likely to have been unanticipated, it is not surprising that this route has the lowest probability of a return. In contrast, many of those leaving home for temporary conditions such as schooling or service in the military probably hoped to return (safely) and did not view their stint away from home as a "life course transition" at all. How large are these differences? There is a clear negative relationship between the age young adults left home and the proportion who return (Figure 3.2). More than 40 percent of those leaving home at age 18 or younger return home, with only a slight falling off to about 37 percent among those leaving at age 19 or 20. The proportion returning home drops below about 30 percent for those who left at age 21 or 22 and below 25 percent for those leaving at age 23 or 24, with continued reductions for the few who left in their mid- or late 20s.[1]

There are also large differences in the likelihood of returning by route taken out of the home, with most routes varying substantially from each other. It is clear that people who left home to get married had decisively lower rates of returning home than any other route (Figure 3.3). They were only half as likely to return to live with their parents for four months or more than those who left home to attend school (the reference category). There were no differences between those who left to attend school and those who left either just to be independent or to establish a nontraditional family. (Most of those were single parents but some were cohabiting.) Those who left to take a job were somewhat more likely to return than those who left for school (15 percent). The least permanent route, however, was leaving home to join the military. Those who left home to serve in the military (and survived to be interviewed in the NSFH) had about 50 percent greater relative odds of returning home than those who went away to school.

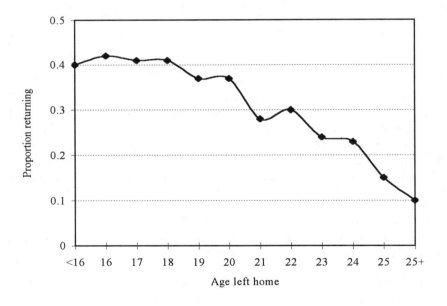

Figure 3.2. Proportion Returning Home, by Age Left Home
SOURCE: Calculated by the authors from the NSFH.

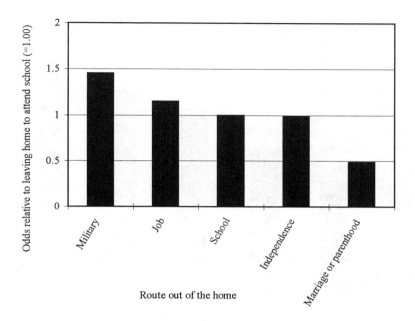

Figure 3.3. Relative Odds of Returning Home by Route Taken
SOURCE: Calculated from Table A.3 in the appendix.

These differences in returning home by route taken actually combine two phenomena: How likely people are to return at all (at any duration after leaving) and how long they stayed away. In most cases, these two phenomena work in concert. However, the two semiautonomous routes—college and the military—operate differently, reflecting the fact that they tend to have built-in "finishing" times.

The case of the military is the most dramatic. In these data, those who reported that they returned after leaving home to join the armed services stayed away longer than any category of returnees, with a median duration away from home of 3.5 years, even though overall, they had the highest likelihood of return (Figure 3.4). Hence, their relative odds of returning home understate the proportions who actually return. They stay away for quite a while but then are very likely to return (58 percent). Evidently, the experience of living in a military base, often far from home, provides less opportunity to establish a separate residence after military service than the towns adjacent to residential colleges. In turn, the latter is a no more (in) secure route out of the home than the kinds of employment young people find in early adulthood or the uncommitted relationships with lovers and friends common at this age.

A similar pattern, although much less dramatic, occurs for the school inde-

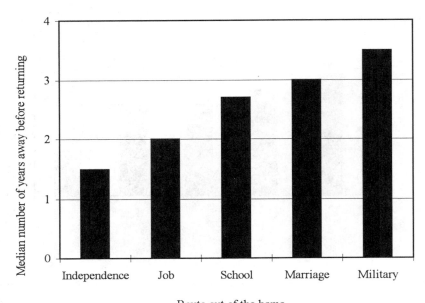

Figure 3.4. Median Duration Away from Home among Those Who Returned
by the Route Left
SOURCE: Calculated by the authors from the NSFH.

pendence comparison. Although the relative odds of returning home for those who took these two routes are the same, this arises because those who go away to school remain away from home considerably longer than do those who left to be independent but were more likely to eventually return. School leavers who returned home had been away for a median duration of 2.7 years, compared with only 1.5 years for those who left for independence, the route with the shortest average duration away. The eventual proportion who returned, however, was greater for school leavers than for those who left to be independent (45 percent vs. 39 percent, respectively).

Overall, then, it appears that there could be a close connection between changes in patterns of leaving home and those in returning home. Because young people leave the parental home over a relatively brief age range—mostly between ages 17 and 22—and the rates of returning home are reduced by nearly half between the youngest and oldest of these ages, the decline in age at leaving home (which has only been partially reversed) could have had a strong effect on the likelihood of returning home. Furthermore, the big differences in the rate of return between those who left home for marriage and those who left home for independence, and the great shifts between these two reasons for leaving home that have occurred over the 20th century, could also have made contribution. We now turn to these questions directly and ascertain how much change there really has been in returning home and when it occurred.

INCREASES IN RETURNING HOME: CONNECTIONS TO ROUTES OUT OF THE HOME

How has the likelihood of returning home changed over time? There has been a clear increase in the proportion who returned home with each younger nest-leaving cohort (Figure 3.5). The cohort that came of age prior to the Great Depression of the 1930s had odds of returning home for four months or more about half the level of the Vietnam cohort (who reached age 18 between 1966 and 1972). In contrast, the most recent cohort that has had sufficient time to leave and return home was 5 percent more likely to return home.[2]

Translating these relative odds into proportions reveals that the percentage returning home has increased from barely 20 percent in the oldest cohort to

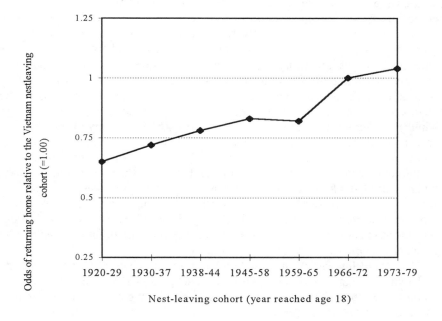

Figure 3.5. Odds of Returning Home, by Nest-Leaving Cohort
SOURCE: Calculated from Table A.3 in the appendix.

more than 40 percent. Much of the increase, however, occurred by the cohort reaching adulthood about the time of World War II (to 34 percent), with very small increases for the next two nest-leaving cohorts (those reaching age 18 between 1945 and 1965). There was a major jump in the odds of returning home for the Vietnam cohort, who came of age between 1966 and 1972, but that level has held steady since then. The increase in returning home for the 1973 to 1979 nest-leaving cohort was not statistically significant. The public perception of increases in returning home, which was not expressed until the late 1980s, was actually well behind the changes in actual behavior.

Thus, there has been a dramatic increase over time in rates of returning home over the 20th century. Much of the change occurred between the 1920s and World War II, with less change in the more recent decades, which was also the period of the major decline in age at leaving home. How much of the increase in returning home is the result of changes in the leaving-home process itself, resulting either from the overall decline in age at leaving home or from the decline in marriage as a route out of the home? How much does it reflect the increase in the fragility of marriage and, hence, in the relationships between men and women? How much of the increase reflects a change in the relationships between parents and children, as they negotiate the tenuous stages of "independence" in young adulthood?

Perhaps these factors are relatively unimportant. The increase in returning home and its connections to leaving home may reflect other factors that are more likely to leave home at an early age to attend college and have a relatively attractive home to return to (Bianchi 1987). This may be particularly important because educational levels have been increasing over time. In contrast, some factors might mask the link between leaving and returning home. Young adults growing up in nontraditional families may be very likely to leave home early and unlikely to return home, and such families are increasing.

Hence, our first question is, How does controlling for changes in background factors (parental education and family structure, ethnicity, and ethnic origin) and for changes in nest-leaving pattern (age of leaving home and the route taken) influence the overall trend in returning home? Is much of the trend in returning home is the result of these changes? Our analysis indicates that we were correct to expect that these factors would be influential, although much of the upward trend remains (Figure 3.6).

The solid line shows the simple relationship between nest-leaving cohort and returning home, with no controls for background factors or nest-leaving pattern. We then show a line that includes only background controls for the other factors whose changes have been reshaping young adulthood in the United States in the 20th century. These factors have a small effect on reducing the rate of increase in returning home, primarily by raising the predicted level of returning home for the first four nest-leaving cohorts. For these early cohorts, there was a high proportion of foreign-born. For them, once the lower

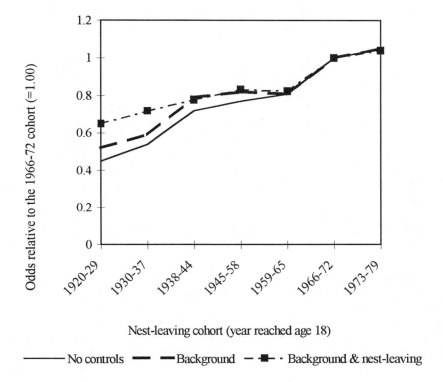

Figure 3.6. Effects of Controlling Background Characteristics and Nest-Leaving Pattern on the Odds of Returning Home
SOURCE: Calculated by the authors from the NSFH.

rate of returning home of immigrants is controlled, the overall level of returning home increases.

The third line shows the predicted odds of returning home adding the two nest-leaving measures (age at leaving home and route taken out of the home). These have a strong effect, as well, although their total effect is concentrated in the two oldest cohorts. This result suggests that the major effect of changes in leaving home on changes in returning home is due to the significantly older ages at leaving home of the cohorts who came of age during the Great Depression and earlier. Because the age at leaving home was already very low for the World War II cohort, the further age declines that continued until the Vietnam cohort (and that reversed thereafter) had relatively little effect.

FACTORS INFLUENCING THE INCREASING RATE OF RETURNING HOME

These patterns reflect only the additive effects of route and assume that the effect of route out of the home on returning was constant over the whole period. We know that young marriages are more likely to break up in the more recent period than earlier in this century so that changes in male-female relationships might have contributed to the recent trend in returning home. The problems young adults have been having in the job market, with the increase in "lousy jobs," may also have contributed to increases in the "failures" who return home. Furthermore, the parent-child relationship itself might have changed, if young adults who leave "just" to be independent have become more likely to return home.

We test these hypotheses to determine whether the overall increase in returning home is simply an artifact of the changes in these underlying dynamics. We do this by allowing the effects of nest-leaving cohort to vary by the route taken out of the home. (Given the concentrated years that military service was an important route, we did not test this interaction.) We present the results of two regressions that focus on change in returning home (Figure 3.7). The first regression appears as a single line, labeled "Basic I" (the highest of the four). This is simply the same pattern of "increases in returning home" over time that we documented after controls for background and nest-leaving variables had been included (Figure 3.6), except that we have "smoothed" time by using a continuous specification. The second regression appears as three lines, labeled (in descending order on the left side of the figure) "Basic II," "Independence," and "Marriage."[3]

The lines for the second regression make it clear that there have been changes in the odds of returning home for several important routes, although the basic pattern of increase remains but is considerably softened. There have been substantial increases in returning home for those who left home for marriage. Much more dramatic, however, is the increase in returning home among those who left home for independence.

What is *not* there is a line for change in the odds of returning for those who left home to take a job, because there was no significant interaction. The "lousy jobs" young adults are taking in the recent period are evidently not that much more lousy than young people took as a first job after leaving home in the past. Changes in returning home among those leaving home to take a job has not made a significant, disproportionate contribution to the overall increase in returning home. There has been an increase in returning home among those leaving for jobs, as there has been among nearly all routes taken. However, only the marriage and independence routes have increased more rapidly to a statistically significant extent.

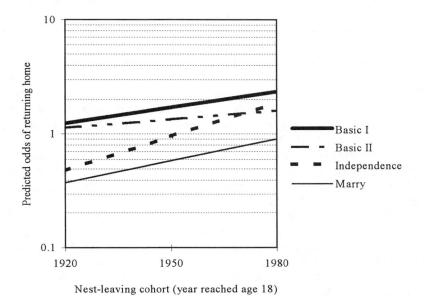

Figure 3.7. Modeling Changes in Returning Home, by Route Left
SOURCE: Calculated by the authors from the NSFH.

In contrast, increases in marital instability have contributed significantly to the likelihood of returning home, as indicated by the lowest line. This pattern shows the increase in the likelihood of returning home among those who left home to marry. This change alone accounted for nearly 20 percent of the increase in the likelihood that young adults return home. Nevertheless, the probability of returning home for those who left for marriage remains well below that of those who left home for other reasons.

The increase in the likelihood of returning home among those who reported independence-related reasons for their departure was even greater than that for marriage and contributed even more to the increase in young adults returning home. The odds of returning home for those who left just to be independent or to cohabit have increased more than three times as rapidly as the overall average (comparing the slopes of the "Independence" and "Basic II lines) and nearly twice as much as the increase in returning home among those who left for marriage (comparing the slope of the "independence" line with the "marriage" line). Among the early cohorts, those who left to be independent were little more likely to return than those who left to marry. By the most recent cohorts, those who left home to be independent were even more likely to return home than those who left to attend school.

Nevertheless, the increases in returning home from marriage and from independence are not the whole story. The slope on "Basic II," which combines those who left to attend school, serve in the military, and take a job, is increasing over time. The increase is statistically significant, although only about half as fast as when the effects of the increases in returning home from marriage and independence were included (comparing the "Basic I" and "Basic II" lines). This dimension of the parent-child relationship—that is, coming home again—appears to be changing, as the leaving-home transition has become more reversible over time. Perhaps as a product of some combination of increased need and increased willingness to do so on the part of the young adults and/or their parents, the boundaries between the parental home and the households formed by their children have become more permeable.

The likelihood of returning home for each nest-leaving route out of the parental home examined separately shows some sign of increase, with one exception. As we noted above, there has been an increase in returning home even for those who left to take a job, but it is no greater than that for school. There has been no increase over time in the odds of returning home, however, among those who left home to join the military. Young adults who left home to join the armed services have been the most likely to return home in every era of the 20th century, whether they served during years of war or peace, depression or prosperity (and whether the cohort was 98 percent male or only 90 percent male). Evidently, there is a strong normative expectation that returning home from the military requires family support in the transition to civilian life. The semiautonomy of the military, in contrast to going away to college, does not appear to provide the basis for independence from the parental home.

RETURNING HOME AND THE LIFE COURSE OF YOUNG ADULTS AND THEIR PARENTS

Returning home in young adulthood to live for more than a few months, although clearly not a new phenomenon, has increased substantially in the 20th century. It has gone from a relatively rare event to one experienced by nearly half of all those leaving home (and by their parents). The leaving-home transition has become more renewable, less a one-way street, and more like circular migration. Not only can young adults return home, it has increasingly become normative to do so. And we have shown that this return is in large part a reflection of the contexts in which they first leave their parental homes.

Our research has shown that this substantial cohort change in the life course transitions of early adulthood is linked in multiple ways to changes in the leaving-home transition itself. The long-term decline in age at leaving home made a contribution to the increase in returning early in the century, because those who leave home at a young age are more likely to return. With the rise in age at leaving home of the past two decades, however, age at leaving home is not a key factor in accounting for the most recent increase in returning home. More important in the recent period has been the increase in alternatives to marriage as a route out of the home. Leaving to attend school, take a job, or just to be independent all have higher probabilities of returning home than leaving to get married. Young adults have increasingly been leaving home to cohabit or simply to be independent. These routes have become even more reversible in the last decades of the 20th century.

We had expected that with the rise in divorce, marriage itself would be an increasingly precarious route out of the home. This is indeed the case, but it contributed relatively little to the overall increase in returning home. We also had expected that leaving home to take a job might have become more precarious as well, based on the argument that the jobs young adults first take when they leave home have increasingly become lousy jobs. However, we found no disproportionate increase over time in the probability of returning home for those who left home via this route. The route that has made the greatest contribution to the increase in returning home is not tied to any of the "normal" life course events of getting married or taking a job. Instead, the increase in returning home is almost a "just because" reason—leaving home to be independent. Independence apparently has become enough of a reason for leaving home early, as young adults have increasingly defined the end of high school as the latest one should remain residentially dependent. Their parents, the first cohort that had themselves left home at very young ages during World War II and the baby boom, apparently have agreed.

How then should we understand this most recent reversal in the complex set of behaviors involving households and families? The constellation of family changes that began in all the industrialized countries in the 1960s and 1970s has been called "antifamily," based on its combination of late and nonmarriage, cohabitation, out-of-wedlock childbearing and single parenting, and nonfamily living early (and later) in adulthood. Some describe recent cohorts in terms of "postmaterialism" and the emergence of "higher-order needs" for self-fulfillment and individual autonomy, rooted in increased affluence and continued secularization (Lesthaeghe 1988; Lesthaeghe and Meekers 1986).

The fact that young people who left home to be independent can now return home if necessary, however, appears to be a "pro-family" change. Earlier in the 20th century, the only "good" reasons to leave home were those approved and often controlled by parents—that is, marriage, jobs, education, and military service. It was therefore easier for young adults to return home, if necessary. Young adults who did not have a good reason, who just wanted to be independent, could not count on the welcome of the "prodigal son" (or daughter) and, indeed, rarely returned home. By the end of the 20th century, however, young adults could make forays into independence and know that the parental home still served as insurance, a "safety net."

Perhaps as parents' lives extend, increasing their joint survival with their children, particularly when both generations are adults, their relationships may take on a more egalitarian and elastic, flexible character. Exchanges of support may increasingly respond to particular situations rather than to a rigid life course schedule or to overwhelming disasters. It is ironic, however, that not long after the first demographic transition (the declines in mortality and fertility) created the possibility for adults to experience an extended empty-nest period late in their lives, the nest is being refilled by young adults returning home. The family in this second demographic transition is thereby being reconfigured and redefined.

Young adults return home to live with parents who are less familiar than their children with this "backward" transition. But not all that unfamiliar: a substantial proportion of young people have returned home throughout most of the 20th century. Even among the earliest nest-leaving cohorts, nearly one-fourth returned home to live at some point after leaving. Thus, an increasing proportion of contemporary young adults are returning home to parents who themselves have had the experience of returning home. Evidently the meaning of leaving home "to live in my own place" has changed dramatically over the 20th century, at least in terms of its link to returning home. Earlier in the century, it seems to have meant "if you leave my roof, don't come back"; simple independence for no obvious reason occurred only in situations of great friction—or it generated friction. Parents evidently increasingly agree with (and support) the idea that young people should leave home to have their own place, even when there is no obvious reason. Few intergenerational rifts result over this reason for leaving home. Under these circumstances, the need for independence appears to be cancelable if something doesn't work out. Young adults can (and do) come home again from "independence" as do those leaving for any (other) short-term purpose. And parents increasingly are leaving the door open, because they know what it is like to have the option of returning home.

NOTES

1. There is a somewhat puzzling irregularity in the relationship with age. Those who left home at ages that are odd numbers (17, 19, 21, 23) are somewhat less likely to return home than those who left home at even ages (16, 18, 20, 22, 24). This appears to be some sort of digit preference. We know from other evidence that there was a tendency in these data to round down the ages at leaving home, making it appear that respondents left home at an earlier age than they did (Goldscheider, Biddlecom, and St. Clair 1994). This would suggest that those who left home at an even age were rounding their ages down to an odd age (e.g., from 20 to 19) so that return rates for 19-year-olds

were depressed by the presence of some who were actually age 20 when they left home; those who left home at an odd numbered age were less likely to round their ages down,

2.   The nest-leaving cohort of the 1980s were 30 percent more likely to return home.   However, we consider this level to be exaggerated.   This cohort was still very young at the survey date so that returnees disproportionately represented very early nest-leavers who have a higher rate of returning home.

3. "Basic II" is actually plotted for school (the reference category in the regression), but neither the slopes nor the intercept values for "job" differed significantly from those for school.   It does not include the higher intercept value of "military."   There are no substantive differences in any of the other effects between these two models.   Race, class, and gender continue to have no important effects, once parental family structure, age, and route of leaving home are taken into account.

CHAPTER 4

Runaways and Stay-at-Homes

As the 20th turns toward the 21st century, people concerned about the age when young adults leave home as a *problem* in our society are most likely to think about delayed nest-leaving—those who stay home "too long." When the question reaches the popular press, the focus is always on the "shocking" proportions of 23-year-olds, or 27-year-olds, who are living in the parental home.[1] They are sometimes referred to as "Peter Pans" because they "won't grow up." Scholars have taken much the same approach, referring to staying at home as a "young adult syndrome" (Schnaiberg and Goldenberg 1989) and using titles for their studies such as "Still in the Nest" (Cherlin, Scabini, and Rossi 1997b), "Adult Children: A Source of Stress for Elderly Couple's Marriages?" (Suitor and Pillemer 1987), "The Cluttered Nest" (Boyd and Pryor 1989), and "Will the Children Ever Leave" (Ward and Spitze 1996).

The focus of this concern would be very surprising to the scholars who thought and wrote about unusual patterns of leaving home in the 1950s and 1960s. For them, the concern was about leaving home *too early*. They studied what they called "runaways" or, sometimes, "throwaways." These authors were mostly social workers and psychologists who interviewed and reported on samples of teenagers living in various forms of temporary, congregate living quarters, such as homeless shelters. (For reviews of the literature of this period, see Brenton 1978; Christie 1997; and Payne 1995.) These young people who left home at an early age were the social problem. There was no concern at that time with those who might stay in the parental home "too long."

It was never clear what the source was of this interest in leaving home too early. Were there more young people leaving home very early during that period, which then declined later in the century? Did the problem end because few social programs after that period included funds for research? Or was there a fundamental frustration with the scientific problems of such research? Such studies provide no information on the population at risk to run away. There is no way to know whether the fact that many runaways came from broken homes, poverty backgrounds, or particular disadvantaged racial minorities means that marital breakup, minority status, or poverty increases the likelihood of running away (i.e., many children from broken, poor, or minority homes do *not* run away). Nevertheless, the interest died and was buried so deeply that when early studies of leaving home first emerged, primarily in the 1980s (as we discussed in Chapter 1), the view taken by most researchers was that leaving home was a healthy sign of increasing adult status and independence; there was never any concern expressed about leaving home "too soon."

The National Survey of Families and Households (NSFH) data we analyze allow us for the first time to answer questions about who leaves home at relatively young ages—or at relatively old ages. We can establish the factors associated with leaving home very early—or very late. These results should inform us which is the relatively more problematic nest-leaving pattern: leaving home at very young ages or staying home until an older age.

EARLY VERSUS LATE NEST-LEAVING

Why might young people remain in the parental home well past the time they have become adults in the eyes of the law (usually age 18), and why is this of such concern? We have already noted (Chapter 1) that nest-leaving among young adults has been viewed in much of the research literature as a beneficial response to the long-term growth in economic resources, increasing privacy for adjacent generations (Michael, Fuchs, and Scott 1980; Goldscheider and Goldscheider 1987). As an area of family study, leaving the parental home is thus a celebration of increasing independence and a sign of social adulthood. Nest-leaving is rarely framed in the larger context of the ways family members are *interdependent*, supporting and receiving support from each other. The increasing link between separating from the parental home and becoming an "adult" has reinforced the sense that anything that speeds the process is beneficial. Even as a response to problematic family relationships resulting from changes in family structure, leaving home at a young age has been viewed as the result of the earlier development of "a sense of self as separate from family, thus making it easier for children to initiate the transition to independence" (Aquilino 1991:1009).

Late nest-leaving, then, becomes associated with the "postponement of adulthood" among young persons and the delay in the transition to the empty nest of their parents. Postponement of growing up and the delay in the independence that parents seem to want for their children might also be the result of the increased financial ability to provide an attractive home with private space available for children. There seems to be a general understanding that increased parental affluence has made staying home very attractive—the "feathered nest" (an issue we address in more detail in Chapter 8). This suggests that those in families with more resources will be more likely to remain at home until a later age, although it is also the case that parents with resources can subsidize independence and purchase privacy for themselves and their children. Sons might be particularly likely to remain at home. They are much less likely to contribute to the care and maintenance of the parental home than are daughters (Chapter 7). Their failure to grow up seems to be of particular concern to parents and other observers.

The enthusiasm for early nest-leaving in the recent research literature (and the public press) is prevalent despite the fact that leaving home *early* is likely to be problematic. Leaving home at a very young age, particularly when not in conjunction with attending a residential school away from home, has been shown to have a variety of negative consequences for the trajectory of young adults into successful career patterns and stable families. Many of those who leave home early miss the additional time needed to complete an academic program, to establish a base of savings, or to test a new relationship. Leaving home at an early age has been associated with lower educational attainment (White and Lacy 1997) and lower educational aspirations (Goldscheider and Goldscheider 1993). Other research has suggested that early residential independence reduces young adults' orientations toward traditional family roles, because it delays marriage and fosters less traditional attitudes toward marriage and family life (Waite, Goldscheider, and Witsberger 1986). Thus, early nest-leaving could reduce a young adult's likelihood of achieving a satisfying and supportive family life as an adult.

Furthermore, when the median age at leaving home is younger than 20, much of very early nest-leaving necessarily involves those who are *not* yet adults—those in their mid-teens. For this group, leaving home is more likely to mean dropping out of high school than losing the opportunity to graduate from college, with a severe loss of lifetime earning potential (Levy 1987). Leaving home at this pre-adult age is also likely to involve entering exploitative sexual relationships, even prostitution (Farrow et al., 1993), rather than simply reflecting the delay in the entrance to enduring, mutually supportive family relationships.

What factors might lead to such early nest-leaving? One of the strongest findings of research both in the runaway and nest-leaving traditions is that family disruption in the parental household is likely to result in leaving home early (Aquilino 1991; Brenton 1978; Goldscheider and Goldscheider 1993; Mitchell, Wister, and Burch 1989; Peron, Lapierre-Adamcyk, and Morissette 1986; Steinmetz 1987; White and Booth 1985; Zhao, Rajulton, and Ravanera 1993). In addition, analyses of runaways suggest that very young leavers are particularly likely to be girls, from poor families, and members of minority groups who are economically disadvantaged. Hence, both the research on runaways—leaving too young—and the theorizing on leaving late suggest substantial continuities in the nest-leaving process over age. Among the very young and among those who have remained home until older ages, females and those living in less affluent families should be more likely to leave home.

We analyze the data from the NSFH to document the changes over time in leaving early and leaving late. We link the timing of leaving home within the life course with specific time periods in the United States as we reconstruct the survey data to capture what happened in the past (Chapter 2). We then examine the characteristics of the early and late leavers, specifying the economic and family contexts that shape these change patterns over time.

CHANGES IN LEAVING EARLY AND LEAVING LATE

We have already described the general contours of the age pattern of leaving home, documenting the decline in age at leaving home between the 1920s and the early 1970s, followed by an increase (Chapter 2). These overall trends fit the experience of late leavers but not of early leavers. A quarter of young adults who came of age during the 1920s and 1930s remained at home until ages 23 to 24. This pattern of late nest-leaving was nearly eliminated by the mobilization of young adults during World War II and the early marriage pattern of the baby boom periods and the youth movements of the Vietnam era. Only after the Vietnam war ended (1973) did leaving at later ages begin to appear again.

Leaving home very early, however, did not follow a complementary pattern. If it had mirrored the pattern of late leaving, there would have been a great increase in early leaving during the height of the baby boom and a decline in the more recent period. This is not what happened. The proportions who left home prior to age 16 fluctuated extensively, if narrowly, between 3 and 7 percent of each cohort. These fluctuations occurred around an overall slow and gradual decline (Figure 4.1).

One of the high points of leaving at such a young age occurred during the immediate post-World War II years when nest-leaving was particularly early, suggesting consistency between the overall age trend and leaving young. Another high point appears among the oldest cohorts, however, when nest-leaving ages were quite late. During that early period, then, there was considerable heterogeneity—spread—in the ages at leaving home. In contrast, the major period of declining ages at leaving home (from the post-World War II period until the Vietnam era) was marked by declining, not increasing, proportions leaving home very early. The trend line reached the low point of barely 3 percent who left home prior to age 16 for the Vietnam nest-leaving cohort. Members of that cohort left home earlier than any cohort before or since. Hence, although many young adults left home early during this period, almost none left their parents' home *very* early. There appeared to be a great concentration in the ages that young adults left home in this nest-leaving cohort. Among the most recent cohorts, however, there has again been an increase in the heterogeneity of the ages that young adults leave home and a decrease in the concentration of ages of leaving home. Thus, even as the average ages at leaving home have been increasing, the proportions leaving home at extremely young ages have increased as well.

The trend during the post-World War II period is consistent with an economic explanation. Increased affluence during the relatively egalitarian 1960s allowed early nest-leaving among those who had reached adulthood, while protecting the most vulnerable. The reverses in this pattern during the last quarter of the 20th century have been part of the increases in economic inequality and actual declines in income for the lower 80 percent of the income distribution (Danziger and Gottschalk 1995). These economic reversals are likely to have constrained all but the poorest to remain *in* their parental home. The intense pressures that poverty puts on families located at the bottom of the economic class structure forced the youngest members out of the household at early ages. If this economic argument was the entire story, the economic depression of the 1930s does not fit. Perhaps it is not only the economic conditions but the combination of economic and family patterns that together resulted in the patterns of the 1930s (when traditional family structure was dominant). One pattern emerges clearly: when scholars of the 1950s through the 1970s were studying runaways, the phenomenon was decreasing, not increasing. For the two most recent decades, when the proportions leaving home early were increasing, the phenomenon had surprisingly passed out of

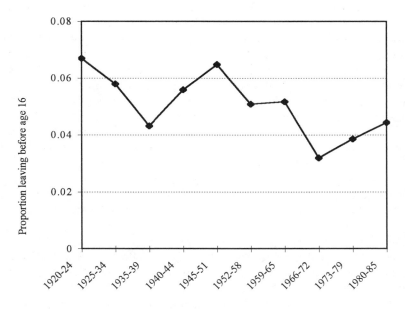

Nest-leaving cohort (year reached age 18)

Figure 4.1. Proportions Leaving Home Very Young (< 16) by Nest-Leaving Cohort
SOURCE: Calculated by the authors from the NSFH.

public concern to be replaced by a concern over young adults living in the parental home too long.

WHO LEAVES HOME EARLY AND WHO LEAVES HOME LATE?

We expected continuities in the nest-leaving process as it unfolds from the mid-teens (age 15) to the late 20s, particularly by gender and social class. Specifically, we expected daughters rather than sons to be among those who left home both at the very young ages and at older ages. We also anticipated that the poor would leave home at early and at late ages compared with the more affluent. We found some continuities over the nest-leaving process, to be sure, but there are also major differences as well. The factors that influence leaving home at an early age are often quite different from the factors associated with delayed nest-leaving. These differences portray the process at work in some quite unexpected ways.

In Table A.4 in the appendix we provide the data to answer the questions, Who leaves home early? and Who leaves home late? These data show the details of our analysis of leaving home, comparing results for all nest-leavers, for those at risk of leaving between age 15 and 16 (young), and for two groups of later leavers—those at risk of leaving between ages 23 and 25 (older) and those who remained at risk at age 25 (oldest). These results allow us to compare the factors affecting both overall leaving home and leaving for two routes—independence and marriage—for runaways and stay-at-homes. We focus on these two routes because attending college is too age-circumscribed to analyze in this way; most young adults go away to college between ages 17 and 18. Too few left home to cohabit or head a single-parent family or to enter the military to obtain estimates for separate age groups. We also do not present information on leaving home to take a job, because few consistent patterns appeared and it is unclear how to interpret leaving home to take a job among 15-year-olds.

Our focus is therefore on two critical pathways out of the home: marriage and independence. Very young marriages are quite fragile. Leaving home for independence at age 15 or 16 is too young to reasonably expect children to have established any financial basis for independence. Leaving home at such a young age to be independent appears more like running away than like a residential transition to independent adulthood. In contrast, those who leave home to get married at age 24, or at age 27, seem quite prudent, even if they (and their friends) wondered why they had not left home sooner, perhaps to be independent of parents and families.

The time pattern of leaving very young and among the oldest nest-leavers has fluctuated relatively little, suggesting major continuity in the nest-leaving process. The general pattern we described earlier (Chapter 2) characterizes only those leaving at more central ages. Thus, for example, the overall likelihood of leaving home among those in the pre-World War II cohorts (those who reached age 18 prior to 1938) was only 60 percent that of the Vietnam cohort (1959-1972). When we restrict the model to the risk of leaving between ages 15 and 16, we observe that the pre-World War II cohorts were almost exactly as likely to leave home as the Vietnam cohort (.99). Among those who remained home through age 25, the result is the same: The pre-World War II cohorts were also almost exactly as likely to leave as the Vietnam cohort (1.05). In contrast, those who had remained at home through age 22 show odds of leaving home between age 23 and 25 that fluctuate exactly like the total, indicating that they have participated in the major nest-leaving trends that affected leaving home from age 17 to age 22. Only the very youngest and very oldest nest-leavers show such great stability and are similar on this dimension. But are they similar on other dimensions? Do gender, parental resources, childhood family structure, and minority status have the same effects on leaving early and leaving late?

DO GIRLS LEAVE HOME EARLY AND BOYS STAY HOME LATE?

Are girls more likely to leave home very early, as some of the limited studies of runaways found? Are boys more likely to remain in the parental home later into adulthood enjoying the comforts of the parental home and their mother's cooking, as popular perceptions of the stay-at-homes suggest? Our results suggest that the studies of runaways may have been correct—among those at risk to leave home between ages 15 and 16, girls are 46 percent more likely to leave than boys (Figure 4.2). However, our results indicate that this pattern reflects the fact that although some girls marry at those ages, almost no boys do (resulting in an odds ratio in favor of girls of 14:1 for marriage at this age).

If more girls appeared in the children's shelters, this might also reflect the fact that for most of the century, it was easier for teenage boys than it was for girls to get legal work and to support themselves, primarily through unskilled labor. Without an income or a supportive family and with limited opportunities for work, many adolescent girls were probably forced to turn to prostitution to support themselves. (This had also become the case for adolescent boys by the end of the 20th century, with the decline in the availability of other employment.) Presumably, most of those very young married "women" would not have appeared in shelters and would not have been defined as a "social problem."

Hence, the studies of runaways were "correct" about girls being more likely than boys to leave home very early but adduced the wrong reasons for the gender pattern. What about those who remained with their parents until older ages? Are sons who have reached the age of 23—or 26—and are still living in their parents' home more likely to remain there? We find very little evidence to support this stereotype. At each age, the differences between males and females are small and insignificant. If anything, daughters are more likely than

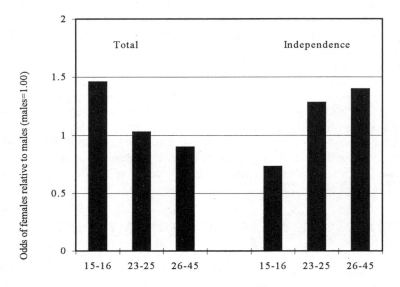

Age at which risk of leaving home is assessed

Figure 4.2. Gender Differences in Leaving Home Very Early, Later, and Very Late, Overall and for Independence
SOURCE: Calculated from Table A.4 in the appendix.

sons to remain among those still at home after age 25 (with odds only 90 percent those of males). This may reflect the fewer opportunities young women have to support themselves in the labor market. For most of this period, women who reached age 25 unmarried were much less likely to eventually marry than otherwise comparable men. Far from being cared for, daughters living in their parents' home at these later ages were doing their share, and likely more than their share, of caring for their parent(s).

When we consider leaving home just to be independent, however, the picture shifts. The data indicate that the "runaway" studies were incorrect, and perhaps the public perception of at least some stay-at-homes might be closer to the mark. Among the very young leavers, boys are much more likely than girls to leave home for this reason. Among those at risk of leaving home at a very young age, girls had less than three-quarters the odds of boys of giving this reason. In contrast, sons are conspicuously unlikely to leave home via the independence route among those at risk of leaving home after age 22. Among those living at home after this age, daughters were 30 to 40 percent more likely to remain in their parents' home compared with sons. It seems plausible that already adult sons have less need to leave their parents home to be independent.

Parents supervise their sons less than their daughters and expect sons to carry out fewer household responsibilities that interfere with their independence than they do for daughters.

THE FEATHERED NEST: PARENTAL RESOURCES AND LEAVING HOME EARLY OR LATE

Both research on runaways and the popular perception of young adults staying home to enjoy their parents' feathered nest suggest that the more resources parents have, the less likely their children will be to leave home—whether at a younger or at an older age. We will explore this issue in much more detail later (Chapter 8), with a particular focus on the role of parental resources on leaving home to attend college. Here, however, our focus will be on the ages well before, and well after, the normal ages for going away to college as a pathway out of the home.

We consider two dimensions underlying parental social class. We first measure the combined educational levels of parents. We also use a separate measure of occupational prestige ranking, which reflects the relative standing of jobs parents held when our respondents were growing up. (For more details on these measures, see Chapter 8.)

The general pattern of effects for each measure is similar. The effects for parental education are sharper, however, so we will focus our discussion on those. As the runaway theorists and social workers understood, each measure of social class shows that parental resources sharply reduce the likelihood of leaving home very young. The effect of parental resources shifts dramatically, however, over the transition to adulthood, becoming positive, not negative. This means that among those still at home at older ages, having parents with higher-ranked occupations or with more education makes them *more* likely to leave home, not less.

The magnitude of the reversal in the effects of parental education is clear, not just for overall leaving home but also for the two routes that we examined in detail (Figure 4.3). An additional year of parental education reduces the likelihood that a very young person (age 15 to 16) leaves home either for independence or for marriage. The strongest effects appear for marriage, with an odds ratio of 0.9 for each additional year of education. This means that a young person whose parents have four more years of school than do the parents of an otherwise similar friend has odds of leaving home for marriage less than three-quarters those of their friend (0.9^4). The effect is nearly as strong for leaving home for independence (with a reduction of .92 for each additional year). In short, the data show that parental resources protect strongly against leaving home very—and perhaps too—young.

The protective effect of parental resources on leaving home very young contrasts sharply with their effects on leaving home after age 22, and

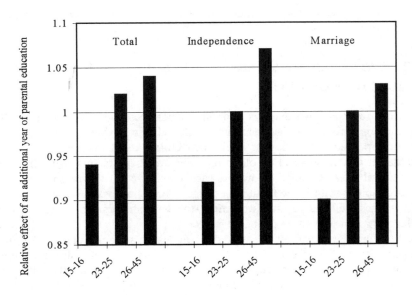

Age at which risk of leaving home is assessed

Figure 4.3. The Effect of Parental Education on Leaving Home Early and Late, Overall and for Independence and Marriage

SOURCE: Calculated from Table A.4 in the appendix.

particularly after age 25. Among those who have remained home up to these ages, the more resources parents have in terms of occupation and education, the more, not less, likely they are to leave home. The largest effect is on leaving home for independence, but there is also a strong and significant effect for leaving home in conjunction with getting married. Among those past age 25, each additional year of parental education increases the odds of leaving home to get married by 3 percent and of leaving home for independence by 7 percent.

Of course, the explanation for this pattern may simply be that the children of the more successful have more resources themselves in terms of educational credentials and job contacts, making it more feasible for them to leave home. However, it is also possible that, just as parents use their resources to protect their children as much as they can, including against early nest-leaving, they also use their resources to subsidize their children's transitions to adulthood. Over time, parental assistance may include their helping out their newly married child with gifts of furniture, a down payment on a house, and child care costs. The even stronger effect on independence than on marriage suggests that parents may also provide help with the rent of a separate apartment, providing privacy both for their children and for themselves.

We cannot separate these two possibilities with the data available, because we do not know what the respondents were earning during their nest-leaving years. However, studies of leaving home for the recent period that include measures of both parental and young adult incomes suggest that not all the effects of parental resources on their children's nest-leaving at older ages is indirect through the characteristics of their children. A significant part of the effect of parental resources is direct, suggesting that parents do subsidize their children's residential independence (Avery, Goldscheider, and Speare 1992; Whittington and Peters 1996). It is likely that the use of parental resources also characterized intergenerational support earlier in the 20th century. Whatever the mechanism, however, emerging clearly from the evidence is that parental resources are not retaining their adult children in the home. If they are contributing to their children's greater residential quality, helping them to enjoy a more richly feathered nest than they could afford on their own, they are likely to be doing so in a separate place of residence.

THE EFFECTS OF HAVING SIBLINGS ON LEAVING HOME EARLY OR LATE

In most theorizing on the effects of parental resources on their children's attainments, the concern is not only about the extent of the parents' resources but also on how many children they have among whom to divide their resources. This is sometimes called "the resource dilution hypothesis." Parental resources, both money and time, are finite. Hence, it is usually the case that the more that is given to one child, the less is available to others. This may not always be true, however. One can imagine circumstances in which those with large families spend more time with the family group as a whole, whereas those with fewer children spend more time in work or non-child-related leisure. In this case, each child actually gets more parental attention in large families than in small ones.

In addition to time and money, siblings are also likely to compete for space in the parental home, reducing privacy, not only for their parents but also for their brothers and sisters. Is the effect of siblings on leaving home (early or late) different from the effect of more direct measures of parental resources?

The data show that siblings have a strong, positive, and consistent effect on the likelihood of leaving home. The more siblings a person has, the more likely she or he is to leave home. The effects of siblings on leaving home operate almost totally consistently, whether we are considering leaving home at a young or an older age and whether we are examining the effects on the overall probability of leaving home or leaving home to independence or to get married (Figure 4.4). Because we do not know where the siblings are living, we cannot tell directly whether brothers and sisters push their siblings out (through reducing the resources in the parental home) or pull them out (perhaps by example).

Hence, when we are considering leaving home at an early age, the effects of having more siblings are consistent with having parents with fewer resources. Those with more siblings act like those whose parents have fewer resources, being more likely to leave home. At older ages, however, the effects of having more siblings are *not* consistent with the effects of parental resources on leaving home. Those with more siblings are like those with more parental resources, not less, in being more likely to leave. If parents are using their resources to encourage their older adult children to leave home, then having more children does not reduce this effect.

We think these results are consistent with a somewhat different interpretation. The parental income derived from having higher-status occupations can be used either at home or toward a separate apartment, but parental time is less easily divided across households. Furthermore, when parents have a few children or only one child, the child becomes more valuable, perhaps as companionship, for many parents (although to achieve an empty nest some might push hardest on the last child). It seems likely that when there

Figure 4.4. The Effect of Having More Siblings on Leaving Home Early, and Late, Overall and for Independence and Marriage

SOURCE: Calculated from Table A.4 in the appendix.

are few or no other siblings living at home, young adults would have relatively little need for independence, because they are more likely to be treated as another adult by their parent(s) than when there are a number of children living at home or in the vicinity.

It is also possible that by the time they are adults, some children were contributing resources to their parents' home. These contributions might include both domestic time (e.g., physical tasks and emotional support) and even earnings. In such cases, the fewer children there are among which to divide these resources, the more important the contribution of each child to the maintenance of the parental household. Hence, it might be more difficult for children with few or no siblings to leave home. Many of those whose transition to adulthood is being measured in these data grew up in a time when unmarried children felt an obligation to maintain a home for a widowed parent. A frequent theme of novels of the 1930s and 1940s was that this obligation of children to parents often resulted in intergenerational conflicts and romantic difficulties.

Our results suggest that older children who remained home may have felt constrained from leaving home for *independence* by the lack of siblings, but the romantic dilemma must have been rare, however, because they were not constrained by the number of siblings from leaving home to get married. This was the one exception in the results for siblings. Having more siblings increases the odds of leaving home for independence at each age, whether very young (ages 15 to 16), relatively older (ages 23 to 25), or even older (over age 26). In contrast, their effect on leaving home to get married was not consistent. Although the effects of siblings was positive (and at least marginally significant) for very young children and for those just past the normal nest-leaving ages, the number of siblings no longer had an effect on those who had passed age 25 and were still living at home.

Some researchers have speculated that much of the great increase in leaving home that occurred during the 1950s to 1970s period was the result of an increase in the number of siblings produced during the baby boom. Furthermore, the slowdown of nest-leaving during the 1980s followed the "baby bust" and the lower fertility of the 1970s (Pitkin and Masnick 1988). When we examined changes over time in nest-leaving, the patterns are essentially unaffected whether or not we include controls for number of siblings. Hence, changing fertility patterns and, thereby, increases in the number of siblings could have contributed extremely little to the overall trend in nest-leaving. Nevertheless, their insight was correct at the level of families: The more siblings in families, the more rapidly young adults leave home.

FAMILY STRUCTURE AND LEAVING HOME EARLY OR LATE

The results that we presented showing the effects of siblings on early and late nest-leaving raise another question: How does childhood family structure affect the timing of leaving home? In particular, does the structure of the parental family increase leaving home so young that it is essentially running away? The structure of the family, in addition to the number of siblings and the allocation of resources, is another important feature that may have implications for when young adults leave home. The literature on the problematics of early nest-leaving in the context of runaways suggests that unstable or dysfunctional families may "push" children out of the home at young ages. We have reconstructed the data in such a way as to investigate the impact of the divorce revolution. Specifically, we can explore the attendant complexities of remarriage on leaving at young and at older ages and the effects on children of those who were never married.

The data show that the experiences of growing up in nontraditional families during childhood, and particularly families involving a stepparent, normally have their strongest effects very early in the transition to adulthood. Having a stepparent sharply accelerates leaving home for those between ages 15 and 16. The increase characterizes both the paths of marriage and of independence that we have examined in detail. We shall subsequently discuss the broader effects of family structure on the other routes out of the home—and particularly its effect on *not* leaving home to attend college—as well as its effects on returning home (Chapter 6). The effect of living in any family that is not a two-parent, stable family encourages leaving home at all ages, consistent with previous research (summarized in Chapter 6). Our results, however, refine this finding and suggest that most of the increase in the odds of leaving home occurs in stepparent families (and those that involve stepsiblings). Moreover, much of the effect on nest-leaving is on leaving home at very young ages. There were no consistent effects of family structure among those leaving at later ages. Evidently, if a nontraditional family structure has not led a young adult to leave home by age 21, it does not have nearly as powerful an effect at later ages.

Adolescents whose families gained a stepparent before they were age 12 show the general pattern most clearly. For them, adding a stepparent increased their odds of leaving home to be independent by 70 percent; adding a stepparent increased the odds of leaving home to get married by 90 percent, with a drop-off after age 16 (Figure 4.5). Some part of the declining effect of acquiring a stepparent is likely to be the result of the stabilizing effects of the passage of time on the family. Within a few years, the effect on children of living in a stable reconstituted family closely resembles those living in a stable two-parent family.

The only dimension of experiencing a nontraditional family structure in childhood that is not primarily limited to relatively young potential nest-leavers is the presence of stepsiblings. Both very early nest-leaving and very late nest-leaving is increased when there is an indication that the respondent lived at some point in childhood with stepsiblings, although there is some evidence that

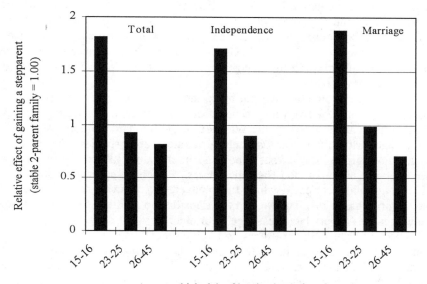

Figure 4.5. The Effect of Gaining a Stepparent Before Age 12 on Leaving Home
Early and Late, Overall and for Independence and Marriage
SOURCE: Calculated from Table A.4 in the appendix.

stepsiblings matter less at the normal ages of leaving home (Table A.4 in the
appendix). This result parallels our finding for siblings shown previously. At
all ages, those who grow up with more siblings (and evidently, with
stepsiblings as well) are more likely to leave home. It is clear from these
findings that there is more to family structure than the relationships between
parents. The presence of other children (or other young adults) in the
household has a powerful effect on the domestic scene.

MINORITY GROUP STATUS AND THE TIMING OF LEAVING HOME

Many forces affect what happens in families, both inside and outside the
front door. Ethnicity is an important source of pressure on families, normally
affecting many of the choices individuals make about their family lives. The
effect occurs because ethnicity often implies both restricted access to
opportunities and some particular family norms and preferences. Research on
runaways had suggested that minority group members—particularly American

Blacks—were likely to appear in the shelters that they were studying. Other evidence has suggested that at least in the relatively recent period, Black and Hispanic young adults are less likely to leave home than non-Hispanic whites (Goldscheider and Goldscheider 1993). We will address the question of the stability of these patterns over the 20th century in a subsequent chapter (Chapter 9). The question we pose here is, Given the discrimination faced by minority groups, are adolescents in these most vulnerable families particularly likely to leave home very early?

Our results show that far from being more likely to run away from home (leaving at ages 15 or 16), young people from both Black and Hispanic families are less likely than non-Hispanic Whites to leave the parental home at such a young age, with differences particularly marked for Hispanics (Figure 4.6). Both ethnic groups show what appears to be a simple life course pattern of leaving home later than non-Hispanic Whites. They have particularly low rates of leaving home very early, which then converge to, or even surpass, those of the majority group by a later age in the transition to adulthood. In each case, convergence is at very late ages—age 25 or older.

Hispanics are only two-thirds as likely as non-Hispanic Whites to leave home at ages 15 to 16. Among those still at home at age 23, they are only 80 percent as likely to leave. Only among those older than age 25 do we observe considerably higher rates of leaving home among Hispanics than for non-Hispanic Whites (odds ratio of 1.57). Although the same pattern appears for leaving home for independence, this pattern is most conspicuous when we consider leaving home in conjunction with marriage. Hispanics are very unlikely to marry early, despite common stereotypes. Hispanics have only half the odds of non-Hispanic Whites of leaving home to get married in their mid-teens. There is relatively little difference for those still at home after age 22 over the subsequent three years of age. There is some slight indication from the data that Hispanics are still less likely to leave home for marriage at these ages, as they are overall. After age 25, however, among those still living at home, Hispanics are 44 percent more likely to leave home for marriage than non-Hispanic Whites.

Blacks show the same pattern as Hispanics overall with lower rates of leaving home very young and eventual convergence to the White pattern at later ages. The distinctiveness of Black Americans in leaving home is greater in terms of route out of the home than life course timing. Unlike the Hispanic pattern, differences between Blacks and Whites in leaving home for independence and marriage are essentially maintained at each age. Young Black adults are more likely than non-Hispanic Whites to leave home for independence-related reasons. This is the case both among the very young (although the difference is relatively small—15 percent—and not statistically significant) and among older young adults still living in their parents' home. Furthermore, the pattern of being less likely to leave home for marriage that is most characteristic of Blacks overall is maintained at each age, although it

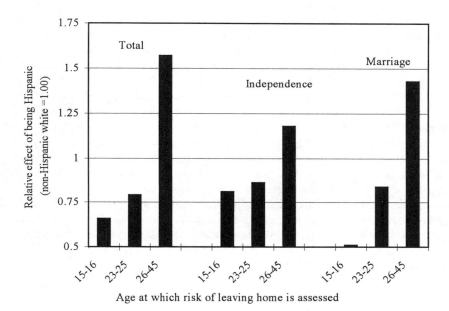

Figure 4.6. The Effects of Being Hispanic on Leaving Home Early and Late, Overall and for Independence and Marriage
SOURCE: Calculated from Table A.4 in the appendix.

attenuates over the life course. Like Hispanics, Black adolescents are only about half as likely to leave home to get married compared with non-Hispanic Whites in their mid-teens. Blacks increase only slightly thereafter, reaching 60 percent of the non-Hispanic White level at ages 23 to 25, and 70 percent of the non-Hispanic White level after age 25 (Table A.4 in the appendix).

These findings point to two important correctives in the research literature. First, the image held by many Whites that disadvantaged minority young adults leave home early, and in particular, marry at early ages, is clearly fallacious. It is non-Hispanic Whites (and as we shall document in Chapter 9, primarily non-Hispanic Whites who are Fundamentalist Protestants), who are marked by early family formation, not disadvantaged minorities.

The second point emerging from these data is that Blacks and Hispanics show quite different patterns of family distinctiveness. As we have documented, Hispanics are different from non-Hispanic Whites primarily in the timing of leaving home. They leave home at a later age than the pattern shown by non-Hispanic Whites. As a result, more Hispanics are still living at home in their mid-20s. These young adults remain part of the normal Hispanic nest-leaving process, with an open marriage market and likely few special circumstances keeping them at home. It is the non-Hispanic adults in their mid-20s, not teenagers, who are less likely to leave for marriage than Hispanics. These adults have remained at home until after their marriage market has nearly closed and at a time when most potential partners—those of the "appropriate" age and with other characteristics that make them eligible for marriage—have made other choices.

Blacks, in contrast, although somewhat slower than non-Hispanic Whites to leave home, are most distinctive in terms of the pathways they take out of the home. Black-White differences are fairly consistent among early, later, and even very late leavers. They are more likely to remain with their parents when they are quite young (they do *not* run away nearly as much as non-Hispanic Whites) as well as when they are older. The parent-child coresidential bond appears to be strong throughout at least the period of young adulthood, stronger than it is for non-Hispanic Whites. In contrast, marriage, the more committed pair-bond, appears quite weak, relative to non-Hispanic Whites (and Hispanics, who get there eventually). We shall reconsider these patterns in their historical contexts to determine when these ethnic patterns first emerged in America in a subsequent analysis (Chapter 9).

CONCLUDING OBSERVATIONS

There seems to be little concern about runaways and throwaways in the 1990s. Much more concern is expressed about the "syndrome" of those who are still in the nest at older ages, failing somehow to grow up and stressing out their parents. The evidence available suggests that this focus is badly off the mark. There has been an increase in the 1980s and 1990s of children leaving their parental home at much too early ages, often in response to what appears to be their family's abandonment of them. They appear to leave home to escape a changed or an unsupportive home. They are unlikely to find much long-term comfort in the jobs they take, the friends they make, or the families they start on their own. If anything, adolescents living in nonfamily settings become problems for themselves and their communities and are likely not to find their way to healthy relationships as their life course unfolds. In contrast, children in their mid- to late 20s living at home more often than not have the continuing support of family members. They often use the resources of the parental household to look for a job in a very changed economic market, to expand their educational training, and to learn how to live interdependently with their families.

Who is likely to runaway from families at an early age? And who is more likely to leave the parental household at a late age? The evidence that we presented suggests that girls are more likely than boys to be runaways and daughters are more likely to leave home to be independent at later ages than are their brothers. We suspect that this gender difference is strongly related to the ways in which sons and daughters are differentially raised in families, with the latter more likely to be given domestic responsibilities (like cleaning house, cooking, and caring for younger siblings) than sons. Daughters are also likely to be more controlled when living in their parents' house than are sons. Often, this means that there are fewer "costs" for sons than for daughters to remain in their parents' home and more benefits for daughters to leave home searching for the independence that their brothers have found at less cost at home.

We have also documented that having more parental resources retains younger children at home until they are more able to cope with independence whereas poverty increases the likelihood that young children leave home at early ages. Money seems to protect the young from leaving before they are ready, while facilitating the independence of children at a later age, when they are ready. For both older and younger children, then, family resources can be used to provide the support children need, either through coresidence or through subsidizing a separate residence.

If having resources strengthens a family's ability to support their children, having a functioning family that provides access to those resources is no less important. We found that experiencing some nontraditional family environment in childhood has its strongest impact extremely early in the transition to adulthood—during mid-adolescence. This is particularly the case in stepparent families. Those with a stepparent leave home at early ages; having stepsiblings results in leaving home both at very early ages and very late ages.

Having more siblings also reduces young adults' access to their parents' resources. Siblings increase the likelihood of leaving home, at early or later ages, or leaving in conjunction with marriage or to be independent. Having more siblings is similar, at least in terms of leaving home very young, to having fewer resources. The differences in their effects for later nest-leaving, however, is more puzzling. More detailed research will have to be carried out to sort out why having more resources facilitates leaving at a later age, but having more siblings not only does not offset this effect but in fact enhances it. We suspect that first and last born children may be treated differently and that the effects might differ for sons and daughters. The proximity to the parental residence where children live after they have left home and the relative age and health of parents are also likely to be important considerations in understanding how parents use their resources and the access children have to them. More research focused on these issues would be useful to clarify these complexities.

Although resources strongly shape the likelihood of leaving home early and late, values matter as well. We have no direct measures of these values, given our focus on reconstructing data for past generations. Our findings for American Black and Hispanic families, however, are consistent with the argument that some family values are able to balance the effects of poor resources on nest-leaving patterns (Chapter 9). Young people from disadvantaged minority families are *less* likely to leave home early and converge with non-Hispanic Whites only after age 25, if at all. These findings clearly challenge prevailing stereotypes about the weaknesses of disadvantaged minority families. Somehow, the values that reinforce family support of young children from these minority groups overcome the effects of pushes from economic disadvantage, albeit with different strategies. Hispanics avoid leaving home except in conjunction with marriage, whereas Blacks delay leaving, given their avoidance of marriage. It seems to us that the values that parents have are likely to play a critical role in the decisions that young adults make as they consider leaving home early or later, whether shaped by their ethnic histories or by other sources of values about the importance of supporting their children during their transition to adulthood.

NOTE

1. Many popular articles have reviewed these patterns. See, for example, Estess (1994), Gross (1991), McPhillips (1994), Perin (1995).

CHAPTER 5

The Changing Role of Regional Communities

The United States is a big country. It did not complete its current shape until the 20th century, with the consolidation of its continental identity in 1912 (when Arizona was added to the roll of states) and the later additions of Alaska and Hawaii in 1959 and 1960. The different regions of the country thus have very different histories, both in terms of their settlement with European-origin populations and in terms of their incorporation in the country as a whole.

Although the shape was pretty much set, the various regions of the country had very different experiences even in the 20th century, changing them relative to each other. During the first half of this century, the agrarian South declined economically; subsequently, the "new South" emerged in the latter half of the century. The industrial Midwest boomed during much of the century and then suffered a sharp decline so that its decaying cities were increasingly described as the "rust belt." The movement of resources, mass culture, and young and old people continued to strengthen the far West throughout the century, shining as the "sun belt" to the eyes of potential migrants, scholars, and pundits alike.

At the same time, however, the 20th century saw an enormous growth and diffusion of mass culture. It began with the creation of radio networks early in the century, took root with the national distribution of films, and then exploded with the enormous popularity of network television. The growth in mass culture produced the potential to reduce regional differences, as the adventures of the same families entered nearly every home in the country, from Luci and Desi in the 1950s to *All in the Family* in the 1970s and the Seinfeld "family" of the 1990s, to be watched at the same time and then discussed with friends, family, and fellow workers across the country the next morning.

The patterns we have described so far in leaving and returning home have been for the nation as a whole. Have these nest-leaving patterns been shaped by regional variation? How are changes in leaving and returning home linked with regional changes around the country? Some pathways out of the home, such as the rise in leaving home for independence and nontraditional family formation, have grown explosively. These trends, like other fads that have swept the country, might have been quite uneven in their initial impact. Furthermore, the major pathways out of the parental home involve going away to school, getting married, or getting a job. All of these paths out of the nest are embedded in community contexts, and thus subject to local variation.

The type of community young adults grow up in shapes the availability of educational institutions, potential marriage partners, housing, and occupational and career possibilities. Young adults with job opportunities close to home because they live in a large or booming community do not need to leave home to earn a salary nearly as much as young adults whose communities have few or appropriate economic opportunities for them. Young adults living near a range of educational institutions can continue in school while remaining at home, and thus might be less likely to leave home for this reason than those living a greater distance from such institutions. Small and economically depressed communities often have little social life for young people, either because most potential partners had to go elsewhere to find work or there were few partners to begin with, restricting the chances of finding someone to marry and create a home with.

In addition to limiting what is possible, communities also shape what is preferred in the routes taken out of the home, as in other aspects of life. One of the strongest findings of analyses of leaving home for the contemporary period is that "family values"—attitudes about the importance of remaining close to parents and of the role of marriage in adult lives—have as much affect on the nest-leaving process as measures of resources (Goldscheider and Goldscheider 1993). We have no direct measures of attitudinal changes in this study, so we depend on indirect indicators, such as religious affiliation and ethnicity (Chapters 9 and 10). Communities, however, can also serve as indirect indicators of common values. Young people are likely to be influenced by the ideas and decisions of their peers about moving out of their parent's home to be independent or go to college or to stay home until they get married. Hence, the timing of the transition to adulthood and the specific paths young people take out of their home are likely to be shaped by the communities in which they grow up for this reason as well.

We shall focus in this chapter on the *region* where young adults grew up as our indicator of the opportunities and values of the community of residence that may influence when young adults leave home and what paths they take. Although much larger than a "neighborhood," it is almost never possible to measure the latter with the data available (cf. White 1987). The National Survey of Family and Households (NSFH) data file that we use to retrospectively reconstruct nest-leaving patterns over the 20th century provided information on the region, but not the neighborhood, that young adults lived in when they were growing up.

THE MEANING OF REGIONS AND REGIONAL CHANGE

We treat regional variation as one important social or community context shaping family relationships. These family relationships encompass intergenerational relations with parents, male-female relationships, and the centrality of marriage in adulthood. These are one set of ways that region of socialization is linked to the timing of leaving home and the routes taken. Region of residence also reflects the community resources available, the types of job opportunities that characterize different areas of the country, and the availability of educational institutions in these areas. The extent of opportunities available on these dimensions, however, has changed in many regions of the country. The decline and then rise of the Southern region, the boom and then decline in the Midwest, and the ongoing boom (despite short-term difficulties) of the Pacific region have changed these places relative to the established, industrial East. The changing fortunes of these regions have also affected their investments in educational institutions, with a long history of weak educational systems in the South changing late in the century. In contrast, a vast system of smaller and larger universities and community colleges began to be constructed in the Western region during the 1960s.

Regions vary in terms of the extent of familism and the resultant family and peer pressures likely to influence remaining in the parental home until marriage. The West has long been characterized as an area of strong "individualism," with early marriage and independence from parents and high levels of divorce (Castleton and Goldscheider 1989). In contrast, the South has been marked by early and stable marriage (Goldscheider and Waite 1991). To the extent that these family values are characteristic of areas, they will influence relationships between parents and children.

These two community-level effects—structural and cultural—are likely to be most influential at critical junctures in the life course. Thus, community and regional differences should be particularly important factors when young adults are growing up and faced with decisions about leaving their parents' home and the route to take out of the home. In short, we treat the region where young adults spent their formative years as a community-level indicator of the underlying broad themes that have been based on individual characteristics. Among these, the economic, educational, and family formation connections are the most critical. In this sense, region or community of residence is the "macrolevel" counterpart to "microlevel" characteristics of individuals.

Furthermore, as the characteristics of individuals have changed over the 20th century (with great increases in the affluence but decreases in the stability of the homes in which young people have grown up) and as the meanings of other characteristics have changed (with the gender revolution, the civil rights movement, and secularization), so, too, we expect that the effects of region have changed over the century. Some changes, such as the diffusion of a national culture, should have led to the diminishing of regional differences in the norms of leaving home, as for other dimensions of social life. Other changes, including the great shifts of regionally based economic opportunities, such as the rise of the West, the fall and rise of the South, and the rise and fall of the Midwest, may also have shifted the pattern of regional differences in the nest-leaving process. However, it is not clear whether the forces resulting in convergence among regions into a national pattern have had stronger effects on changes in the transition to adulthood than the forces leading to continued, even if shifting, regional variation.

Our understanding of regional variation, therefore, goes beyond the assertion that region is an important differentiator of the transition to adulthood. Regions have specific characteristics that should affect young adults' timing and routes out of the home. Three major features of regions will be emphasized in our examination of the evidence: (1) Some regions of the country developed a strong tradition of private college education, often designed as residential institutions in rural settings. This should lead to higher rates of going away from home to attend college relative to regions without such a tradition, and particularly relative to regions with a strong network of local and community institutions built in urban areas. (2) Plentiful economic opportunities should reduce the need for young adults to leave home to find a job. (3) Regions with a long tradition of parent-child independence and family innovation should have higher rates of leaving home both for independence and for nontraditional family formation than those with a strong emphasis on family cohesion and the centrality and stability of marriage.

The regional units that we are able to identify retrospectively are crude, because they cover areas that are larger and more heterogeneous than is ideal. Regions, therefore, are only approximate indicators of community. Nevertheless, we argue that these broad areas capture more than the characteristics of individuals and shape the broader social environment of young adults. How do the regions of the United States fit these expectations?

WHICH REGIONS?

We began our analyses of regional differences in the timing of nest-leaving and the routes taken out of the home with the nine regions defined by the U.S. Bureau of the Census. Based in part on our understanding of how regional differences are likely to shape leaving home over the 20th century, the regional results from previous research on nest-leaving in the 1980s (Goldscheider and Goldscheider 1993), and the patterns we actually found, we have recategorized them into five regional groupings: a central core area that includes the South; two regions to its west (Pacific and Mountain); and two regions to its north and east (the eastern Midwest and Mid-Atlantic, and New England. (See Map 5.1.)

THE TRADITIONAL CORE

The traditional core region of the United States includes the South (the east-south central and the south Atlantic regions, from Virginia to Alabama) and the Western portions of the Midwest (the west-north central and the west-south central regions, from Louisiana north to North Dakota). These four regions are contiguous geographically. Although the South has a very different history from the western portions of the Midwest, they all (still) have disproportionately agrarian economies.

The agrarian history of the traditional core region has meant a higher level of involvement by children in the household economy in the South (Goldscheider and Waite 1991), a pattern that has also been found in farm areas in the Great Plains states, in the western portion of this constructed region (White and Brinkerhoff 1981). Although the southern regions of the United States have been characterized as having a more gender-segregated culture, this appeared in our analyses only in a pattern of early leaving home to marriage, which was also the case in the western portions of this area, particularly the west-south central region. When we examine the regional patterns in multivariate analysis, we use this first category as our reference category for the other four regions, two to its west and two to its northeast.

THE PACIFIC AND MOUNTAIN REGIONS

The western region includes the coastal (Pacific) and the interior (Mountain) regions, which are similar in some respects but quite different in others. In addition to experiencing a boom in economic growth in the 1970s and 1980s, both are considered areas with a greater stress on individualism (including female autonomy). The Pacific area, however (which includes Oregon and Washington, although it is dominated in terms of population by California), differed in several important ways from the states of the western interior (Colorado, Utah, Nevada, Idaho, Wyoming, Montana, Arizona and New Mexico). The coastal states, with their large cities and dense networks of suburbs, place greater emphasis on forms of behavior that are less family oriented. The Mountain region is much less densely populated; the predominately Mormon areas of Utah and Idaho reinforce familism through gender segregation. In our context, this should encourage children's early independence from parents through marriage (Castleton and Goldscheider 1989).

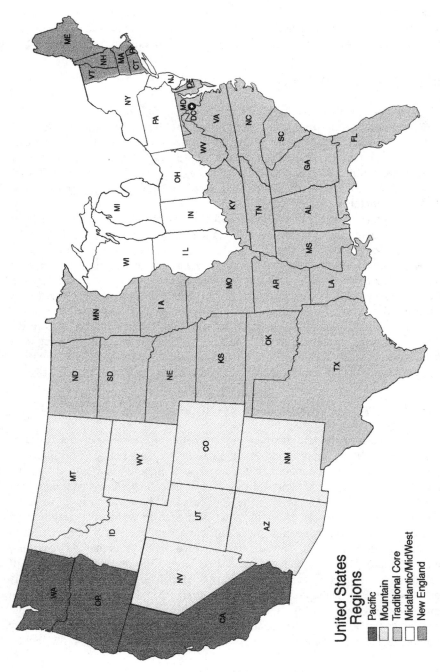

Map 5.1 United States Regions

Although the tradition of individualism in the West appears long-standing, its translation into delays in marriage and remarriage is very recent in California. California went from one of the more early marrying states in the 1950s to one of the latest in the 1980s (Castleton and Goldscheider 1989). Hence, we were not surprised to find that the Pacific census region had distinctive patterns of nest-leaving compared with the other major Western region, and we have therefore kept them separate.

NEW ENGLAND AND THE MID-ATLANTIC/MIDWEST

The two areas to the west of the "traditional core" region are balanced (geographically) by two areas to its north and east, one that is also a combination of census regions, and one that, like the Pacific, remained distinctive throughout our analyses. These are New England and the Mid-Atlantic/Midwest, which combines both these census regions.

The Mid-Atlantic/Midwest region is the heart of the industrial East, from New York, New Jersey, and Pennsylvania to Ohio, Indiana, Michigan, Illinois, and Wisconsin. These regions were not distinctive from each other in family and nest-leaving patterns late in the 20th century (Goldscheider and Goldscheider 1993; Goldscheider and Waite 1991). However, these analyses largely reflected regions' characteristics of these areas after their peak as centers of industrial activities had passed. Since the 1960s, these regions have experienced economic declines and slow growth in manufacturing and related sectors of employment (Frey and Speare 1988). As a result, the fraction of families living in poverty has increased, whereas regional poverty rates in the South and West have declined (see Chase-Lansdale and Gordon 1996). Hence, there may have been substantial change in nest-leaving patterns over the 20th century for this region, particularly in leaving home to take a job.

The census bureau grouped together the six states of New England as a single region. Dominated in population size by Massachusetts and its megacity, Boston (which extends into Southern Maine and New Hampshire) on the east, and by the Connecticut satellite cities and suburbs of New York City on the west, the region is distinctive in its large number of old, 19th-century industrial cities. It also is characterized by the substantial immigrant populations that were drawn to the region during their years of rapid growth at the beginning of the century.

The New England region also has a long history of higher-than-average educational levels, with a rich network of private residential colleges, many in rural areas. In the 1980s, it had a high age at marriage and high proportions who expected residential independence for young adults, both parents and young adults (Goldscheider and Goldscheider 1993). We therefore anticipate that the education route out of the nest will be higher among those who have been raised in New England; leaving home to marriage is likely to be lower there than among those raised in other regions of the United States. As a highly urban region, we also expect that fewer would need to leave home to get a job.

REGIONAL DIFFERENCES IN ROUTES OUT OF THE HOME

We observe some clear regional differences in the patterns of leaving home. Most of these differences are in the routes taken out of the home rather than in overall timing (similar to patterns we will document for ethnicity and religion in Chapters 9 and 10). Hence, regional differences in nest-leaving processes are primarily shaped by the unfolding structure of the adult lives of young people rather than by their residential relationships with their parents. This is not the full story, however, because there are also regional differences in the likelihood of returning home (Table A.5 in the appendix).

The regional differences in route out of the parental home are consistent with previous research focusing on marriage (Goldscheider and Goldscheider 1993; Goldscheider and Waite 1991). Large differences appear as well for other routes, but not always where we most expected them. Regional differences are less marked for leaving home for a job or to attend school, which we had expected based on differences in educational and job opportunities (although some do appear), than they are for the new routes that are more closely tied to differences in family values, such as leaving home to be independent or to form a nontraditional family. There are also large, puzzling regional differences in leaving home to join the military. We examine first the routes related to new family values—marriage, independence, and nontraditional family formation—followed by the more institutionally related routes of job, school, and the military.

Marriage. Those in the "traditional core," which includes the South, leave most rapidly for the marriage route out of the home (Figure 5.1). None of the other regional groupings have higher probabilities of leaving home via this route, although the Mountain region, the area immediately to the west of the western part of this "traditional core," comes close (and in fact, is not different statistically from the traditional core).

The likelihood of leaving home for marriage drops for each region further from the traditional core, both for the regional groupings to the west and those to the northeast. Those raised in the western regional groupings, however, are more likely to take this route at a given age than the two eastern ones. This leaves New England with the lowest level of leaving home via this route, less than three-quarters the odds of those who grew up in the South.

Independence. In contrast to its traditional pattern in terms of leaving home for marriage, those in the "traditional core" are intermediate in the likelihood of leaving home for one of the newest routes out of the home, independence, occupying the middle point in the west-to-east gradient (Figure

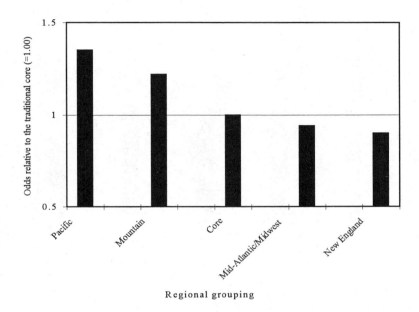

Figure 5.1. Regional Differences in Leaving Home for Marriage
SOURCE: From Table A.5 in the appendix.

5.2). Those in the Pacific region are the most likely to leave home via this route, with levels fully 35 percent higher than those in the traditional core. The Mountain region is not far behind; young adults there are 22 percent more likely to take this route than those in the traditional core.

Those in New England are less likely than those in any other region to leave home at a given age via this route. Neither of the two regions to the east, however, are distinctively below the level of those in the traditional core as those to the west are above the level. The odds that young adults in New England leave home by this route are 90 percent the level of those in the traditional core, which is not a statistically significantly difference. The two western regions are clearly distinctive on this "new" route out of the home.

Nontraditional Family Formation. Much larger differences appear for the other "new route" out of the home, leaving to form a nontraditional family via cohabitation or single parenthood, with a pattern much like that we saw for marriage, with the peripheral regions increasingly different from the core (Figure 5.3). In this case, however, the pattern is reversed. Those in the core are the least likely to take this route out of the parental home. The differences are huge. Young adults in both the Pacific and New England regions are about

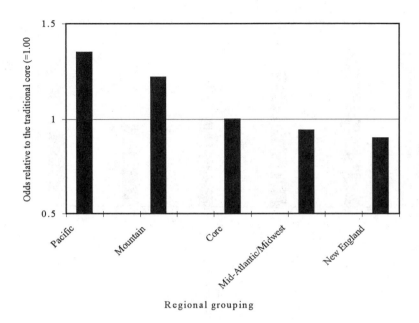

Figure 5.2. Regional Differences in Leaving Home for Independence
SOURCE: From Table A.5 in appendix.

2.5 times as likely to leave their parental home in this manner at a given age as are those in the traditional core. New England is particularly distinctive relative to its nearest neighbor, the Mid-Atlantic/Midwest region, where young adults are less than a quarter more likely to leave home via this route than those in the traditional core, a difference that is not statistically significant. The Mountain area much more closely approaches the level of the Pacific region than is the case for the two regions to the east.

The development of new "family values" in parent-child relationships (independence) and the substitution of new patterns for old in male-female relationships (marriage and nontraditional family formation) have clearly characterized different regions of the United States. The two routes most tied to the changing relationships between men and women radiate from the traditional core, supplanting more traditional family forms with less traditional family forms. In contrast, the gradient of change in parent-child relationships follows much more closely the history of European settlement of the country, a pattern dominated by young adults leaving their parents to make a home in the West. It almost seems as if those who remained in the East were those not looking so hard for independence from their families, whereas those who went to the West continue to need to do so, even when there is no longer a westward

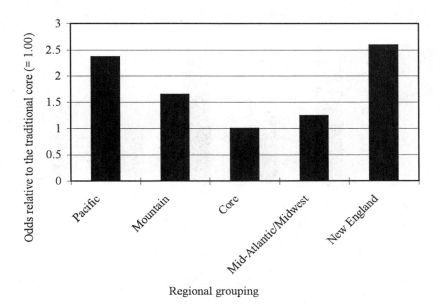

Figure 5.3. Regional Differences in Leaving Home to Cohabit or Head a Single-Parent Family
SOURCE: From Table A.5 in the appendix.

frontier to follow.

Jobs. The regional pattern of leaving home to take a job resembles that of leaving home for independence, although less sharply (Figure 5.4). In this case, however, the two eastern regions are most distinctive, with odds of leaving home via this route only 60 percent to 70 percent of the level of those in both the traditional core and the Pacific regions. The Mountain region is something of an exception, although the difference is only marginally significant.

This parallel between leaving home for independence and leaving for a job suggests that there is a more general regional pattern, one based on whether leaving home is structured more around family reasons or around nonfamily reasons. For the former, whether the new family is traditional or nontraditional, innovation increases out from the core area. For the latter, whether the nonfamily route is for a job or just for independence, the gradient is west to east. The fact that the pattern for leaving for a job is less sharp than that for independence might reflect the constraints of job availability: One can always construct independence by leaving home, but leaving home for a job

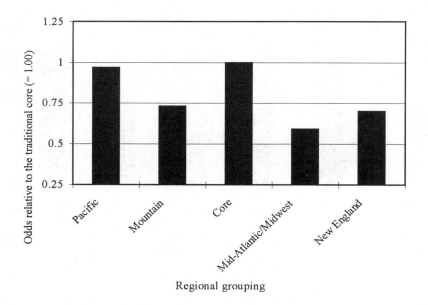

Figure 5.4. Regional Differences in Leaving Home for a Job
SOURCE: From Table A.5 in the appendix.

requires that there be one.

The regional pattern in leaving home for a job, however, also parallels regional differences in urban concentration. This may simply mean that in the East, there is less reason to leave home to take a job; the distances are shorter and the public transportation better. Young adults living in the East, like their parents, can just commute to their jobs. They need a better reason to leave home, and if not to form a new family, then for something else, such as college or the military.

College. At least for those having grown up in New England, one way to leave home without establishing a family is to go away to school. This region is quite distinctive in its use of this route, particularly relative both to its nearest neighbor, the Mid-Atlantic/Midwest, and also to the Pacific region (Figure 5.5). Those living in the Mid-Atlantic/Midwest area have only about three-quarters the likelihood of taking this route out of the home at a given age; those growing up in the Pacific region have only two-thirds the likelihood of those in the traditional core.

New England's ivy-aura distinctiveness, however, is shared both with the traditional core, which includes the South, and with the Mountain region. It may be that the Pacific and Mid-Atlantic/Midwest regions are distinctive in developing a rich network of local institutions that allowed extensive commuting, from the network of institutions in New York City, Philadelphia, Detroit, and Chicago to the community colleges that dot the California cities and suburbs. We should be able to clarify this puzzle in a later section, when we examine changes over time in regional differences in routes out of the home.

Military Service. There are also large regional differences in military service as a route out of the home. We find this quite surprising, because most young adults who experienced military service as their first home away from home did so during periods of mass conscription. Young adults growing up in the traditional core area, as well as in the area to its immediate north and east, the Mid-Atlantic/Midwest regions, have the lowest likelihood of leaving home to the military, whereas both New England and the Mountain regions stand out as areas of higher levels, with the Pacific region at a somewhat intermediate level (Figure 5.6).

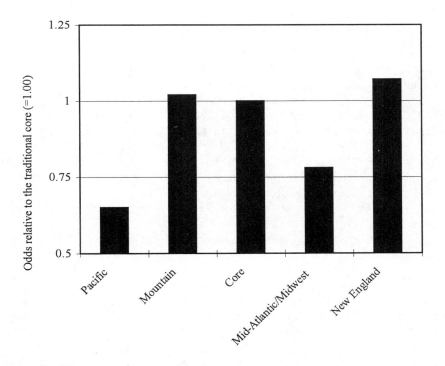

Figure 5.5. Regional Differences in Leaving Home for School
SOURCE: From Table A.5 in the appendix.

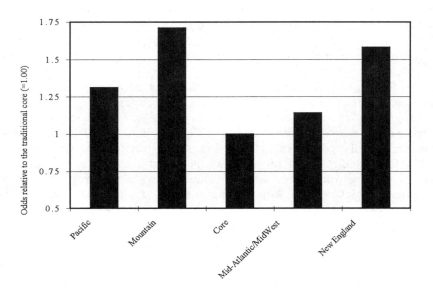

Figure 5.6. Regional Differences in Leaving Home for the Military
SOURCE: From Table A.5 in the appendix.

The Mountain area has a strong military tradition, as the area most recently "pacified" for European-origin settlement, which might be consistent with choosing a military route. The South, however, also has a strong military tradition, but those growing up there have been unlikely to take this route (perhaps because it is the "wrong" army, at least for some unreconstructed Southerners). Those growing up in New England, which would seem to have had neither a violent nor a wild-and-woolly tradition, in contrast, are particularly likely to take this route.

The answer to these puzzling findings may rest with a pattern we will document later (Chapter 8), which suggests that differences in education may be a contributing factor. The traditional core, and particularly the South, had a lower level of education than the other regions during most of the 20th century, and particularly than New England. There have also been large pockets of populations with little education in the Mid-Atlantic and Midwest states during much of the century. Given that the armed services screen out the least educated, even if young adults in these two regions had responded to the call to fight in equal numbers, they might have had more difficulty in getting into the army or the other branches of the service, returning home quickly rather than later or not at all.

REGIONAL DIFFERENCES IN RETURNING HOME

As was the case for leaving home, regional differences in returning home focus our attention on differences in returning home among the specific routes taken out of the home, because there are no overall differences by region in the overall likelihood of returning home. Among the routes we examined, there were a small number of significant differences, but we were more surprised by those we did not find than by those we found.

We had expected that there would be a higher likelihood of returning home from marriage in the Pacific region than in the traditional core, given the very different rates of divorce in the two regions and the connection between divorce and returning to the parental home. But we found no regional differences in returning home from marriage (Table A.5 in the appendix). Evidently, although divorce does frequently lead to returns home, in areas where divorce is high, young people who do divorce are less likely to return than those who do so where divorce is low. This suggests that there is a connection between increased divorce and a search for independence, which would not be found in the parental home. It also suggests that where divorce is rare, and hence particularly deviant, young people nevertheless can still return home.

The most consistent finding of regional differences in rates of returning to the nest appears for the Mid-Atlantic/Midwest area (Figure 5.7). Those growing up there were significantly more likely to return from most forms of nonfamily living than were those who grew up in the traditional core or in other regions of the country. Young adults from the Mid-Atlantic/Midwest area were about 25 percent more likely to return home if they left for school, the military, or a job. Those in this region were similar to others from other regions in the likelihood of returning home from independence.

This result is particularly interesting because those who grew up in the Mid-Atlantic/Midwest region have also been slower than others in the country to leave home, the only overall regional difference. This may reflect the economic difficulties this region has faced in the past few decades (whose members dominate our overall results). If so, we should observe this pattern in our analysis of regional changes over time in leaving home.

Two of these three nonfamily routes that lead to higher rates of return among those from the Mid-Atlantic/Midwest area—leaving home for the military and for a job—also have higher rates of returning for other regions. Those in New England are significantly more likely to return from each, with relative probabilities of returning home nearly 50 percent greater than those in the traditional core. This does not make them particularly distinctive among regions in returning after leaving for a job, because all regions are more likely to do so than the traditional core area. Those from New England are the most likely of all regions, however, to return after military service. It is unclear why this should be the case.

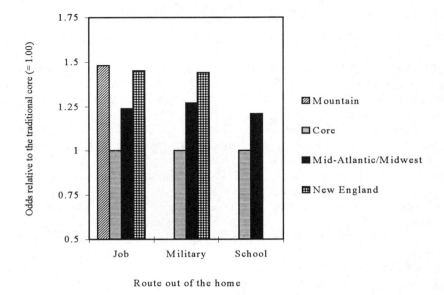

Figure 5.7. Regional Differences in Returning Home by Route Left
SOURCE: From Table A.5 in the appendix.

CHANGES OVER TIME IN REGIONAL NEST-LEAVING PATTERNS

How stable have these patterns of regional differences been over the 20th century? To what extent have there been shifts over time that reflect changes in economic opportunities as the West increasingly led, the Midwest rose and fell, and the South fell and rose? How much do changes over time reflect the homogenizing effects of mass culture? Our results suggest that both the overall regional patterns and their shifts are much more sensitive to regional changes in values than in economic opportunities, with a story that is largely, but not wholly, one of regional convergence in leaving-home patterns over time.

Our expectation that there would be significant changes over time in regional patterns of nest-leaving tied to job and schooling opportunities is not borne out by the evidence in any way. The decline in the structure of job opportunities in the Mid-Atlantic/Midwest area over the last several decades has not resulted in a change in the regional pattern of leaving the parental home in search of jobs. Those who grew up in this area have been among the least likely to leave home in search of employment throughout the entire period (data not presented). This finding suggests that the issue in leaving home is the persistence of the density of job opportunities, which has remained high in these older industrial areas, rather than relative shifts over time.

We were also surprised to see that the regional differences that appeared in leaving home to attend school have also been stable over the period. Young adults in the Pacific region were unlikely to leave home to attend college both before their rich network of local and community colleges was developed and subsequently. This route out of the home was also low throughout the period in the Mid-Atlantic/Midwest, although this might also reflect the long-standing availability of college education in their city college systems, particularly characteristic of New York. The tradition of "going away to school" is evidently a deeply embedded one and not particularly responsive to changes in the opportunities to attend college while remaining at home.

Much larger regional changes appear when we turn to routes out of the home tied more directly to differences in values about parent-child and male-female relationships. The emergence of independence as an adequate reason for leaving home clearly occurred first in the Pacific (Figure 5.8). Among the oldest nest-leaving cohorts (those of the Great Depression and before), this route was extremely rare, and no region was distinctive in choosing it.

During the early years of the great growth in this route, however, the Pacific region held a dominant position, consistent with the pattern we saw in the overall regional differences in leaving home for independence. During these years (the cohorts who reached age 18 between 1938 and 1972), young adults in this region had about twice the likelihood of taking this route than did those either in the traditional core or in the other regions. For the two most recent cohorts, however, this was no longer the case; the other regions have "caught up" so that there has been substantial regional convergence in this route out of the parental home.

A similar pattern characterizes the route out of the home to nontraditional family formation via either cohabitation or single parenthood. Data not presented in tabular form show the strong bicoastal pattern of high levels on the West and the Northeast, with lower levels in the Mountain and Mid-Atlantic/Midwest areas and the lowest in the traditional core. These regional differences are substantial, greater than 2:1. There have been great declines among all of the regions relative to the traditional core area over the period. These regional declines imply that the most recent growth in this route out of the home has been greatest in the states of the traditional core. For the youngest cohort (who reached age 18 in 1980 or later), there were no regional differences that were either very large or statistically significant.

A somewhat more complex story appears, however, when we consider regional changes in leaving home for marriage. This is the most traditional route out of the home, tied to the most fundamental relationship between men and women. Patterns over time in leaving home to marriage show some regional differences that are long-standing but others that are changing dramatically. Hence, not only has there not been convergence in regional patterns of leaving home for marriage, there has been divergence.

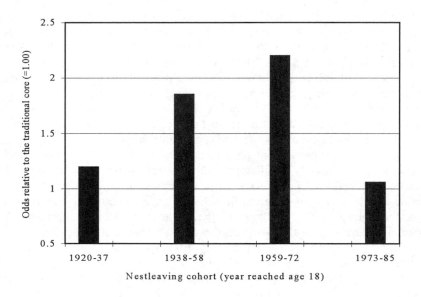

Figure 5.8. The Rise and Fall of Independence Route in the Pacific Region
SOURCE: Calculated by the authors from the NSFH.

The eastern areas have remained stable relative to the traditional core throughout the period. The level we observed earlier for New England, which was about three-quarters that of the traditional core, was similar among the older and younger cohorts. This is also the case for the Mid-Atlantic/Midwest area (data not presented). The story changes, however, when we consider the parts of the country west of the traditional core. The Pacific region has diverged both from the traditional core regions and from the Mountain region.

For the first half of the century, young adults in the Pacific region were as likely to take this route out of the home as those in the traditional core (Figure 5.9) and, hence, much more likely to do so than young adults in the eastern states. The decline in leaving home for marriage among those in the Pacific region began with the 1959 to 1972 nest-leaving cohorts, who were about 85 percent as likely to take this route as those in the traditional core regions. The trends intensified among the younger, post-Vietnam cohorts (1973+), who were less than three-quarters as likely to take this route. It appears therefore that those who grew up in the western region of the United States have led the revolution in the decline in marriage as the route out of the home, a revolution that shows no sign of ending. It is part of a pattern of increased regional polarization rather than convergence.

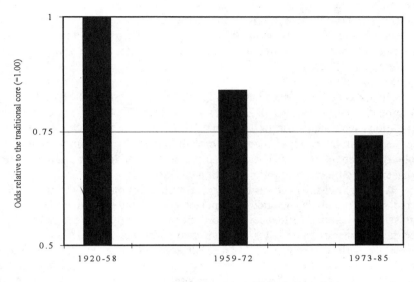

Figure 5.9. The Pacific Region Leads the Decline in Nest-Leaving for Marriage
SOURCE: Calculated by the authors from the NSFH.

This pattern of change in leaving home for marriage is consistent with research showing that those in the western region, and in California in particular, have anticipated major parts of both the marriage and the fertility revolutions (Castleton and Goldscheider 1989). It is not clear, however, whether the other regions will catch up to those in the Pacific region on this dimension, as they appear to on others. If that becomes the trend among other regions, the national decline in leaving home for marriage will intensify greatly. Whether because of the economic power now concentrated in the West or, more likely, because of the power to shape mass culture that is even more concentrated there, this seems highly likely.

CONCLUDING OBSERVATIONS

Our review of the evidence on regional variation in leaving home over the 20th century suggests that the "cultural" set of factors (defined in terms of the specific histories of the various regions of the country, particularly the South and West) seems to be more important in interpreting these regional differences than were economic changes; the trends in nest-leaving do not appear to be correlated with regional economic changes. On most dimensions of the nest-leaving process, persons growing up in other regions of the country have caught up to the pattern characterizing the Pacific and Western regions so that the pattern of those growing up in the West is no longer distinctive. This convergence appears to be a classic case of cultural diffusion—a pattern of nest-leaving that was initially important only in one region of the country moving across regions to characterize other areas.

Enhancing this "cultural" story are the negative findings on changes over time in looking for jobs as a factor in the regional patterns of nest-leaving. Despite the large regional differences in the growth of jobs, these economic conditions have had little or no effect on changes in the patterns of leaving home in search of employment. We shall pursue this cultural argument in subsequent chapters when we focus more sharply at linking individual-level measures of ethnicity and religion with nest-leaving.

When we consider the variety of social influences on family changes, rarely have social scientists included regional or areal contexts. In large part, this omission of regional influences is based on the assumption that areal units are too heterogeneous to reveal any significant influence or that their impact is subsumed within other factors. As a result, we have often focused our inquiries solely on individual-based characteristics (e.g., age, sex, or education) or have focused on family-level factors (e.g., parental income or family structure). As we have demonstrated in this chapter, regional contexts are among the factors that shape changes and variations in the transition to adulthood. These factors take on importance in considering the nest-leaving process in addition to, but not synonymous with, the influence of individual- and family-level factors.

When we have information only on either the neighborhood where people live when they are growing up or on their individual characteristics, it is difficult to separate their effects. In large part, areal and individual characteristics are highly correlated, even when they are not identical. When data on both areal and individual characteristics are available, we can begin to disentangle the relative importance of social and community level contexts from individual variation as we analyze the factors involved in the transitions to adulthood. At least for nest-leaving, one conclusion is inescapable: The communities where people are raised have important influences on the decisions they make about their relationships with their families. From the inferences we have drawn, it appears that regional factors are more likely to be cultural in the broad sense that we have used the concept culture rather than narrowly economic.

CHAPTER 6

Who Left Whom? The Effects of Childhood Family Structure

O̲ur first look at the links between the changes in leaving and returning home and the other "revolutions" of the 20th century focuses on changes in family structure, because this revolution is fundamental to the family itself. The growth in divorce and remarriage in the United States has increased the complexity of the homes in which young people grow up and from which they leave to establish households of their own in their transition to adulthood. Divorce deprives them of one parent in the home and normally reduces their access to the non-coresident parent. A parent's remarriage introduces a new parental figure in the household. Given the parallel growth of unmarried parenthood, increasingly some children are growing up in homes where their two biological parents have never regularly lived.

These experiences affect the lives of parents as well and may force them to reduce their investments in their children's future. They may also change the ways parents relate to their children. As we noted earlier, leaving home is a household decision involving both children and parents (Chapter 1). Hence, decisions about when children leave their home to begin to live independently of parents may strongly reflect these changes in parent-child relationships that loom so large in the lives of many children. These changes may also affect the routes that young adults take out of the home. They may become wary of marriage and decide instead to cohabit; they may need to be independent rather than waiting until they are ready to take an appropriate job. If instead of having the resources to leave home to attend school (the "intermediate" form of independence that represents an investment in their futures), they may need to find some other institutional setting that will support them "for free" and join the military. Once they leave, there may be the option to return home when the

99

relationship, job, school program, or military stint has ended. But they may find it more difficult to return to live again in their parent's home, a home they may perceive to have left them.

In this chapter, we explore the links between the structure of the parental families young people grew up in and the transition they make to residential adulthood. We analyze how the changing family patterns that characterize the households where children grow up affect the decisions that young people (and their parents) make about leaving and returning home. Are young adults who have experienced nontraditional family forms in childhood (particularly divorce, remarriage, and unmarried parenthood) more likely to leave home and less likely to return than those who grew up in stable two-parent families? Does their experience shape the route they take out of the home, affecting their likelihood of leaving home for marriage or cohabitation, for school or the military, for a job or just to be independent?

Furthermore, does the type or timing of the family structural experience differentially shape the nest-leaving process? Is the major source of differences among family types stability of the family environment or changes in the structure of the family, no matter what its structure (because many children are growing up in homes in which their mother never marries)? Does it matter whether the disruption of family life happened early or later in childhood? And perhaps of greatest importance, because the revolution in marital instability shows no signs of ebbing, are the effects on young people's lives attenuating as the experience becomes more common, more normal? Or are its effects increasing, perhaps, because the "back-up" relatives, the grandparents and others who often provide support during difficult times to children in disrupted families, have become overwhelmed by the increase in disruption as it enters their lives from even more directions?

The answers to these questions provide important insight into the importance of the parental family in launching the next generation into an adult trajectory toward stable and successful work and family roles. As we documented earlier (Chapter 4), those who experienced family disruption, particularly stepparent families and those with stepsiblings, are very likely to leave home extremely young (before age 17), especially to early marriage and independence. Here, we will examine the issues more broadly, considering family structure in detail and documenting its effects on cohabitation and military service, its intensifying effects on marriage, and its powerful (though perhaps weakening) effects on going away to college.

CHANGES IN FAMILY STRUCTURE AND NEST LEAVING

What have been the patterns of change in family structure, and how might the changes affect the timing of leaving home, the route taken, and/or the likelihood of return? Might some of the decline in the age at leaving home that emerged in the post-World War II period and intensified through the

Vietnam cohort be the result of the divorce revolution? How many of the changes that we documented earlier in leaving and returning home (Chapters 2 and 3) might be the result of this "revolution"?

A close look at trends in childhood family structure shows that very few changes in leaving (or returning) home can be linked with the growth of the divorce revolution. Most of the decline in age at leaving home took place before any major increase in the experience of family disruption. In fact, the cohorts that have been the most affected by the divorce revolution, those who came of age after 1973, are actually those who have been leaving home later (Figure 6.1). Because experiencing family disruption increases "running away" or leaving home at a young age, the recent increases in young adults living with parents might have been even more dramatic if families had remained as stable as they were in the past.

These data show that it is important not to exaggerate the extent to which families have changed. The experiences of the early cohorts were not so very stable. Even for the most recent two cohorts, the decreases in stability had not—yet—been that extreme. Among the older cohorts (those who came of age before 1972), there are very few differences. The proportions who experienced a stable two-biological-parent family fluctuated between 73 percent and 77 percent, and the other categories also fluctuated within a narrow range.

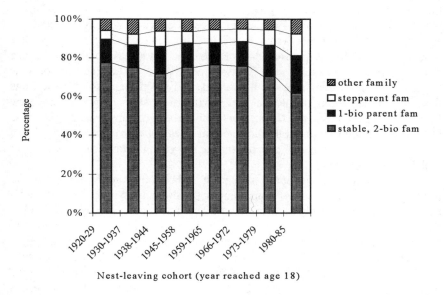

Figure 6.1. Family Structure by Nest-Leaving Cohort
SOURCE: Calculated by the authors from the NSFH.

Although divorce was certainly increasing during most of this period, mortality was decreasing so that about as many gained in stability as lost.

The two most recent cohorts, however, show the new trend quite distinctly, with increases in both single-parent and stepparent families. Whereas about 12 percent among the older cohorts grew up with a single parent, this had reached nearly 20 percent for those who came of age after 1980. Similarly, the experience of having a stepparent, which was rarely more than 5 percent among the older cohorts, had exceeded 10 percent for the youngest cohort. Both of these cohorts, however, had parents who married quite early in the divorce revolution, because they were born in the years around 1960, a period of fairly low divorce rates. Those who are coming of age even later in the 20th century and in the early years of the next century will have very different backgrounds on this dimension, increasing the importance of understanding these effects within each cohort. Our results on the effects of family structure on leaving home early suggest that the divorce revolution may have even more problematic dimensions than have been apparent so far.

Although nest-leaving among young adults has been viewed in much of the research literature as a normal life course transition—a beneficial response to the growth in resources allowing privacy for both generations and a "signal" of adulthood—analyzing the effects of family structure makes it clear that when young people leave home, it is not always because they were being "pulled" by the opportunities afforded by greater resources. It just as often may be the result of a "push" out of a difficult or nonsupportive home environment, an environment that may not welcome a returning adult needing refueling after time away, which has become one of the key ways that young adults use returning home (DaVanzo and Goldscheider 1990). The addition of new parental figures to their parent's household, and the presence of new siblings there, may make young people feel that leaving to, or staying away in, any new home is better than living in their parental home. No matter how risky, a home of their own might be preferable to one that does not provide the resources of attention, love, and material support that many young people can count on in their parental homes.

This view of leaving home as a push rather than simply a response to normal adult development is consistent with research showing that parental family disruption not only increases nest-leaving at young ages (Chapter 4) but also increases less stable forms of family formation, including cohabitation, premarital pregnancy, and unmarried parenthood (Cherlin, et al. 1995; Goldscheider and Waite 1991; Thornton 1991). We will extend these results further in order to see which routes out of the parental home are most affected by parental family structure and whether those routes are likely to lead to less stable and successful adult roles. Among young adults who are forming new families, we distinguish between marriage and cohabitation; among those leaving to semiautonomous quarters, we distinguish between attending college and joining the military; and among those leaving to a nonfamilial independent residence, we distinguish between those who left to obtain employment and those who left just to be independent. Analyzing the various routes out of the home in the context of parental disruption during childhood focuses attention on situations likely to be linked with continued parental investment (marriage and college) from those less likely to attract resources from parents (military service and cohabitation). If family disruption also decreases returning home, and particularly returning home from those routes that look more like escape routes than like decisions taken with mature consideration, this will strengthen our concern that at least some portion of the early nest-leaving that accompanies family disruption is more than ordinarily problematic in the transition to adulthood.

MEASURING CHILDHOOD FAMILY STRUCTURE

We were able to construct an unusually detailed set of types of family structure for our analysis of leaving home. Among the respondents in the National Survey of Families and Households (NSFH), those had not lived with both biological (or adoptive) parents from birth to age 19 or until they left home were asked a detailed series of questions to determine with whom they lived at each age. We used this information to address two types of concerns about family structure that have emerged in the research literature: (1) At what time did the structure of families change in children's lives and if it did, discovering that a critical time is at the beginning of adolescence, which we took to be age 12, and (2) when there was a change, what sort of structure—two-parent, one-parent, or none—emerged. From myriad possibilities, we identified seven family types with enough cases and large enough differences to provide stable results.

1.   Families with stable, two biological (or adoptive) parents
2.   Other stable family forms, mostly unmarried mothers
3.   Families broken by divorce or widowhood with no remarriage (for whom timing did not matter)
4.   Families with a stepparent introduced before the respondent reached age 12, which were stable after that change
5.   Families with a stepparent introduced after the respondent reached age 12 and that were stable after that age
6.   Other family histories (such as living with other relatives or nonrelatives) that were stable after the respondent reached age 12
7.   Other family histories that included changes after the respondent reached age 12

We also included a separate measure of the presence of step- or half-siblings. Our detailed analyses indicated that the presence of such siblings had an independent effect on leaving home that differed little by family structure. This effect even characterized those who were raised by two biological parents, one of whom had brought a child from a previous marriage to the household.

FAMILY STRUCTURE AND LEAVING AND RETURNING HOME

The effects of growing up in families with a nontraditional family structure on leaving home suggest a consistent pattern of reduced parental investment in their children's lives. These effects resemble the effects of having parents with lower socioeconomic status or having many siblings (Chapter 8). The general pattern is of increased odds of leaving the parental home for the least supportive family situations (cohabitation and unmarried parenthood). Moreover, the data show that among those who left home in the context of parental family disruption, there are decreased odds of leaving to attend school. However, there are higher probabilities of leaving to the semiautonomous arrangements that provide less investment in future earnings (the military), and for the least productive reasons for nonfamily living (independence rather than employment). These patterns emerge for nearly every measure of nontraditional family structure. However, the patterns would be much less clear if the specific routes out of the home were not distinguished. (The detailed results of the analysis of leaving and returning home by specific routes for these family structural types are presented in Table A.6.1 in the appendix).

The most dramatic effects on nest leaving, overall, are associated with acquiring a stepparent or stepsiblings. Young people who grew up in stepfamilies experienced increased odds of leaving home of 20 to 25 percent, depending on whether the stepparent entered the family before or after they had their 12th birthday (Figure 6.2). An additional significant increase of similar size characterizes those whose family experiences in childhood included living with half- or stepsiblings. In contrast, single-parent families, whether stable or resulting from divorce, do not appear to accelerate leaving home at all and are not significantly different from those whose experience has been of stable two-parent families. Other nontraditional forms also do not differ from single parent or stable two-parent families in their effects on the overall probabilities of leaving home.

FAMILY STRUCTURE AND ROUTES TAKEN OUT OF THE HOME

These similarities in overall leaving home for all but stepfamilies, however, do not consistently reflect similar underlying differences in the routes taken. When routes out of the parental home are considered, it becomes clear that there are also many more differences among the various types of nontraditional family structures. Subdividing leaving home among the routes taken shows clearly that simply analyzing the overall timing of leaving home can be seriously misleading, because some routes are accelerated, whereas others are depressed.

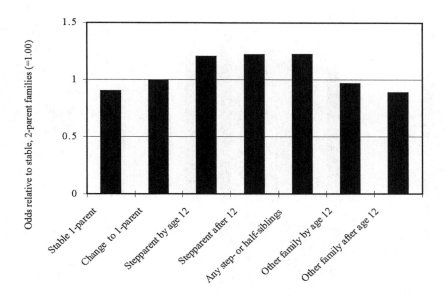

Figure 6.2. Effect of Family Structure on Leaving Home
SOURCE: From Table A.6 in the appendix.

Semiautonomy: College and the Armed Services

We first consider the semi-independent routes out of the parental home—to attend college and to serve in the armed services. These are often considered semi-independent, or semiautonomous, because in most cases, the living situation is not a private home or apartment but, instead, some form of group quarters. In some data sources, those who leave home to one of these semiautonomous quarters are not considered to have "left home." How they are treated in the study of leaving home, and particularly for those studying the effects of family structure, however, clearly matters. Each shows strong effects—but very different ones. Those who did not grow up in a stable two-parent home are only 50 percent to 75 percent as likely to leave home to attend college as those who did (controlling for the other factors in our models, including measures of family resources). More than 20 percent of young adults who grew up in families with both biological parents left home to attend college compared with only 10 to 15 percent of young adults from other types of families. In contrast, the military was a particularly favored route, at least among those with stepparents and/or stepsiblings (Figure 6.3).

There is much more variation among types of family structure for leaving home to go away to college. The evidence indicates that the number of

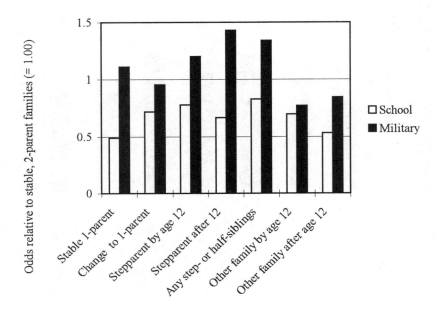

Figure 6.3. Effects of Family Structure on Leaving Home to School and the Military
SOURCE: From Table A.6 in the appendix.

coresident parents and how long they have lived together have important influences on leaving home to college. The contributions of a non-coresident parent may also be important. Those whose experience of family disruption ended before age 12, whether the result was a stable remarriage or some other family form, have somewhat higher odds of leaving home to attend college than do those who were still experiencing family instability as adolescents. This finding suggests that nonparental members (either a stepparent or some other relative) in a family that has been stable because age 12 make some contribution to these young adults. This distinction did not matter for single-parent families. Among single-parent families, the large difference is between those who became single-parents through divorce and those who never married. Although the latter is more "stable," at least on the dimension of parental coresidence, children in disrupted families may gain because the absent parent is making at least some financial contribution to the children and to the household, although not enough to erase the impact of the disruption.

The popularity of the military among the children of nontraditional families is an even more unexpected finding. (It seems unlikely that the armed services selectively recruit such people, although when they portray themselves as a supportive family, this may be the result.) We examined this result in more detail, in part because we wondered about the effect of this pattern on the armed services. We found that the effect of family structure is relatively powerful only in periods when relatively few enlist (Figure 6.4). Among cohorts for whom military service was rare as a route out of the home (< 15 percent of men), those from nontraditional families were nearly three times as likely to take this pathway as those from stable two-parent families. (This enlistment level characterizes both the oldest—pre-1938—and youngest—post-1973—cohorts.) In contrast, there was almost no difference by family structure during World War II, when more than 30 percent of young men left home to serve in the military.

Nonfamily Independence: Leaving to Take a Job or Just to be Independent

Leaving home to enter college, and usually also the military, requires some planning and organization. So, too, does leaving home to take a job. Leaving just to be independent—to be on one's own or to have one's own place—can be done on the spur of the moment. We have already documented that gaining a stepparent in childhood substantially increases young people's likelihood of

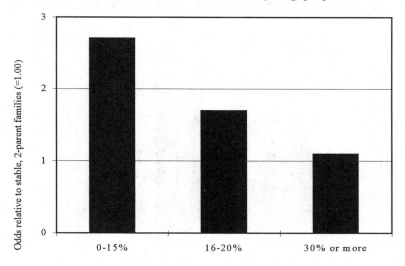

Proportion who left home to join the military ("draft" level)

Figure 6.4. Inverse Relationship Between the Effects of Stepfamilies on Leaving Home to join the Military and the "Draft" Level
SOURCE: Calculated by the authors from the NSFH.

leaving home at a very young age (15 or 16) via this route (Chapter 4). In this section, we consider the effects of all the varieties of nontraditional family structures on leaving home to independence and compare them with leaving to take a job—the two routes to nonfamily, total residential independence.

Like leaving home to join the armed services, leaving home to take a job and to be independent are much more likely among those who experienced some sort of nontraditional family structure in childhood (Figure 6.5). The most powerful effects, across the most forms of nontraditional family structures, are for the independence route. Leaving home to take a job is only accelerated significantly only among those with stepparents (whether they joined the family before or after the respondent had reached age 12) and stepsiblings.

The strongest effect of family structure on leaving home for independence occurs among the recent stepparent type. Leaving home via this route is nearly 80 percent more rapid than among those from stable two-parent families. Whereas about 18 percent of those with stable two-parent families took the independence route out of the home, this was the choice of about one-third of those from families that gained a stepparent after age 12.

The experience of a longer-term stepparent increases this route somewhat less, about the same as having stepsiblings (about 50 percent) and being from

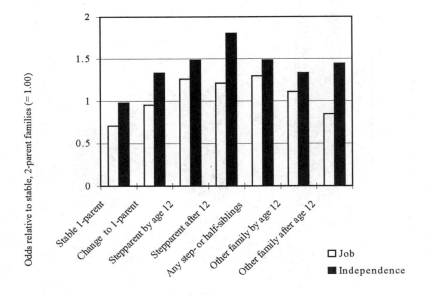

Figure 6.5. Effects of Family Structure on Leaving Home for a Job or Independence
SOURCE: From Table A.6 in the appendix.

other families who experienced a change after age 12, and slightly more than coming from families that became single-parent at some point. The major contrasting nontraditional family effect on independence is for those from stable, one-parent families, who are no more likely to take this route than those from stable two-parent families. This suggests that for most forms of nontraditional family structure, the parental home feels less like their own place than it does for children from stable two-biological-parent families—or for those who have grown up in a stable single-parent home.

Overall, then, when considering these four reasons for leaving home that are not linked to new family formation, those who did not grow up in stable two-parent homes are less likely to leave home for education but more likely to leave to join the military, get a job, or particularly just to be independent. These effects partially offset each other in the analysis of overall leaving home. When they are separated, the data show clearly that although nontraditional family structures accelerate leaving home to nonfamily living arrangements, this occurs despite the fact that children in stable two-parent families are more likely to leave home to go away to college. Thus, not only the timing of leaving home but the contexts or the routes taken allow us to understand the effects of family structure on the nestleaving process. For routes that require the most planning and parental investment—college—children from nontraditional families are at a disadvantage. But for those routes that do not require parental investment, the less the level of planning needed, the more likely young people who had nontraditional family structures in childhood are to take them.

FAMILY INDEPENDENCE: LEAVING TO COHABIT OR TO GET MARRIED

But what of our "new family" routes out of the home—marriage and cohabitation or single parenthood? They require more than planning; they require cooperation with a partner. In the case of single parenthood, the partner's cooperation might have been brief, but because most in the "cohabitation-single parenthood" category actually were cohabiting when they first left home, we will normally refer to this category simply as "cohabitation" and think of it in these terms. Furthermore, perhaps there are always partners of some sort to be found, given that we found an extremely powerful effect on leaving home to very early marriage (between age 15 and 16) among those with stepparents (Chapter 4). However, there is also some evidence that the children in families that have experienced disruption are more averse to marriage than those who grew up in stable families. We also found that the positive effect of stepparents on early marriage dropped off dramatically as children grew up (Chapter 4). How does the wider range of nontraditional family forms affect the likelihood of leaving home for marriage over all ages? Do they differ in their effects on the less traditional types of new family formation, cohabitation and single parenthood?

Our analysis shows that overall, positive effects on marriage appear only for stepparent (and stepsibling) families. However, there are much stronger, and more consistently powerful, effects on leaving home to cohabit or to head a single-parent family (Figure 6.6). The greatest proportionate impact is nearly always on the less conventional family forms rather than on marriage. Nevertheless, even a small increase in the odds of leaving home to get married can translate into major effects, whereas even a doubling or trebling of the odds of leaving home to cohabit can have little overall effect, because marriage is a far more common route out of the home (38 percent took this route compared with 3 percent who left to cohabit or head a single-parent family). Thus, the odds ratio of leaving home for marriage among those with a long-term stepparent is 1.37, the strongest effect of family structure on this route. The effect of a recent stepparent on leaving home to cohabit is 2.75, the strongest effect of family structure on this route. The relative impact on cohabitation is thus much larger. In absolute terms, however, the proportion leaving to marriage increased from 36 percent to 49 percent among those with a long standing stepparent—an increase of 13 percentage points—whereas the proportion leaving to cohabit increased from 3 percent to 8 percent among those with a recent stepparent—an increase of "only" 5 percentage points.

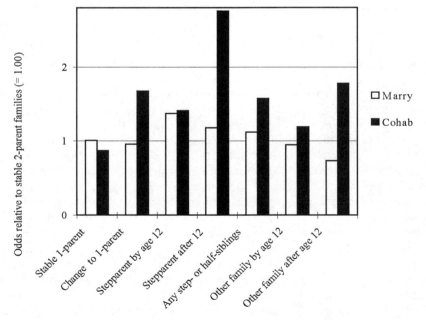

Figure 6.6. Effect of Family Structure on Leaving Home for Marriage or Cohabitation
SOURCE: From Table A.6 in the appendix.

Change in family structure, particularly recent change (after age 12), has the greatest impact on cohabitation. Relative to those growing up in a stable two-parent family, the odds of taking the cohabitation route are 78 percent greater for those who experienced changes in adolescence that brought them to some "other" family form but only 19 percent greater if this change took place before age 12. Similarly, as we noted above, a recent stepparent increases the odds of leaving home to cohabit by 178 percent, whereas having this experience prior to adolescence results in an increase of only 41 percent. The effects of family instability leading to a single-parent family (normally divorce) were less sensitive to timing, with an overall increase in leaving to cohabitation of 67 percent. Only those from stable one-parent families do not show this strong effect.

These findings are consistent with, and contribute to, research focusing on the factors underlying becoming a single parent or becoming dependent on welfare (McLanahan and Bumpass 1988). Studies have interpreted these patterns as reflecting reduced parental time investment in children via monitoring their activities and companions, with the result that there is an increased likelihood of precocious sexual relationships. It is more difficult to interpret the increase in the likelihood of marriage in this way, although the extent that these marriages are initiated by pregnancy would reinforce such an interpretation. It is possible, however, that marriage, with or without pregnancy, is simply another route out of a difficult situation, another way to get "one's own place." If this is the case, young adults who have experienced family instability are essentially leaving home any way they can, whether or not they are emotionally or financially ready to do so. The home is the problem; they are not leaving because they are somehow, precociously "ready." This interpretation is reinforced by the results of the analyses on leaving home at an early age (Chapter 4). We now turn to evidence on returning home to explore this interpretation further.

RETURNING HOME

Returning home, whether viewed as an indication of "failure" or simply as a useful "refueling" step in the uncertain transition to adulthood, should normally be thought of as a step that primarily benefits the prodigal child. Few parents in this modern economy can compel children who are functioning independently to return home. Those whose childhoods were marked by nontraditional families should have the greatest need to return home. They disproportionately took the most risky routes out of the home, at least in terms of their likely contribution to stable and secure adult roles—that is, to the military rather than to college, to independence rather than to take a job, to cohabitation rather than to marriage. The evidence, however, suggests that this is not the case, because they are much less likely to return home. The parental homes for many of them provide too few resources, or resources at too high a cost, to be worth returning to.

The effects of the different family structures on returning home parallel those on leaving home, with a few exceptions (Figure 6.7). All are less likely to return home than are young adults who grew up in stable two-parent homes. Those with single parents are more likely to return home than those with stepparents (about 85 percent vs. about 70 percent the likelihood of returning home compared with children who grew up in stable two-parent families). In turn, they are more likely to return home than those who experienced multiple changes or lived for a time in nonparental families (who were only about 50 percent as likely to return home as those who had no experience of a nontraditional family).

In the case of returning home, it does not seem to matter how old they were when the stepparent arrived or when the final change in these nonparental families occurred (the increase in likelihood of returning home among this latter group is not significant). An interesting exception to the general pattern of effects on leaving home appears for stepsiblings, whose presence has no significant effect on rates of returning home. Perhaps they are no longer there, or if they are, are still so young that even if their parent's absorption in them made it easy, or even necessary to leave home, they are less a barrier to returning than is a problematic relationship with parents or stepparents.

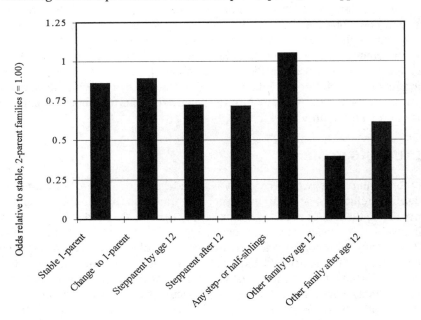

Figure 6.7. Effect of Family Structure on Returning Home
SOURCE: From Table A.6 in the appendix.

ARE THERE CHANGES IN THE EFFECTS OF FAMILY STRUCTURE?

Our detailed review of the effects of nontraditional family structures on leaving and returning home ended on a relatively benign note (maybe stepsiblings are not so bad, after all). However, it is difficult to escape the general conclusion that on a wide range of outcomes, experiencing one or another of these nontraditional family forms is problematic for young people making their transition to adulthood. This general conclusion increases the need to assess whether there have been changes over time in these patterns. As these experiences of family disruptions and instability become more common, have their impacts on the transition to adulthood lessened or have their effects intensified?

In the following section, we review the results of our analyses of change in the effects of family structure. Overall, we find great stability, which should be a source of concern, given the increased numbers of young adults in the most recent periods who have been exposed to these risks. In two key areas, however, we present some findings that indicate that on one dimension, things are getting better, much better; on another dimension, they may be getting worse. These dimensions are leaving home for college among stepchildren and leaving home for marriage among the children of single parents.

THE DECREASING EFFECTS OF STEPFAMILIES ON COLLEGE

One of the strongest findings in the "consequences of family structure" literature has been that those in stable two-parent families are the most likely to continue in school, either to finish high school or to go on to college (McLanahan and Bumpass 1988). In those studies, stepfamilies are normally as problematic, and sometimes more problematic, than single-parent families. Our results show that, at least when attending college is framed within the context of a route out of the home, this problem is becoming far less acute.

Among the oldest cohorts, those who came of age during World War II or earlier, the effects of having a stepparent sometime during childhood were dramatic—those who had this experience were barely 30 percent as likely to take this route as those with stable, two-parent families (Figure 6.8). Among the cohorts who came of age between the end of the second world war and the Vietnam war, the deficit had decreased but was still substantial. Children in stepfamilies were about three-quarters as likely to leave home to attend college as those in stable two-parent families. For the two most recent cohorts, however (1973-79 and 1980+), there was no discernible effect at all.

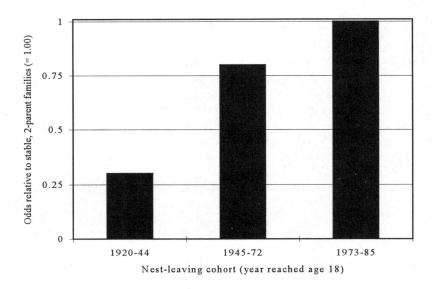

Figure 6.8. The Decreasing Effect of Stepfamilies on Leaving Home for College
SOURCE: Calculated by the authors from the NSFH.

Clearly, the costs in terms of leaving home to attend college have decreased enormously. Among the earliest cohorts, when college attendance was extremely rare, it seems that the small chance one might have had was essentially wiped out by this family structure experience. It is not necessarily the case, however, that the attenuation of the stepparent effect reflects greater willingness on the part of stepparents to assume these costs. The post-1970 period saw an enormous expansion in the willingness of colleges themselves to provide financial aid. We will see later that having received public assistance in childhood has also become much less a problem over time for this route out of the home that is so critical for later economic success (Chapter 8). Much more research is needed about the ways that stepparents—and non-coresident parents—find to contribute to children's educational attainment.

THE CHANGING EFFECT OF SINGLE PARENTS ON MARRIAGE

Another common finding in the research literature on the consequences of family structure is the precocious rate of family formation (and early sexuality) shown by many who grew up in disrupted families. Our analyses of cohort change in the likelihood of leaving home to get married show that, at least among those who grew up in single-parent homes (either through divorce, widowhood, or never marriage), this has been a rapidly evolving situation (Figure 6.9). The cohorts who came of age during World War II or before were about 40 percent more likely to leave home via marriage at a given age than were those who had a stable two-parent family. There were no statistically significant differences for the cohorts coming of age between 1945 and 1972. Among the most recent cohorts, children from single-parent families were significantly less likely to leave home for marriage (about 80 percent) relative to those from stable homes.

Part of what has been happening to marriage rates among very young adults is that cohabitation has increasingly served as a substitute. Cohabitation was nearly nonexistent in the reports of these respondents who grew up in the years before the end of World War II, and remained so through most of the 1960s. This very low rate of reported cohabitation makes it difficult to test for intercohort change in leaving home to cohabit. These results suggest that the children of family disruption have led the expansion of cohabitation because that time, by increasingly avoiding marriage as their route out of the home to a new family.

Hence, on this dimension, at least, it is clear that the effects of family structure, although changing, remain potent (as they do on most of the other routes out of the home). Where there are other institutions that provide

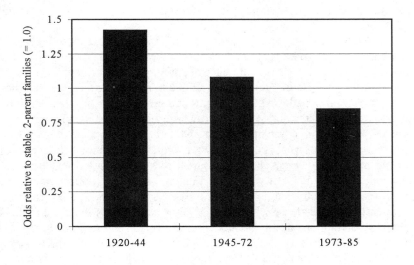

Nest-leaving cohort (year reached age 18)

Figure 6.9. Changing Effect of Growing Up in a Single-Parent Family on Leaving Home for Marriage
SOURCE: Calculated by the authors from the NSFH.

alternative sources of support, however, the effects can be offset. The commitment by the nation's private and public colleges to provide financial aid to students in need is one such source of support, making it more possible for them to experience success in their economic lives as adults. Perhaps as the divorce revolution progresses, parents and others will find ways to provide the supports needed to increase the likelihood that their children also experience stable and successful family lives.

CONCLUDING OBSERVATIONS

We have shown that instability in parental presence in the homes that increasing proportions of young adults experienced in childhood is linked with nest-leaving and returning patterns. Leaving home under these circumstances appears to be a more difficult transition to successful work and family roles. All forms of nontraditional family structures reduce the likelihood that young adults have the opportunity to leave home to attend college and reduce the likelihood that they return to the parental home. The most powerful effects are associated with gaining a stepparent, particularly during adolescence rather than earlier, and with having stepsiblings. Nearly every route out of the home is accelerated by these experiences, particularly leaving for independence, to enter the military, and to take a job. There are also strong increases in leaving home linked with nontraditional family formation via cohabitation or single parenthood.

Our results linking family disruption and leaving home closely resemble the impact of lower parental social class and having more siblings on these processes (Chapter 8). But the influence of parental family structure on leaving home is stronger. Both family and social class patterns suggest that nest-leaving timing and pathways reflect parental investments in their children. Having two parents in a stable family structure, like having parents with more resources and having fewer siblings to share them with, appears to provide children with more of what is needed for a successful launching into adulthood. They are more likely to get the educational investments they need to obtain a secure and successful career trajectory. Young adults can remain home until they are ready to establish a home of their own via marriage or some other form of residential independence. Those with other experiences during childhood, particularly disruptions during adolescence, are very likely to leave home at an early age any way they can. They are likely to move into family relationships that provide less support and less stability. They often leave simply to independence at such young ages that it resembles running away from home.

Clearly, it is important to conduct analyses that connect both the economic and family pathways to adulthood. These issues are firmly linked throughout adulthood but particularly at this critical juncture of the life course. It is likely that these linkages are made early, reflecting patterns of parental investment when their children are growing up. As young people make the transition to adulthood, the family decisions and economic outcomes in their parents' lives influence parental investment in children. In turn, these investments carry over generationally in the progress that young adults make on their own economic and family pathways.

The links between the type of families that children experience when they are growing up and the paths they take out of the nest are powerful. But just as all families are not the same, so all children are not the same. We now turn to another powerful revolution and explore how changes in gender roles are linked to the routes sons and daughters take in their transition to adulthood.

CHAPTER 7

Sons and Daughters

Among the most dramatic family changes of the 20th century are those linked with the ongoing gender revolution. Women's roles outside the home have been transformed with the ubiquitous growth in their employment in offices and factories, in the professions, and in technical jobs. This expansion of work-related activities has occurred among both married and single women and includes those with and without young children at home. Research has documented that there has been an overall increase in the labor force participation of women from around 20 percent to more than 50 percent over the 20th century and a 10-fold increase among married women between 1890 and 1980, starting from a low of 5 percent (Goldin 1990, Table 2.1).

The growth in paid employment opportunities for women is closely linked as a cause and a consequence with their increased educational attainment. Increasing education enriches the personal and family lives of women irrespective of their employment status. The importance of education, however, is more clearly evident for those who expect to be employed outside the home, because those with higher levels of education normally earn considerably more than those who are less educated.

Links between this growth in women's employment and their family lives—and the family lives of men—are much less clear than the connections between employment and education (even before we consider the more complicated links to leaving and returning home in early adulthood). The primary response to the increased employment of married women has been the growth in the "second shift," in that most married women continue to perform their household's domestic tasks along with their work outside the home (Hochschild 1989).

Because of the connection between working outside the home and the economic independence of women, many have argued that the increased level of female employment in the paid labor force is behind the decline in fertility

119

and the growth in delayed marriage, cohabitation, divorce, and out-of-wedlock childbearing (e.g., Cherlin 1996). The evidence connecting the increased labor force participation of women and these family-related changes, however, is neither clear nor consistent. Others argue that the causal arrow is from family processes to employment rather than the other way around, suggesting, for example, that the trend toward cohabitation or divorce requires women to work (Johnson and Skinner 1986). It may be, however, that an examination of a different dimension of family behavior might shed light on the ongoing controversy about the impact of working on women's family life. We have already suggested that leaving the parental home is a link between two types of family relationships (Chapter 1). First, there have been changes in the parent-child relationship and the ways that parents relate differently to sons than to daughters. Second, there have been changes in the relationships between adult males and females, whose negotiations are shaped by their values about union formation and parenthood and about career and home. Thus, our analysis of gender differences in the nest-leaving process has the potential to clarify some of the ways the gender revolution is affecting the family.

The nature of the gender revolution is not the only source of complexity. It is also the case that the progress in reducing the gap between men and women, boys and girls, sons and daughters across the 20th century has been anything but smooth. There have been periods over the last century when the social and economic gaps between men and women have narrowed considerably and other times when gaps have remained unchanged or even increased. One of the most dramatic changes in the gender gap occurred in the first two decades after World War II, when, in the midst of the baby boom, women, whose educational levels had been increasing throughout the century, actually lost ground on some dimensions. The proportions of women among college students, which had reached 47 percent in 1920, had fallen back by 1957 to 35 percent. The share of women receiving doctorates dropped from 17 percent in 1920 to 10 percent in 1957 (Newcomer 1959). Our focus on changes in gender gaps over time in leaving and returning home is likely to provide some insight into this unusual baby boom period.

Our first questions focus on gender differences in the routes taken out of the parental home—and the likelihood that sons and daughters will return home. The results of this analysis will prepare us for a more thorough examination of how changes in the nest-leaving process have influenced the early life courses of men and women. Together, the evidence that we can reconstruct for the 20th century will allow us to clarify whether men and women have become more similar to each other in this aspect of family relationships and to identify the critical timing in the historical convergence between men and women. We shall also be able to identify in what contexts and time periods gender differences have changed more rapidly or whether the gender gap in some areas has remained stable or has widened over the 20th century.

GENDER GAPS IN LEAVING AND RETURNING HOME

The period between late adolescence and early middle age is characterized by the greatest gender differentiation in social roles and attitudes over the entire life course. The social roles of younger girls and boys in the home and particularly in school are relatively similar, even if their play is often quite gender segregated. Similarly, the lives of men and women converge later in adulthood and become more similar after the years of raising small children end and as their work schedules become increasingly identical. How do patterns of leaving and returning home fit into this life course picture? We begin our analysis of the gender gap by examining the timing and routes taken by young men and women.

WOMEN AND MEN LEAVING HOME

Consistent with its life course location in late adolescence and early adulthood, patterns of leaving home among women and men are quite distinctive. Surprisingly, there is relatively little difference in men's and women's likelihood of leaving home (Figure 7.1). The bar on the chart labeled "overall" indicates that women leave home about 7 percent more rapidly than men. But overall timing conceals wide gender differences in the likelihood of leaving home by a given route. Women marry earlier than men and hence are nearly three times as likely as men to take this route out of the home at a given age. Consistent with their somewhat earlier family formation schedule, women are also more than twice as likely as men to leave home to begin a nontraditional family, either through cohabitation or single parenthood.

At the other extreme of gender role specialization, nearly all those who left home to join the military are men. Women were only 3 percent as likely to leave home in conjunction with military service as men during the 20th century. The other routes out of the home, however, show much less gender differentiation. Leaving the parental home to take a job was disproportionately male during this period, but women were nearly two-thirds as likely as men to leave home via this route at any specific age. Leaving home to attend school was equally balanced between young men and women, and women were actually 10 percent more likely than young men to leave home just to be independent. With the significant increase in this route out of the home starting for the nest-leaving cohorts of the 1960s and the parallel decline in the marriage, job, and military service routes (Chapter 2), it appears likely that the pattern of overall differences between men and women may have diminished as well. We shall investigate changes over time in the timing and the pathways out of the home in a subsequent section of this chapter, after we explore gender differences in the rates of returning home and some contextual factors influencing both leaving and returning home.

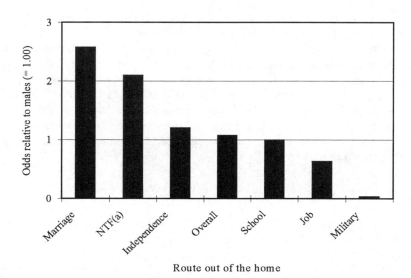

Route out of the home

(a) Nontraditional family.

Figure 7.1. Gender Differences in Leaving Home by Each Route
SOURCE: Calculated from Table A.2 in the appendix.

MEN AND WOMEN RETURNING HOME

If the main differences between men and women are in the specific paths taken out of the parental home and not in the timing of leaving home, what about returning home? The evidence suggests that there was much less difference between men and women in returning home over this period than for leaving home. Generally, women are considerably less likely to return home than men, when we control for a set of background characteristics such as race/ethnicity, nest-leaving cohort, and the family structure and social class of parents. However, this reflects the greater likelihood of women leaving home to marriage, which has the lowest rate of returning home (Chapter 3). When the gender differences in pathways taken out of the home are controlled, the gap between rates of returning home among women and men reduces essentially to zero. Nevertheless, there are considerable differences in men's and women's likelihood of returning from each of the major routes taken out of the parental home. These gender differences in returning by the specific pathways taken out of the home provide important insights about the relationship between leaving and returning home and, more generally, the transition to adulthood of men and women.

Gender differences in the likelihood of leaving home by a given route are closely mirrored by gender differences in the likelihood of returning home, given the pathway taken. This connection suggests that there is a normative element in the relationship between leaving and returning home: Those who take a route out of the home that is unexpected among those of their gender (i.e., one that is not normative) have perhaps burned their bridges more thoroughly than those whose nest-leaving route fits more closely to expected gender patterns. Even the exceptions tend to reinforce this notion.

Women are more likely than men to return home if they left for marriage, the most "female" route out of the parental home. Similarly, men are more likely to return home than otherwise comparable women if they left to enter the military (Figure 7.2). Part of women's greater likelihood of returning to their parents' home after leaving to get married may reflect greater need. This need may be particularly intense if women have young children living with them who require the care of grandparents and whose care during the marriage may have hindered the career progress of mothers. Nevertheless, for those gender-distinctive routes, the gender most likely to take it is the most likely to return. The pattern of similarities is much broader than this, extending to include returning home from having left for a job and for independence. Nontraditional family formation in conjunction with leaving home is the major exception.

The "echo" pattern of women being more likely to return than men among those who took "female" routes and men being more likely to return than women among those who took "male" routes is considerably dampened, because overall, gender differences in rates of returning are less dramatic than differences between women and men in the routes taken out of the parental home. Women are about 50 percent more likely than men to return home if they left to marry (compared with the nearly threefold female advantage in taking this route out of the home). Women are 65 percent as likely to return if they left to join the military (compared with the minuscule proportions who took this route). The gender gap in the leave-return relationship is also muted for those who left to take a job: Women who left home via this route are about 80 percent as likely to return as otherwise comparable men, compared with their reduced likelihood of leaving by this route of 65 percent. The "muting" of the echo is absent only where gender differences in leaving were particularly weak; there is essentially no gender leave-return gap for those who left for independence, with women 10 percent more likely than men to take this route and about 10 percent more likely than men to return home from the independence route. There is one minor exception to this pattern of similarity in the gender differences between leaving and returning—leaving for school—and one major one—leaving in conjunction with forming a nontraditional family. Women are about 15 percent more likely than men to return home if

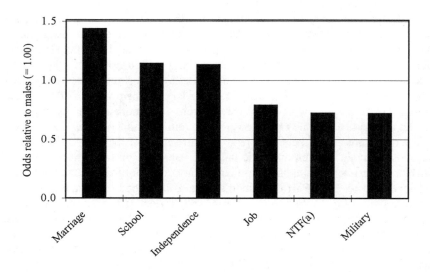

Route out of the home

(a) Nontraditional family.

Figure 7.2. Gender Differences in Returning Home by Route Out of Home
SOURCE: From Table A.3 in the appendix.

they left to attend school, even though young men and women were approximately equal in having taken this route out of the home. This gender pattern may reflect the greater likelihood that, in contrast to women, men will complete their educational program. It might also be the result of the greater value of men's educational attainment in the workplace.

Much more dramatic, however, is the gap between men and women in the likelihood of leaving and returning home from the nontraditional family pathways of cohabitation and single parenthood. Women, as we documented (Figure 7.1), are much more likely to take this route out of the home than men (indeed, more than twice as likely). However, women are considerably less likely to return home if they left to these forms of family formation (only 72 percent as likely as otherwise comparable men). If children were part of married women's greater likelihood of returning home, this should also be the case here, because some proportion of the women taking this route out of their parents' home are mothers (and not all women returning home after having left home to get married are mothers).

Clearly, during much of the 20th century, nonmarital cohabitation and unmarried parenthood were stigmatized. In the past, few parents were likely to be very approving of their children—sons or daughters—leaving home to form nontraditional families. However, stigma per se could not be a major factor accounting for these patterns, because rates of returning home among those leaving to form such nontraditional families are quite high (Chapter 3). What seems more likely is that the stigma attaches disproportionately to daughters. If, in general, it is easier to "change your mind" after leaving home to take a more common pathway for your gender, the greater likelihood that women will take the route to nontraditional family formation did not establish this route as "normative" for their parents. "Prodigal" daughters may have a more difficult time returning home than "prodigal" sons. The parental home is often a very different place for sons than for daughters. The parents' double standards may be only one dimension of the ways the home pushes the transition to adulthood of sons and daughters in different directions. It shapes the routes sons and daughters take when they leave the parental home and the probabilities of returning home from the pathways they select.

GENDER DIFFERENCES IN CONTEXT

What are the ways that the parental home can really be a different place for daughters than for sons? In turn, how does the context of the parental home influence the timing and routes out of the home among their children? Clearly, parents can make an enormous difference in the lives of their children in their differential expectations for and treatment of their sons and daughters. Even the most egalitarian parents, however, soon learn that the larger society shapes the lives of their sons and daughters in different ways. Our goal here is to explore these differences by assessing how changes in the context of the family might affect the life course of young men and women differently. In particular, we shall investigate whether these gender differences imply a tendency toward gender convergence or divergence in the pathways out of the nest over time. We examine the effects of three family contexts for understanding their effects on sons and daughters: (1) the structure of the family when children are growing up, (2) the resources available to the family at the time in the life course when sons and daughters are making decisions about leaving home, and (3) indicators of family attitudes and values likely to influence the decisions that young adults make about their residential relationship to their parents.

FAMILY STRUCTURE

We are able to explore two dimensions of family structure with the data available from the National Survey of Families and Households (NSFH): (1) whether having brothers or sisters matters in shaping the process of leaving home and (2) how divorce might influence young people's lives and the decisions they make about leaving home. We have already documented that experiencing change in the parental family, both parental separation and particularly parental remarriage, has a profound influence on the leaving- and returning-home process. Separation and remarriage sharply increases the likelihood of leaving home and reduces rates of returning home (Chapter 6). Having more siblings increases the probability of leaving home. We now ask, Does it matter whether these siblings are brothers or sisters? Do changes in parental family structure differentially affect the leaving home patterns of sons and daughters?

Brothers and Sisters. There were almost no differences overall in the effects of having siblings on the nest-leaving patterns of young men compared with young women. Relatively few effects, as well, were shaped by the sex of their siblings. Two findings, however, stand out, because they are part of an important process by which the family influences the next generation. The first is the effects of siblings on leaving home to attend college. Having more siblings reduces the likelihood that young adults leave home to attend college. Moreover, siblings have a greater effect on boys than on girls, and what particularly matters is having brothers. A second effect of siblings is on leaving home to join the military service. In contrast to going away to college, sisters have the greatest effect on leaving home in conjunction with military service. Having sisters reduces the odds that both young men and women leave home to enlist in the military and has a particularly powerful impact on young women (Figure 7.3).

Each additional sister (and for women, each additional brother) reduces the probability that young adults will leave home to attend college by a small but consistent and significant amount—about 2 percent. As a result, having a large family can cumulate to a moderately large effect. Brothers, however, reduce the likelihood that young men leave home to attend college about four times as much as do sisters. Many families invest more resources in their sons than in their daughters, particularly for educational purposes. This differential investment for sons and daughters could be part of the explanation of the impact of brothers on sons. However, it is puzzling that no such substitution influences young women's likelihood of taking this most egalitarian of all pathways out of their parent's home.

An even stronger difference emerged for the military route out of the home. As we documented earlier, this route is the most gender differentiated, with daughters only about 3 percent as likely as sons to leave home by this route. Having more brothers increases the likelihood that both young men and women leave home via this route; having more sisters reduces it, particularly for women. Young women who have one sister are only two-thirds as likely to leave via this route as those with no sister; those with two sisters are less than half (46 percent or .68 X .68) as likely to take this route as those with no sister. Clearly, the presence of more brothers or sisters shapes the family context that young adults experience when they grow up, as it does the family lives of their parents.

Parental Family Structure. A second family context that relates to gender differences is growing up with divorced parents. The specific combination of sons and daughters in families influences whether the marriage of parents lasts. Research has shown that divorce is more likely when there are daughters living at home than when there are sons, perhaps reflecting some men's greater involvement with their sons than with their daughters (Morgan et al. 1989). In turn, the marital stability of the family differentially influences the nest-leaving pathways of the sons and daughters who experience the separation and remarriage of their parents during their childhood. Although the differences are not large, daughters in such families are considerably more likely than sons to leave home overall (12 percent compared with 5 percent in stable two-parent families). This is the case primarily because the gender difference is reduced for several of the pathways that are disproportionately male—to take a job and for military service (Figure 7.4).

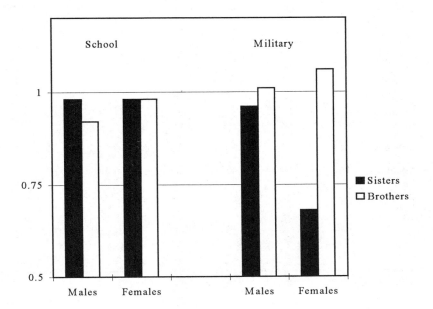

Figure 7.3. Differences in the Effects of Additional Brothers and Sisters on Men's and Women's Leaving Home for School and Military Service
SOURCE: Calculated by the authors using NSFH in a multivariate competing risks hazards analysis of leaving home, controlling for leave cohort, ethnicity, family structure and social class.

The overall pattern of gender differences is not altered when family structure is introduced, with one exception—the greater likelihood of daughters leaving home just to be independent only characterizes those in unstable families. Sons and daughters growing up in stable two-parent families do not differ from each other in the probability that they will leave just for independence. Gender differences in nest-leaving emerge primarily in two kinds of nontraditional families—those with stepsiblings and those headed by mothers (Table 7.1). Evidently, both of these family types make daughters need more "space" in ways that are less problematic for sons.

TABLE 7.1. Effect of Parental Family Structure[a] on Leaving Home by Gender and Route Left

Family Structure	*Total*		*Marriage*		*School*	
	Males	Females	Males	Females	Males	Females
Stable 1 parent	0.84	0.93	1.12	1.03	0.68	0.41*
Change to 1 parent	0.97	1.03	1.03	0.94	0.76*	0.71*
Stepfamily <12	1.30*	1.23*	1.25	1.40*	0.75	0.83
Stepfamily 12+	1.16	1.31*	0.82	1.29	0.66	0.71
Other <12	0.95	1.11	0.89	1.14	0.86	0.67
Other 12+	1.14	1.08	0.86	1.00	0.61*	0.51*
Stepsiblings	1.18*	1.31*	1.13	1.16*	0.89	0.81
	Military		*NTF[b]*		*PRI[c]*	
Stable 1 parent	1.01	2.76	1.00	0.83	0.66	1.02
Change to 1 parent	1.01	0.50	1.28	1.87*	1.04	1.30*
Stepfamily <12	1.20	1.38	2.49*	1.12	1.61*	1.34*
Stepfamily 12+	1.42	2.13	2.42	2.75*	1.47*	1.66*
Other <12	0.84	na	1.14	1.16	1.35	1.29
Other 12+	1.09	na	3.36*	1.87*	1.54*	1.52*
Stepsiblings	1.35*	1.53	1.35	1.78*	1.24*	1.67*

* significantly different from 1.0, p < .05.

a. Controlling for leave cohort, ethnicity, and family social class.

b. Nontraditional family.

c . Premarital residential independence.

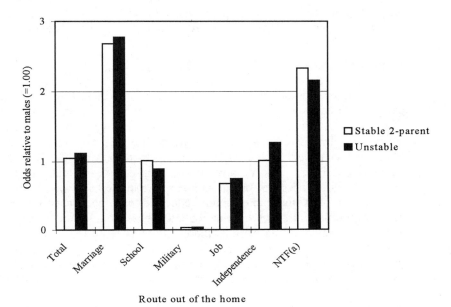

Route out of the home

(a) Nontraditional family.

Figure 7.4. Gender Differences in Leaving Home by Each Route, Stable Two-Parent Families and Other Families.
SOURCE: Calculated by the authors using NSFH in a multivariate competing risks hazards analysis of leaving home, controlling for leave cohort, ethnicity, family structure and social class.

There is some indication from the data that the instability of families when children are growing up disproportionately reduces the likelihood that daughters leave home to attend college. The odds that daughters in nonstable families leave home for college is only 89 percent of the odds of sons in such families compared with identical odds in stable two-parent families. The difference between sons and daughters is not statistically significant, however, and is not particularly consistent among the various types of nonstable families.

Taken together, these connections suggest, at least indirectly, a set of factors that might help to explain our earlier finding that sons are more likely than their sisters to remain in the parental home. The decrease in children's experiences of growing up in stable two-parent families combined with the overall growth in the independence route out of the home appears to be reinforcing young men's greater likelihood than young women to remain in the parental home. It is not clear what is cause and what is effect or how the changing economic context of the 1990s is linked to these changing gender patterns. The data show, however, that two shifts in family processes are linked to changes in the nest-leaving processes of sons and daughters: (1) the increase in non stable family structure and (2) the increase in leaving home just to be independent, unconnected to marriage or to the formation of new families.

PARENTAL RESOURCES

A consistent finding in research on American family patterns has been that gender differences are less pronounced among those at the upper level of the social hierarchy than among those who are at the lower end. This has been particularly the case among those families with higher parental education and has been documented for the process of nest-leaving as well (Goldscheider and Goldscheider 1993). The negative relationship between parental social class and gender differences may be interpreted in two interrelated ways. First, it has been argued that the more highly educated are more exposed to more egalitarian gender attitudes and that this influences them toward greater gender equality for their children. Second, those with more resources have less need to ration them for their sons but can provide as well for their daughters. Based on these considerations, we expected to find some differences in the effects of social class for sons and daughters, at least for leaving home. (See Chapter 8 for the general finding about social class and nest-leaving). Because our data showed no social class effect or overall gender differences in the rates of returning home, we do not anticipate that these relationships will differ between sons and daughters.

We were somewhat surprised to find that there were almost no gender differences of any kind in the effects of parental social class over the period covered by these data. Even when we focused on the major effect of social class on the leaving home process—that is, leaving home to attend college (Chapter 8)—no gender differences appeared. Daughters left home to attend college more if their families were more educated or had higher occupational prestige in much the same proportions as sons.

There are a few, small but interesting gender differences. The protection from military service that sons from the most highly educated families enjoyed was not evident for daughters. However, because women have never been subject to the military draft, it is not surprising that they did not need to find ways to avoid it. There is a faint echo of the traditional gender division of labor in the effects of parental occupational prestige on leaving home to take a job. The higher the prestige level of parents' occupation, the more likely sons are to take this route but the less likely daughters are to do so.

The most strongly gender-differentiated effect that emerged in our research was one that has not been closely studied—the effect on leaving home among those whose families received public assistance during childhood (Figure 7.5). Traditionally, the effect of this experience has been studied to determine whether there is an "inheritance" pattern among daughters of mothers in unstable families. Specifically, the question has been, are women who grew up

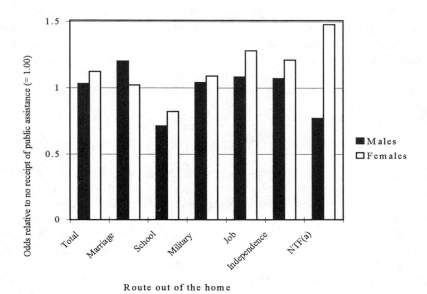

(a) Nontraditional family.

Figure 7.5. Effects of Receiving Public Assistance in Childhood on Men's and Women's Routes Out of Home
SOURCE: Calculated by the authors using NSFH in a multivariate competing risks hazards analysis of leaving home, controlling for leave cohort, ethnicity, family structure and social class.

in families experiencing welfare more likely to shape lives that will lead them onto welfare themselves? Most research has found that this is the case (Leibowitz, Eisen and Chow 1986; McLanahan and Bumpass 1988). Our results are consistent with these findings but show that the effects are much broader than previous arguments had posited.

We shall show that the receipt of public assistance in childhood increases the likelihood that children will leave home (Chapter 8). Our detailed analysis by gender shows that nearly all of the effect of receiving public assistance is on daughters, not on sons. Daughters growing up in families that received public assistance take the path toward more single parenthood or cohabitation relative to marriage. This finding is consistent with the "inheritance" results of previous research. However, receiving public assistance also influences daughters to leave home for nonfamily reasons (i.e., to take a job or just to be independent relative to attending school). It appears that daughters in these families receiving public assistance are leaving home by taking any path they can. It does not appear that they are choosing specifically to replicate their mothers' experiences. If daughters can leave by getting a job or by finding their own space, they do so. If leaving home requires riskier family forms, then they are likely to go that route as well. Whether because they were living with less admirable mother models or with difficult father figures or in contexts of disadvantage and deprivation, households receiving public assistance appear to create situations that are more problematic for daughters than for sons. As a result, daughters are much more likely than sons to leave these home environments at the first opportunity.

FAMILY ATTITUDES AND VALUES

In addition to the different effects of family structure and family resources on sons and daughters, we expect that the *attitudes* and *values* parents hold toward the basic social roles of their sons and daughters should have an important effect on the nest-leaving process. We know that gender role attitudes have a strong effect on the nest-leaving process. Those preferring more gender-segregated roles, net of social class and family structural characteristics, are more likely to remain home until marriage (Goldscheider and Goldscheider 1993). Although this is an important research avenue to pursue, the NSFH survey interviewed the nest-leavers often long after they left home. There were no measures included in the study that tapped either their attitudes when they were growing up or their parents' attitudes during this crucial period when young adults were making decisions about leaving home.

We are therefore limited to using indirect indicators of family attitudes and values in exploring family values associated with gender differences in nest-leaving. We have information on the religious affiliation of parents when young adults were growing up and on birth outside the United States. We begin with gender differences by religion.

We can estimate the religiously based family values likely to be held by respondents' families when they were in this critical life course transition. We are able to consider whether young men and women who have grown up in homes with different religious affiliations have differentially experienced the nest-leaving process. We distinguish families that are Catholic, Jewish, Protestant (either one of the fundamentalist or nonfundamentalist denominations), the Church of Jesus Christ of Latter Day Saints (Mormons), those of "other" religious affiliation (primarily non-Western, such as Buddhist), and those with no affiliation. (See Chapter 10 and the appendix for more details on the definitions of these categories.)

We will show that there were fairly large differences among these groups in nest-leaving processes, reflecting a mixture of group-specific and route-specific patterns (Chapter 10). Those with no religious affiliation leave home relatively early, particularly to the less institutionalized situations (nontraditional family formation and just to be independent); Catholics leave home very late on nearly all routes. Religious differences in leaving home to

TABLE 7.2. Effect of Religious Affiliation[a] in Childhood on Leaving Home by Gender and Route Left

Family Structure	Marriage		School		Military	
	Males	Females	Males	Females	Males	Females
No religious affiliation	0.80	1.05	0.76*	0.82	1.34^	2.00
Catholic	0.90	0.85*	0.84*	0.72	0.93	0.90
Jewish	0.89	0.70*	1.23	0.98	0.55	1.25
LDS (Mormon)	1.48	1.28^	0.84	0.79	0.62^	na
Fundamentalist Protestant	1.62*	1.38*	0.67*	0.61*	0.94	0.60
Other	0.89	0.79	1.15	0.55*	0.78	2.07
Liberal Protestant	1.00	1.00	1.00	1.00	1.00	1.00
	Job		Independence		NTF[b]	
No religious affiliation	1.99*	1.01	1.45*	1.30	1.42	1.53
Catholic	0.80^	0.78^	1.08	1.01	0.72	0.68*
Jewish	0.71	0.27*	1.33	1.21	0.98	0.30
LDS (Mormon)	2.77*	1.06	1.39	0.73	0.68	0.29^
Fundamentalist Protestant	1.21	0.91	1.02	0.92	1.19	0.89
Other	0.99	0.91	1.51	0.93	3.63*	2.18^
Liberal Protestant	1.00	1.00	1.00	1.00	1.00	1.00

* Significantly different from 1.0, p < .05; ^ significantly different from 1.0, .05 < p < .10.

a. Controlling for leave cohort, ethnicity, family structure and social class.
b. Nontraditional family.

get married (at a very early age among Mormons and fundamentalist Protestants; very late among Catholics and also Jews) contribute to overall differences in nest-leaving by religious affiliation. The differences in nest-leaving between men and women within each denomination are largely consistent with these patterns, but some sharp gender differences emerge.

The largest gender differences appear for leaving home to attend school and for nonfamily independence—to take a job or just to be independent (Table 7.2). Women who grew up in families affiliated with "other" religions (primarily non-Western) are significantly less likely to leave home to go to college than those who grew up as liberal Protestants, whereas such men are actually more likely to do so. This pattern results in a particularly sharp gender difference for those affiliated with non-Western religions. Members of these groups may endeavor to keep their daughters more closely linked to the community, to reinforce the likelihood that they marry within the group. There is some suggestion that the same pattern characterizes Jews, although the number of cases is too small to attain statistical significance. We will also show that there are larger gender differences among Jews than among non-Jewish Whites (Chapter 10): leaving home to go to school and for independence is more characteristic of Jewish than non-Jewish sons, whereas there is a greater likelihood that Jewish than non-Jewish daughters will leave home to marriage. These gender differences seem to have narrowed over time more in the general white population than among Jews.

The other major gender difference to emerge is in the likelihood of leaving home to unmarried independence among Mormons and fundamentalist Protestants. For each of these groups, both men and women are highly likely to leave home in conjunction with marriage. If daughters do not leave home to get married, they are very unlikely to leave home by any other route. This is not at all the case for men. The differences are most dramatic for Mormons (Figure 7.6).

Sons in Mormon families are more likely to leave home than daughters via any route, but the differences are largest for taking a job and independence. Evidently, even when daughters are not marrying early, they are much less likely to have, or take, the opportunity to participate in the "mission" type activity so common among sons. Unlike sons, most Mormon daughters marry at young ages and perhaps leave home in conjunction both with marriage and with mission activities. Daughters clearly remain in the parental home for a longer period of time than sons, in part preparing for marriage.

These two rapidly growing groups—and, at least for fundamentalist Protestants, a group that is rapidly diverging from the leaving-home patterns of more liberal Protestants (Chapter 10), are characterized by large gender distinctiveness in the newer routes out of the home—unmarried parenthood and independence. Their pattern of gender differentiation is particularly distinctive when compared with those who grew up in families other than stable two-parent homes and homes that received public assistance, in which daughters differ from sons on just these routes—unmarried parenthood and independence.

In addition to religious affiliation, we briefly examined gender differences in nest-leaving among immigrant groups as an indicator of values. In particular, we separated immigrant groups by whether they were of Western and non-Western origins. Our thinking was that immigrants originating from Western countries would be more likely to share American values than would immigrants from non-Western origins and that gender differences would be more pronounced among the latter. This is generally what we found; if anything, immigrants from Western countries are even less gender differentiated in their routes out of the home than the native-born, but there was

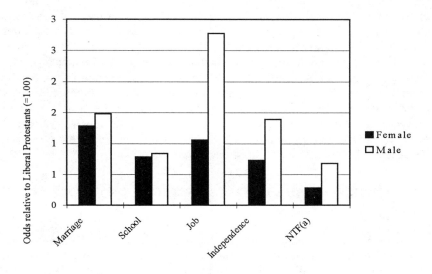

(a) Nontraditional family.

Figure 7.6. Gender Differences by Routes Out of Home by Mormons
SOURCE: From Table 7.2.

a key exception.

Overall, immigrants are dramatically more likely to leave home for a job—as much as three times the level of native-born—and less likely to leave by other routes. Among the nonmarriage routes, nonWestern-origin immigrants have a greater emphasis on marriage than do those from Western origins (although still lower than the native-born) and a lower emphasis on leaving for school than among those of Western origins (Chapter 9). Data that we organized (but do not present) show distinctive gender patterns among both Western and non-Western origin immigrants.

Among Western-origin immigrants, gender differences are generally less than among the native-born, because women from Western countries are over represented on predominately male routes (leaving for a job and for independence, with levels nearly twice those of men from these countries) and men are over represented on the marriage route. For school, however, the one route with the smallest gender difference for the native-born, males greatly predominate over females among those from Western countries. The investment of sending a young adult from a Western country to study abroad in the United States, whether made by parents, businesses, or international organizations, evidently is more likely to be made for males than for females.

The gender pattern among those from non-Western countries also differs from the U.S.-born, as well as from that of immigrants from Western countries, because most of the differences accentuate the gender differences present among the native-born. Among those from non-Western countries, women are relatively more likely than men to leave home for marriage, compared with the native-born, and men are more likely to leave home for a job or to be independent. On the dimension of leaving home to attend school, however, immigrants from non-Western countries, like their counterparts from Western countries and unlike the native-born, favor males over females.

GENDER DIFFERENCES IN NEST-LEAVING OVER THE 20th CENTURY

We now turn to an assessment of what is happening to gender convergence and divergence in the nest-leaving process over the 20th century. Taking the 20th century as a whole, there were considerable—and not fully shared— changes in the nest-leaving experiences of men and women in the United States. In some ways, the swings for men were particularly dramatic. For more than 30 years (1938 to 1972), military service was the route out of the home for between one fifth and one half of each cohort of men (Chapter 2). The post-World War II marriage and baby boom left much less a mark on the nest-leaving pathways of women through the end of the 1950s. About two-thirds of the young women left home to get married during this period, a level that was essentially continuous from the pre-World War II period.

Nevertheless, changes among women have been more fundamental than changes among men. The decline in the marriage route out of the nest for women has been extremely rapid because the post-World War II baby boom, whereas the change in routes for men has been much more gradual and less extreme than for women. Over time, the nest-leaving patterns that men have taken out of the parental home have fluctuated primarily among types of nonfamily living (school, military, and unmarried independence). Changes among women have moved them in the direction of being much more similar to men (increase in school, decrease in marriage).

We can now turn more systematically to two sets of questions about changing gender differences that will directly clarify patterns over time. First, who were the initiators or innovators, men or women, in the changing routes out of the home? Second what is the nature of the relative changes for men and women? In particular, has there been convergence by gender in the routes out of the home? Did both men and women experience changes in the same routes taken out of the nest but at different intensities? Do women follow the male model and converge toward it, or have both men and women changed but in different directions? We answer these questions below by investigating the changing routes of women and men over the course of the 20th century.

The changing gender pattern of leaving home for marriage is sharply evident (Figure 7.7). Although throughout the period, women have been much more likely than men to leave home via this route, the greatest differences were for the World War II cohorts (who reached age 18 between 1938 and 1944) and for the two baby boom cohorts that followed (1945-58 and 1959-65), when the gender gap in leaving home in conjunction with marriage increased to 3:1. There has been much less difference between men and women among the three youngest cohorts, ranging between 2.5:1 and 2:1. This suggests that there might be gender convergence in overall rates of leaving home.

This is not the case, however (Figure 7.8). The effects of marriage on both men's and women's leaving home have waned. Furthermore, the effects of marriage were always different for men and women simply because of gender differences in their ages at marriage. What then has happened over time to the different paths that men and women have taken out of the parental home?

In the earliest period, the young adult years of the cohort that entered their nest-leaving ages before 1930, both men and women were more likely to remain home until marriage. Yet for these cohorts, leaving home differences between men and women were particularly great, because women married so much earlier than men; overall, women were about 30 percent more likely to

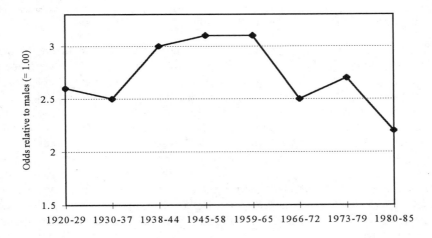

Nest-leaving cohort (year reached age 18)

Figure 7.7. Gender Differences in Leaving Home for Marriage by Nest-Leaving Cohort
SOURCE: Calculated by the authors using NSFH in a multivariate competing risks hazards analysis of leaving home, controlling for leave cohort, ethnicity, family structure and social class.

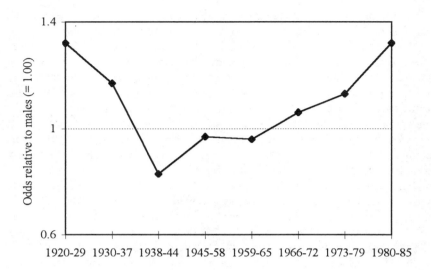

Nest-leaving cohort (year reached age 18)

Figure 7.8. Gender Differences in Leaving Home by Nest-Leaving Cohort
SOURCE: Calculated by the authors using NSFH in a multivariate competing risks hazards analysis of leaving home, controlling for leave cohort, ethnicity, family structure and social class.

leave home than men at any given age. There was some reduction in the gender difference during the nest-leaving cohorts of the 1930s. The Depression years may have delayed marriage for women even more than they did for men.

World War II, however, actually reversed the gender difference, with men more likely to leave home than women. Half of all men left home to serve in the military, often at very young ages; at least some of the women in that cohort waited until the war was over to marry and remained in their parents' home until they did. Men continued to leave home before women among the next two nest-leaving cohorts, likely reflecting both the importance of early military service and the fact that men's marriage ages dropped even more than women's during the baby boom (Cherlin 1992). But in the post-baby boom period, the cohorts that came of age during the Vietnam War, the baby bust, and the 1980s, women have again been leaving home more rapidly than men. Women have diverged from men so rapidly that the gender gap is even larger than it was prior to the economic depression of the 1930s. Does this gender gap continue to reflect the fact that women are more likely to leave home in conjunction with marriage, or is some new gender pattern at work?

No doubt some of the change in the gender gap is not a change at all, given the rapid increase in leaving home to form a nontraditional family via single parenthood or nonmarital cohabitation. This route, like marriage, is disproportionate female (although actually less so than marriage). Two pieces of evidence, however, suggest that the increased speed of women's leaving home relative to men over the last three cohorts is more than just "new wine in old bottles," as it were.

The more indirect evidence is simply logical: With the decline since the baby boom of routes out of the home that are disproportionately male, particularly jobs but also the military, men have lost their gender-specific "excuse" to leave home more than have women. Some of the pattern for women of leaving home early to marriage likely reflected their using marriage in order to leave home, which was evidently less a problem for men. Most homes still expect greater participation in housework and child care of their adolescent daughters than their otherwise comparable sons (Goldscheider and Waite 1991). Parents also more closely supervise their daughters' friends and schedules than they do their sons (Bulcroft, Carmody, and Bulcroft 1996). These gender differences may push at least some daughters out of the home more rapidly than sons.

More direct evidence that the parental home is more congenial to sons than to daughters emerges when we consider gender differences in the proportions returning home over time (Figure 7.9). As we documented in an earlier section, men have usually been more likely than women to return to the parental home after leaving. This reflected, however, the disproportionate use of marriage as a route out of the home among women, the route that continues to be characterized by the lowest rates of returning home among all routes.

The growth of cohabitation obviates this difference, because not only does it have a high rate of return, but the rate of return is actually higher for men than for women. The net result is that for the most recent cohort, the cohort of the 1980s, there have been major changes in the gender pattern of returning home. The rate of returning home had been increasing for both men and women and had substantially converged overall, with almost no differences by sex for the cohorts who came of age between 1959 and 1979. The gender pattern now has diverged, however, with men continuing to increase their rate of returning home but women decreasing their rate of returning home. These changing rates of returning home for men and women over time resemble the time pattern of gender differences in leaving home of a decade or so earlier. Male-female rates of leaving home converged between 1945 and 1965 and then diverged, with women leaving home more rapidly. Taken together, these changes suggest that the increased concentration of men in the parental home is less an artifact of differences in marriage timing or in the timing of other sorts of family formation. Rather, these gender patterns in both leaving and returning home represent a genuine difference in the relationship of men and women to their parental homes.

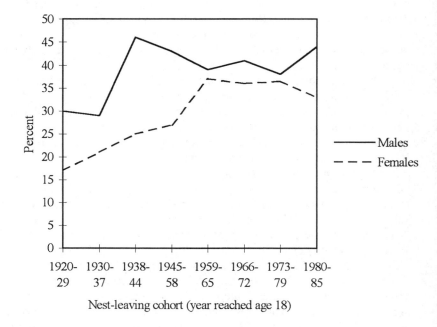

Figure 7.9. Gender Differences in Returning Home by Nest-Leaving Cohort
SOURCE: Calculated by the authors from the NSFH.

RETURNING TO FIRST THEMES

Taking all these results together, how has the gender revolution of the 20th century shaped the nest-leaving patterns of sons and daughters? Has the erosion of the separate spheres of men and women —despite fluctuations of the 1950s—shaped the ways young men and women leave and return home? The answer depends, at least to a certain extent, on whether we think of gender differences narrowly, in terms of the ways parents relate differently to sons and daughters to influence when they leave; or more broadly, in terms of the relationships between men and women as adults and hence, the routes they take out of the home—although, as we have shown, it is not always straightforward to separate the two themes of timing and routes.

The largest gender differences, and the strongest patterns of convergence, focus on the latter—the routes out of the home. In part, this is because the differences in the timing of leaving home, overall, are much smaller than the differences in routes. It is clear, however, that part of the way that parents relate differently to sons than to daughters does shape the nest-leaving experience directly via timing (and of course, parents may do so indirectly as well by reinforcing the importance of marriage for daughters and jobs for sons).

The clearest and most general evidence that parents relate to their children's nest-leaving differentially by sex is the relationship between leaving and returning. We observed a fairly close relationship between rates of return and the popularity of that route for both men and women. Women who left by predominately male routes (to the military or to take a job) were less likely to return than males who took those routes; men who left home by predominately female routes (particularly marriage) were less likely to return than women who took those routes. Although each case could have an idiosyncratic explanation, the general consistency suggests to us that there is a normative element in the nest-leaving process. This normative dimension operates so that children who left home in more approved ways are more welcome, or willing, to return.

The second piece of evidence that the home might be quite different for girls than for boys occurs in stepparent families. Although in stable two-parent families, boys and girls are about equally likely to leave home just to be independent, girls seem to need to use this route more than boys in stepparent families. Most coresident stepparents, of course, are stepfathers, suggesting that in at least some cases, this form of nontraditional family structure has a more negative effect on girls' comfort in their childhood homes than it does on boys. Although this pattern appears to be more the result of the revolution in family structure than a direct consequence of the gender revolution, it highlights the fact that parents do treat their sons differently than they do their daughters.

The strongest effects of the gender revolution per se appear in the convergence of routes out of the home and the increased similarity in their timing. This convergence has been particularly dramatic in the last third of the period that we have examined. This period of time was characterized by two significant changes: increases in leaving home to go away to college and increases in leaving just to be independent. These routes out of the nest came increasingly to replace marriage and leaving for a job (and the military) as the principle routes out of the home for women and men. College, of course, provides both young men and women with the knowledge, credentials, and experiences to allow them to develop successful employment careers. The growth in leaving for independence is a strong statement that many young men and women need to have their own place, independent of their parents. To be independent is sufficient justification for moving out, even if there is no "good reason," such as the draft, a job that requires moving, or a new family. This suggests that young adulthood, the life course period of great gender differentiation, is increasingly being structured in similar ways for men and women.

Our results showing differences among religious groups underline the extent to which the convergence has "come a long way." Nonfundamentalist Protestant and Catholic groups show the greatest gender similarity (with the former leaving home early and the latter leaving home late). The patterns for some other religious groups resemble more closely the gender differentiated patterns of the 1950s. Sons growing up in fundamentalist Protestant and in Mormon homes are much more likely to experience residential independence before marriage than are their sisters. Daughters growing up in homes where the parents have non-Western and Jewish religious traditions were less likely over the period to leave home to attend college than their brothers. The waning of the gender differences in the two largest religious groups should remind us all how far we have come.

CHAPTER 8

Leaving and Returning to the Feathered Nest

A powerful force shaping the history of the American family in much of the 20th century was the massive increase in economic well-being—income, education, wealth—that was particularly marked during three and a half decades around mid-century, 1940 to 1975. This was the period when home ownership and sending children to college became reasonable goals for all Americans, goals attained by many before the expansion of the economy slowed dramatically. The contours of this period are particularly clear in the increase in educational attainment of the parents of our survey group (Figure 8.1), shooting up by nearly four years, an increase of 50 percent, primarily in the post-World War II period.

This was an era when affluence seemed ensured, when America was becoming "the great society," and when the prospects for winning a war against poverty seemed far more realistic than they do at the end of the 20th century. The perception of change during this period of growth were even more intense, because it contrasted so sharply with the previous decade of extreme privation, the Great Depression of the 1930s. World War II was marked by its own privations but also brought the country rapidly to full employment and a strong desire to finally regain the American dream. We are only beginning to understand the meanings of the changing trends since the 1970s—the long slowdown from the mid-1970s through the early 1990s and the more recent partial boom as the 20th century draws to a end.

The period of affluence between World War II and the 1970s shaped many aspects of family life, contributing to a rush toward marriage at an early age and a great increase in births—the "baby boom." It was less clear to everyone what the effects were of increasing economic affluence on patterns of leaving and returning home in 20th century America. On the one hand, increased

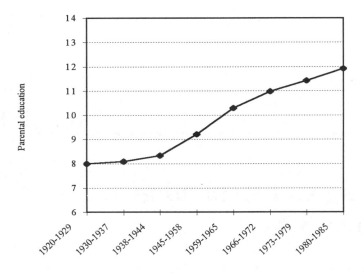

Nest-leaving cohort (year reached age 18)

Figure 8.1. Increases in Parental Education in the 20th Century
SOURCE: Calculated by the authors from the NFSH.

parental resources enhance the potential for young adults to leave home to attend college. This path should decrease the age at leaving home, because attending college away from home is one of the youngest routes out of the home. Affluent parents can provide their children the strongest start toward success, a college education, and at the same time buy their own privacy. On the other hand, there is often a suspicion that parental affluence by itself is an attraction to young adults to remain home for a longer period and to return to the comforts of their parents' "feathered nest" after being away for some time. An affluent parental "nest" might seem quite attractive, particularly in the face of the risks and privations of the struggling period of career development, unstable social and personal relationships, and crowded apartment-style living that most young adults experience. Although we found that increased parental resources actually contributed to the departure of those who had remained home quite late (ages older than 23), particularly to independence, it was also the case that at the very beginning of the nest-leaving stage (ages 15-16), parental resources did retain children in the parental home (Chapter 4). How do resources affect the overall nestleaving process, considering all routes, and how do they affect returning home?

Our first task will be to resolve these various complexities by examining differences in the probability of leaving and returning home by measures of parental social class. These results should provide the first clues about how increases in affluence might have shaped changes in nest-leaving over the 20th century. If we can document a strong social class effect—for example, that those from more educated families leave home earlier and are more likely to return—this could help account for the long-term decline in the age at leaving home and the increase in returning home, though likely not the recent increase in age at leaving home (see Chapters 2 and 3).

It is possible, however, that the effects of social class might have changed over time. There have been periods in the 20th century when "equal opportunity" has been an important value. This might be translated into reduced differences in nest-leaving patterns by parental social class background for some periods. Continuing inequality has appeared to be less a problem to some or even a sign of a healthy society (Herrnstein and Murray 1994).

We have also documented two routes out of the parental home that are relatively "new," in the sense that they have expanded dramatically in their incidence. Leaving home just to be independent was almost never reported among the members of the study who reached adulthood before the 1950s. This route out of the nest has expanded dramatically over the last two decades (as described in Chapter 2). Even more dramatic has been the increase in nontraditional family formation, both as a phenomenon in American society and as a route out of the parental home. The proportion of children born to unmarried mothers has increased from 12 percent to 30 percent between 1960 to 1964 and 1985 to 1989 (Cherlin 1996). Furthermore, the proportion who had cohabited before they married has increased from 11 percent among those who married between 1965 and 1974 to 44 percent among those who married between 1980 and 1984 (Cherlin 1996).

New behavior is often initiated by one segment of the population, which then spreads to others, becoming more widely accepted. Recent research has shown how this process of innovation and diffusion works for the major swings in behavior such as breast-feeding. The more educated were the first to drop the breast-feeding practice in the United States in the 1930s and 1940s. They were the first to take it up again in the 1960 and 1970s, by which time almost no women were breast-feeding their children (Haaga 1988). The more educated have led the recent decline in breast-feeding in response to the great decreases in time taken off from work after childbirth and the increase in the number of weeks mothers have worked during their children's first year (Lindberg 1996). Similarly, the more educated led the increase in fertility of the 1950s baby boom, and led again in the decreased fertility of the baby bust (Rindfuss, Morgan and Swicegood 1988).

This pattern of innovation by the more educated might also characterize trends in leaving home. The children of the more educated may have been in the forefront of the increase in leaving home for independence and nontraditional family formation. A focus of this chapter will be on whether the effects of parental social class on the nest-leaving process have been stable over the 20th century.

PARENTAL SOCIAL CLASS: WHAT IS IT?

The social class of the families where young persons are growing up involves a number of dimensions. We considered in detail two of these in our retrospective reconstruction of the historical record: the educational attainment of parents and their occupational prestige ranking. Each of these dimensions can be assessed for the various nest-leaving cohorts that we have identified at the time when young adults were age 16. This time is of greatest interest, because this is the beginning of the life course stage when leaving home is first considered. Because we are focusing on the longer-term trends, cross-sectional, contemporary information on the social class of the survey respondents is not a valid measure of the conditions and contexts that shaped the decisions when young adults were making decisions about leaving home decades earlier. No retrospective information was obtained on income at the stage when the respondents were still living at home.[1]

In our construction of these social class measures, we included information on both the educational level of the parents and their occupational ranking. In this way, we were able to separate different dimensions of social class and investigate their effects on leaving home. Educational attainment measures the preference or "taste" aspect of social class separately from the resources implied by occupational rank. As we shall show below, each dimension influences leaving home somewhat differently. We treated the level of parental education as taste when resources are statistically controlled. This means that we can estimate the importance of leaving home by particular routes within resource levels. All other things equal, education should reveal the importance of family or independence in the decisions to leave home and should reveal the alternatives of investing in college, independence from parents, or getting a job at similar levels of family resources. And the impact of parental educational levels on leaving home in conjunction with marriage (when resources are the same) should inform us about the changes in the taste or value of forming a new family in conjunction with leaving home.

Similarly, our examination of the net impact of occupation on changes in the timing and routes out of the parental home reveals the influence of financial resources, because occupational levels and income in US households are closely related. This is particularly the case when we control for educational level.

An additional dimension of social class that we can examine retrospectively is whether the family ever received public assistance while the respondent was growing up. This indirectly measures the absence of a wider set of the resources (savings, the contributions of kin) that some families can use to cushion the impact of illness or unemployment whereas others are forced to use public funds. We shall examine the historical changes in leaving home to explore whether the short-term vicissitudes of childhood can be linked to the timing and route out of the parental home.

We constructed the parental occupational prestige ranking using the standard measure of occupations in the National Survey of Families and Households (NSFH). We included the occupational prestige rankings of both parents when the respondent was growing up (or at age 16). We used father's occupational rank alone if an occupation was reported only for him; mother's occupation was used when information was available only for her. We used a combination of the occupational prestige score of both parents when both had an occupation listed, weighting the occupational prestige of fathers double that of mothers (Nock and Rossi 1978). The measurement of education was straightforward except when there was missing information on one of the parents.[2]

All of the analyses of the effects of parental education and occupational prestige assume that young adults have access to the resources that these social class characteristics reflect. Assuming that parents spend time with their children when they were growing up, parental values, preferences, and worldviews resulting from the education they attained become part of the values and attitudes of their children. The mechanism is socialization. Resources that involve the financial contributions of parents to their children can operate differently. Although parents who have more financial resources provide their children with an equivalent lifestyle of investment and consumption, from education to health care, not all do. There are Cinderellas; some children have little access to the resources of their parents.

The economic flow from parents to children has become central in the American stratification system and may also be part of the changing pathways out of the parental home. In particular, financial support from parents may be a key factor in the growth of residential independence before marriage. We do know that parents vary substantially in the extent to which they subsidize their children's lives in young adulthood, even among those with the same level of education and income (Goldscheider and Goldscheider 1991). We do not have retrospective information on these financial flows between the generations. In one study of the nest-leaving cohorts of the 1980s, greater intergenerational financial flows (particularly the subsidies that parents provide to their children for education) increased leaving home before marriage. Such contributions also reduced the probability of early marriage and increased the probability of residential independence. Some of this residential independence was the result of parental financial support of their children to live alone or with housemates. Often, the support was for semiautonomous living arrangements in college dormitories (Goldscheider and Goldscheider 1993).

In some ways, these findings for the cohorts of the 1980s suggest that the pathway out of more affluent parental homes may be through parental investment in the education of their children. As a consequence, the new pattern emerging is of leaving home in conjunction with getting a college education rather than by way of marriage. In turn, the increasing education of the children further delays marriage, hence lengthening the exposure of children to the probabilities of leaving home by other than the marriage route. We shall investigate these patterns of intergenerational relationships indirectly by our retrospective construction of social class measures and their changing connection to measures of the timing and routes out of the parental home.

LEAVING HOME AND PARENTAL SOCIAL CLASS

How, then, do the measures we have reconstructed to capture parental social class affect the timing and routes out of the parental home over time? What is the effect on leaving home of having parents with more education or with higher-ranked occupational prestige?   The evidence points to the following general patterns (Figure 8.2): Those whose parents have more education and those whose parents have higher occupational status are more likely to leave home at any given age during the nest-leaving period. However, the patterns vary by route taken and for each measure of social class. Furthermore, the largest effect on nest-leaving is for parental education, particularly having college-educated parents.

Parents' Education and Leaving Home. Only those whose parents have some exposure to a college education show elevated odds of leaving home, as the height of the bar on the left side of Figure 8.2 indicates. The effect, however, is substantial, with the children of college-educated parents being 20 percent more likely to leave home than those whose parents completed only high school. However, there are no significant differences at all among those whose parents had less than a college education. It did not matter whether parents attended high school but did not complete it or never attended high school. Each of these three lower educational levels had the same effects on leaving home, and each was less than those whose parents had some college education.   The parental education effect on leaving home is dichotomous (college educated or not), not a continuum.

Parents' Occupation and Leaving Home. Somewhat the same pattern appears when we consider parental occupation: Higher occupational prestige is linked with leaving home early. Unlike parental education, however, it is the low end of the occupational prestige ranking, not the higher end, that is distinctive in its effect on nest-leaving. Furthermore, unlike the parental educational effect, the differences between occupational rankings are not great. Young adults whose parents had quite low occupational prestige levels (unskilled laborers) are 94 percent as likely to leave home as those whose parents have even a little higher occupational skill level, as the right side of Figure 8.2 indicates. Once that level is achieved, there is no difference in the likelihood of leaving home among the children of doctors or bank clerks.

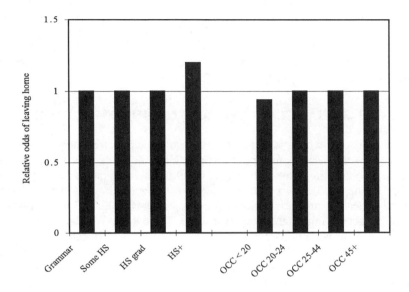

Figure 8.2. Effects of Parental Education and Occupational Prestige on Leaving Home
SOURCE: Calculated by the authors using NSFH controlling for leave cohort, sex, ethnicity, and family structure.

Public Assistance and Leaving Home. Having the experience of receiving public assistance during childhood, which normally is for a short period (although it was a more common experience during the Great Depression of the 1930s and in the past 25 or so years) has relatively little effect on the overall timing of leaving home. And its effect is positive: Those whose parents received public assistance were somewhat more likely to leave home at an early age than others. This is the opposite of the effects of the more enduring measures of social class, in which those who were from families with lower socioeconomic status leave home more slowly, not more rapidly. The difference is small, however: those whose families received public assistance at some time during their childhood were about 6 percent more likely to leave home than those whose families did not.

The real story of public assistance, however, involves a consideration of historical change, gender, and routes taken out of the home. We have already documented that the receipt of public assistance in childhood increases the likelihood that daughters, not sons, take the path toward more single parenthood or cohabitation relative to marriage (Chapter 7). The broader route story, however, is an important part of the effects of public assistance and is also important for sharpening our analysis of the effects of parental education and occupational prestige. It also clarifies how the structure of opportunities has become more and less equal over the 20th century. An analysis of these fluctuations in conjunction with routes taken out of the parental home sheds considerable light on the relationship between social class and changes in leaving and returning home.

PARENTAL SOCIAL CLASS AND ROUTES OUT OF THE HOME

Young people whose parents have attained higher socioeconomic standing leave home somewhat more rapidly overall, but it depends very much on the route taken out of the home. The key is whether the route out of the home was to attend college. To document this, we turn to data that show the effects of parental education and occupational prestige on leaving home for each route, controlling for having taken some other route (Table 8.1). We show the overall effect of each measure of parental social status, rather than in categories, as we did in Figure 8.2. However, for the analysis of the routes taken out of the home, the effects of parental social class are smoother than for the timing of leaving home (data not presented).

Parents' Education and Occupation and Route Taken. These two measures of parental social class have significant effects on nearly every route out of the parental home (the few that are not significant we indicate by an asterisk). In most of the routes taken out of the parental home, however, the effect of social class is negative, delaying leaving home. Most of the positive effect of either measure of parental social class is for leaving home to attend college.

Table 8.1. Effects of Parental Social Class on Leaving Home by Route Taken[a] (1 standard deviation)

Route Out of the Home	Parental Education	Parental Occupation
Total	1.07	1.04
Marriage	0.90	0.91
School	1.82	1.23
Military	1.09	0.80
Job	0.96	0.95*
Independence	1.05	0.93
Nontraditional family	0.96	0.93*

a.   All effects are relative odds, controlling for the other class measure, ethnicity, sex, leave cohort, and family structure.
* Not significantly different from 1.0.

The children of parents with either more education or more occupational prestige leave home to get married significantly more slowly than do the children of lower-status parents. Such children are also slower to leave home to form a nontraditional family or to take a job, although the effects are significant only for parental education in each case. Evidently, parental resources not only increase young people's educational opportunities but also protect them from early marriage. This "protection" does not extend to nontraditional family formation, however, because the effect of parental occupational prestige is not significant and that for parental education is quite small. Each year of parental educational attainment produces odds of leaving home to form such families of .99 relative to those of young adults whose parents have less education. Thus, for example, the children of parents who graduated from high school would be only 96 percent as likely to leave via this route as those whose parents averaged no more than an eighth-grade education.

The only routes increased by these parental social class measures are in response to the greater education of parents, not their higher occupational prestige. The route out of the parental home to independence increases with educational level (although this result is not significant), and there is a significant increase for leaving home to enter the military. By this measure, an additional year of parental education increases the odds of leaving home by enlisting in the military by 2.5 percent. This likely reflects the policies of the armed services, however, and otherwise is something of an exception that proves the rule. During most of its history, the selective service has used tests to screen out applicants unlikely to be useful in military service, tests that those with low education are much more likely to fail. Hence, even if those whose parents had very low levels of education wanted to leave home to join some branch of the armed services, it might not have been possible for many. This case is also the major exception to the smooth pattern of increase or decrease: When parental education is broken into the categories shown in Figure 8.2, the effect on leaving home to join the military resembles an inverted U. Both those whose parents had the lowest level of education (grammar school) and those whose parents had the highest level of education (college) were less likely to leave home via this route than were those whose parents attended high school, whether or not they graduated. Evidently many of the college-educated parents of young adults are able to use their education not only to prevent early marriage but also the losses—of career progress and possibly of life itself—associated with military service.

Public Assistance and Route Taken. We have documented that most of the effects of one's family having received public assistance while one was growing up differ by sex and are significant primarily for daughters, not sons (Chapter 7). However, there is one clear pattern that affected 20th century men as well as women, and it is also consistent with those we have identified for parental educational level and occupational prestige ranking. Having received public assistance in childhood significantly reduces young adults' odds of leaving home to attend college. The effect is relatively strong: Those with this experience were only 75 percent as likely to leave home via this route as those who had not (data not presented). If education is the gateway to opportunity, and it is likely that residential educational institutions offer even more opportunities on average than local and community colleges, this finding is one indication that the United States has not been a place of equal educational opportunity over the 20th century.

The analysis of these three measures of parental social status and their effects of leaving home makes it clear that most of the effects of parental social class are on leaving home to attend college. Other effects of social class are small and in the opposite direction from the major finding, primarily delaying leaving home for marriage and nontraditional family formation. There is no evidence that the children of the affluent resist leaving home in order to enjoy the comforts of the parental nest. Few would argue that delaying marriage and the formation of nontraditional families are important benefits of parental resources, at least for children who still have more education and/or maturity to gain.

A few of these results, however, could be interpreted less positively. The result that children of those with high occupational prestige are less likely to leave home for independence, may be because they have plenty of privacy, perhaps their own rooms, televisions, stereos, VCRs and even microwaves, than those in less comfortable families. And children of high-status families also seem to feel less pressure to leave home to find a job. The effects are small for both measures of parental social class and not significant for occupational prestige. Another way to look at these "delay" results, however, is that it is also likely that children living in more educated families may take more time to do the research needed to find an appropriate job, making a return home less necessary. Thus, even these results do not necessarily indicate that the children of the more affluent are postponing the residential independence of adulthood to enjoy the comforts of their parents' home.

PARENTAL SOCIAL CLASS AND RETURNING HOME

A stronger test of the feathered nest hypothesis would be to investigate if those from higher-status families are more likely to return home. Having access to a more comfortable parental home implies having the kind of home that more money can buy, more prestige requires, and more education provides the taste for greater comfort. We should expect that there should be strong effects of these indicators of parental social class on returning home. The evidence does not support this argument at all.

We examined the effects of parental education, measured both as a continuous variable (in years of education attained) and in school categories (as in Figure 8.2, grammar school through college), and we also analyzed the data in a similar way using measures of parental occupational prestige. We separated these analyses for every route out of the home. Overall, neither measure of parental class background had any significant relationship to returning home (Table 8.2). Neither measure had a statistically significant effect on returning home from marriage, school, the military, a job, or a nontraditional family, routes that vary greatly in their likelihood of return (Chapter 3). It is difficult to have much confidence in the feathered nest hypothesis after assessing these results.

Only one out of all these tests is consistent with the hypothesis: Those who left home just to be independent from the families at the very highest occupational prestige level are somewhat (1.2 times) more likely to return home than other young adults. Although statistically significant at the .05 level, even this result could have occurred by chance, because with 42 tests (two types of parental class, each with three levels to test against a fourth, times seven routes), one or two are likely to appear significant.

The overwhelming conclusion from these results is convincing: If young adults return home, it is not because the physical comforts are so alluring. Other sorts of support clearly increase returning home and are far more important than physical comfort, particularly the comforts of family (Chapter 5). Those from broken families were much less likely to return home than were those whose families had not undergone such stress. These other dimensions of support, however, are evidently just as available in families at all levels of socioeconomic class. Parental social class offers to young adults in the nest-leaving stages of their lives more opportunity to leave under favorable conditions (such as to attend college) and more opportunity not to leave under unfavorable conditions (to an early marriage, to a nontraditional family, and in some instances, to the battlefield). These are the sorts of benefits parents have always passed on to their children when they could. Evidently, most young adults from more affluent families do not use the comforts of the parental feathered nest as an opportunity to live on the cheap or to sponge on their folks.

Have these effects of parental social standing remained the same over time? Have there been periods of time when parental social class background and the avoidance of temporary reverses from ill health or bad luck have had less beneficial consequences than others? Have the effects of social class differed as some segment has led the development of some of the new forms of leaving home, such as nontraditional family formation and independence? We now turn to an examination of how the effects of social class on leaving and returning home have varied over the 20th century.

SOCIAL CLASS, INEQUALITY, AND LEAVING HOME

The United States has always prided itself on being "the land of opportunity" and has celebrated individual achievement based on merit. The

Table 8.2. Effect of Parental Social Class [a] on Returning Home by Route Left

Class	School	Military	Job	Independence	Marry	Cohabit
Parental Education						
Grammar	1.015	1.190	1.176	1.037	1.016	1.092
Some HS	1.041	1.155	1.251	1.111	1.021	1.292
HS	1.000	1.000	1.000	1.000	1.000	1.000
HS+	1.004	1.259	0.908	0.920	0.999	0.825
Occupational prestige score						
<25	1.070	0.975	1.156	0.921	0.931	1.352
25-49	0.954	1.126	1.091	1.034	1.012	1.490
50+	0.917	0.370	1.097	1.283*	1.006	1.022

* p < .05.

a. Controlling for leave cohort, age left, sex, race, ethnicity, religion, region, and childhood family structure.

American dream has been that one can go from log cabin origins to the White House so that one's family background does not predetermine one's position as an adult. Family background and "connections" have always had an important effect on social mobility and achievement, however, even if not a fully determining one, as the proudest self-made business tycoon knows when trying to make things easier for his or her own children. And this possibility has always been more limited for some racial and ethnic groups (see our discussion in Chapter 9).

The weight of family background has varied substantially during the 20th century. In the 1950s and 1960s, the level of inequality of income was reduced substantially, as the growth of the union movement and changes in the structure of the economy opened up a middle-class lifestyle to members of the working classes and the progressive income tax system evened off some of the extremes (Danziger and Gottschalk 1995). These trends reversed later in the century, however, and the level of inequality increased steadily into the 1990s.

These trends are mirrored in the patterns of leaving home, at least via the route that is most closely linked with adult economic success—college attendance. During the Great Depression of the 1930s, young adults whose parents had the lowest level of occupational prestige were little more than half as likely to leave home to attend college than those in the middle category (Figure 8.3).[3] Young adults whose parents had the highest level of occupational prestige ranking were more than twice as likely as those in the middle to leave home for college. By mid-century, these differences had decreased dramatically. The youngest cohort, those who reached age 18 in the 1980s, however, shows a reversal to levels of inequality nearly as great as those of the Great Depression of the 1930s.

The "new" inequality of the 1980s, however, seems to focus on the upper strata. There is less difference in the odds of leaving home to attend college between those in the lowest third and those in the middle third of the parental occupational prestige rankings. There has been, in fact, some suspicion that the residential colleges, particularly private universities but some public ones as well, have been increasing fees and reducing scholarships. The results are that the middle class has little more opportunity than the poor to send their children away to college. This middle-class squeeze is reflected in the data showing the growing similarity of young adults from middle- and lower-class families to leave home to attend college. There has also been some concern that colleges have focused their financial aid budgets on the very poor. Certainly, the 1980s portion of Figure 8.3 is consistent with this concern, because there is much less difference between the lower and middle strata of occupational prestige than there was for the oldest cohorts. The most recent nest-leaving cohort resembles the economic depression cohorts in the extent of inequality only at the top of the social class hierarchy.

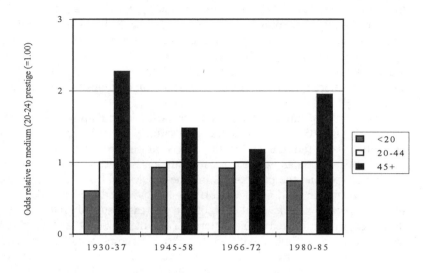

Figure 8.3. Changing Effects of Parental Occupational Prestige Score on Leaving Home for School
SOURCE: Calculated by the authors from the NSFH, controlling as well for sex, ethnicity, and family structure.

Our other measure of parental class background—receipt of public assistance—addresses this issue more directly. As we mentioned earlier, those who reported receiving public assistance at any point during their childhood were less likely to leave home by going way to college. When examined over time, it is clear that having received welfare has become progressively less a problem in the post-World War II period (Figure 8.4). The extent of change is quite dramatic: Those of the youngest nest-leaving cohort whose families received some form of public assistance when they were growing up were no less likely to leave home to attend college than those who had not received assistance.

The public assistance indictor of parental resources—combining as it does both instability (unemployment, health, and divorce crises) and low levels of saving (also salient in financing children's college education, because few can do so from current income alone)—shows a complex trend in its effects on going away to college. The harmful effects of public assistance were greatest in the two decades immediately after World War II. In this period, college education became increasingly important, but the massive increases in funding for higher education (such as the great expansions of the state college systems of California and New York) were not yet in full swing.

For the earliest cohorts (World War II and earlier), few left home via this route. During the war, even the children of the affluent were drawn into the military orbit (Chapter 2). Nearly half the men of the war cohort left home to join the military. Given the nearly parallel, dramatic fall in age at leaving home for young women of this cohort, they likely followed men to take jobs nearby (Modell 1989). Going away to college was simply less relevant to the concerns of young adults during the crises of the war and before it, the economic depression of the 1930s. Each subsequent cohort, however, faced a future in which higher education took on ever increasing importance.

These data confirm that increasingly, access to the opportunity of leaving home to go to college has not been reduced by the experience of having one's family receive public assistance whereas growing up. Among the cohorts coming of age between 1966 and 1979, public assistance still reduced the odds of leaving home to attend school to only 75 percent the level of those whose families had not been on public assistance. For the 1980 cohort, however, there

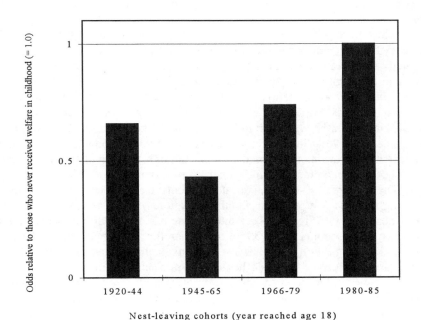

Figure 8.4. Changing Effects of Welfare on Leaving Home for School
SOURCE: Calculated by the authors from the NSFH, controlling sex, ethnicity, and family structure.

were no significant or substantive differences between the two groups. Whether through college scholarships or government programs (e.g., Pell grants), the most economically vulnerable have benefited. On this dimension of potential inequality, then, the major differences are focused primarily between those at the very top and those located below them.

LEAVING HOME AND NONTRADITIONAL FAMILY FORMATION: WHO LED THE GROWTH?

As the analysis of the changes in the leaving-home process showed, the family is subject to the pressures generated in the larger economy. These pressures sometimes change relatively rapidly, as in business cycles (typically of 5 to 7 years' duration) or are the result of longer-term processes of restructuring, as the Industrial Revolution moved to the "postindustrial" economy and then to the contemporary service- and technological-based economy and the "information revolution." These economic changes alter the structure of opportunities so that children are lured to lives their parents never knew or are blocked from following the paths their parents took. Sometimes, however, changes in the family come more indirectly, from the adoption of new ideas and values.

Many have argued that the family changes of the last third of the 20th century have been of this latter sort. These more recent changes are driven less directly by alterations in the economy and more by cultural formulations that weaken the institution of the traditional (patriarchal) family and, at the same time, alter the bonds between parents and children and between men and women. The rise in divorce, and particularly the growth of cohabitation and unmarried parenthood appear to be reactions primarily to such "new ideas" (Lesthaeghe 1995). Initially, "new ideas" are often the province of the more educated, who are more exposed to them through books and travel. Is there evidence of such a process shaping changes in leaving home? There is, indeed.

The children of college-educated parents clearly "led" the growth in leaving home to nontraditional family formation, but just as dramatically they have abandoned it (Figure 8.5). Among those reaching adulthood in the era of the early baby boom (1945-1958), a time when the average parent had barely a ninth-grade education, those whose parents had attended college were 75 percent more likely to have left home to form a nontraditional family through cohabitation or unmarried parenthood (or at least admitted in the late 1980s to having done so) than those whose parents had not attended college.

This route out of the parental home, however, was still extremely rare during that period (less than 1 percent—Chapter 2). Cohabitation and unmarried parenthood perhaps appeared bohemian and daring to the "beat generation" and their college student followers during what are often described as the culturally "gray" years of the early Cold War and the Eisenhower

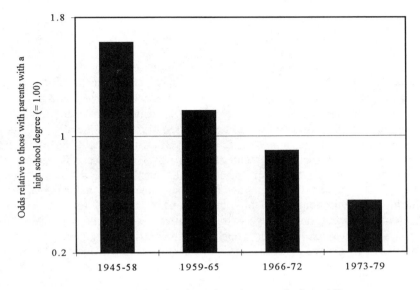

Figure 8.5. Changing Effects of Parental College Education on Leaving Home for Non-Traditional Family Formation
SOURCE: Calculated by the authors from the NSFH, controlling sex, ethnicity, and family structure.

administration. If so, the appeal did not last but was taken up by others. The children of the college educated were still somewhat in the vanguard in the early 1960s, with about 20 percent greater odds of taking this route than were the children of the less educated. However, this time period was still before these nontraditional family forms experienced their greatest growth.

Most of the early studies of cohabitation in the family research literature focused on college students, suggesting the power of the bohemian image. But as these forms entered their explosive growth in the late 1960s and since, the children of college-educated parents increasingly left home by other routes. By the cohort that reached age 18 between 1973 and 1979, young adults with college-educated parents were less than half as likely to leave home via cohabitation and unmarried parenthood than were those whose parents averaged less education (even though the research literature still largely focused on them). Whether because the reality of uncommitted relationships and single parenthood woke them up to their difficulties or because they were no longer outré, young adults from the most educated families have been currently marked by their reluctance to leave home via these routes. They are likely to be the innovators in the rejection of early cohabitation and unmarried parenthood as routes out of the home, as their parental generation were leaders in the early growth of these paths out of their nest.

SOCIAL CLASS AND LEAVING HOME IN THE LATE 20th CENTURY

Like many other aspects of family life, the nest-leaving process is shaped by social class factors. The patterns we have seen over the 20th century, however, were not always those that many had expected. We found almost no evidence for the feathered-nest hypothesis, because there were almost no differences in the timing of leaving home by social class outside of its effects on going away to college, and even fewer on returning home. The major link between parental social class and the leaving home process is through its connection to higher education, which usually means leaving home to attend college. The growth of college attendance may have had a major effect on the timing of leaving home. The high proportions of young adults who live away from home during their college years is a distinctive element of the American nest-leaving process. In other industrialized countries, most young adults live at home during much of their post-high school education (Kiernan 1986). Has the dramatic growth in parental education accounted for much of the decline in age at leaving home between the 1920s and the 1970s (even if it could not have recent increase)? To help us evaluate this possibility, we show differences in median age at leaving home over time by categories of average parental education (Figure 8.6).

If having college-educated parents was the only force shaping the ages at which young adults left home, we would have expected that statistically neutralizing parental educational level would flatten out the time pattern, leaving only the basic differences between parental education groups—that is, those whose parents had more education leaving the parental home earlier than those whose parents had less education. This is clearly not the case. Indeed, it would have been very unlikely that the complexities of the 20th century's impact on families could have been reduced to one background factor. World War II came to all social groups, and ideas about the best time to leave home are shared across the culture. Clearly, each category of parental education shared fairly equally in the overall decline in age at leaving home. It is less clear, however, that they have all shared in the recent increase.

The youngest nest-leaving cohort, those who reached age 18 between 1980 and 1985, seem to be following a different path, reflecting a new "inequality." Most of the increase in age at leaving home has occurred among those whose parents had only a high school education or less, with very little change among those whose parents attended college for at least some period of time. This is a somewhat startling finding, especially because most of the outcry about the increase in the "return to the nest" among young adults has been among the middle class.

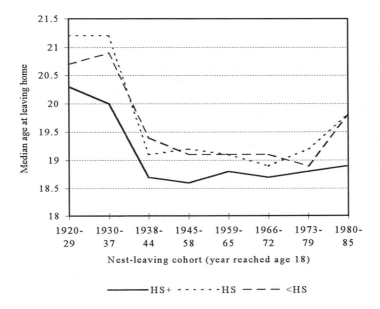

Figure 8.6. Changes in Median Age at Leaving Home by Parental Education
SOURCE: Calculated by the authors from the NSFH.

This finding raises even further doubts about the soundness of the feathered nest hypothesis. Far from its being the children of the affluent who are "refusing to grow up," our findings indicate that it is exactly the opposite: Those who have been having the most difficulty in the new labor market, those from working- and lower-middle-class backgrounds, have been responsible for the delay in leaving home. The links between social stratification and these dimensions of family life remain important, although the complexities of the American social class system and the processes of leaving home have substantially changed over the course of the 20th century. Nevertheless, the social class context of families has not been, and is not now, the sole or even dominant factor in leaving and returning home in 20th century America. There are other powerful social changes that we need to examine to link to the changing trends in leaving home. These changes include religious and ethnic transformations. We now turn to these indicators of changes in family values as the basis for understanding the transition to adulthood.

NOTES

1. For a detailed analysis of the impact of parental education, income and intergenerational income flows, and leaving-home decisions for the cohort of high school students in the early 1980s, see Goldscheider and Goldscheider (1993, chap. 10)

2. In the appendix, we describe the construction of the education measure when there were missing values.

3. We present only patterns for every other nest-leaving cohort, but the missing ones are clearly part of the same trend.

CHAPTER 9

The Shifting Ethnic Mosaic

A critical issue for the understanding of families and family change in the 20th century is the nature and importance of differences by race and ethnicity. The peculiar history of slavery in the United States rendered it one of the most, if not *the* most, racist society in human history (Patterson 1991). Furthermore, and perhaps not totally unrelated, it has attempted to absorb a larger number of immigrants from diverse societies and cultures than any other country. These two phenomena, racism and immigration, have been woven together to create a complex mosaic of groups struggling to create secure family lives on these shores.

In this larger historical context, the events of the 20th century have been particularly dramatic for both the immigrant populations who came to this country voluntarily and those who came as slaves. The century's early years (1900-1924) saw the cresting of a massive wave of immigration, the largest in American history both in absolute and relative terms. Immigration was sharply curtailed, so that relatively few immigrants arrived during the 1925 to 1960 period. Although many factors contributed to this sudden end, a major one was the passage of major restrictive legislation in 1924, which sharply limited immigration from all but a very few national origins (nearly all Western European). The lifting of the restriction of national origin in 1965 (together with other factors) opened the way for large new waves of immigration, which is still ongoing as we near the end of the 20th century. These waves have been dominated by those from Asian and Latin American countries even more culturally different from the United States than earlier immigrant streams. In turn, these immigrant groups have evolved into new large ethnic subpopulations.

The population of Black Americans[1] was also transformed in the 20th century. Although slavery was formally ended during the Civil War (1863), the legislation and practices of nearly a century thereafter ensured not only that few Blacks left the South but also that their lives changed relatively little, remaining an exploited, uneducated, agrarian labor force (Woodward 1966). The closing of immigration, however, brought them new opportunities, particularly during the more-than-full employment period of the World War II.

This led to a massive migration of Blacks out of the South to northern, industrial cities, prepared only for the unskilled, industrial jobs of that time, which unfortunately for them vanished rapidly in the decades that followed. They also suffered great wrenches in both their intergenerational and gender relationships, as migration separated the generations and the partnership of the farming couple came to an abrupt end. This newly visible and often painfully poor and uprooted population became the beneficiaries of many of the "Great Society" initiatives of the 1960s (Chapter 8) and the target of even more programs aimed directly at ending racial discrimination (most notably the Civil Rights Act of 1965). This created new opportunities for many American Blacks, who responded by preparing for and acquiring a large number of middle-class jobs, leading to an extremely rapid growth in this group and a new struggle to adapt their family lives.

Hence, this has been a complex century for both immigrants from abroad and Black migrants from the South. Understanding the complexity of family patterns that has resulted from it has challenged social science research to its core. In this complexity, leaving the parental home in the formation of new households stands as a fulcrum, one point at which gender and generational relationships alike are played out.

BLACKS, HISPANICS, AND ASIANS

A rich body of social science and historical studies has developed over the past several decades seeking to address the complexities of ethnic differences in family patterns, including the nest-leaving process. When we refer to these groups collectively, we will use the term *ethnic*. Categories that seem to be based on race and national origins are each social and cultural constructions. Hence, we use this simple rubric to identify the general category of "racial" and "ethnic" groups.

Much of the research on ethnic groups has focused on Black-White differences. A smaller, but also substantial, set of findings shows that Hispanic and Asian family patterns are distinctive when compared with both White and Black non-Hispanics. In much of this research, Black families are described as being more closely focused on kin ties, particularly between women and their children, but as having weaker bonds between adult men and women. Black families, for example, have been documented to have a high likelihood of family extension (Kramarow 1995). The weakness of the conjugal tie among Blacks is evident in the low proportions of those who marry and in the high risk of divorce among those who do (Farley 1995; Farley and Allen 1987; Jaynes and Williams 1989; Tucker and Mitchell-Kernan 1995), as well as in the high proportion of out-of-wedlock births (McLanahan and Sandefur 1994) and fosterage (McDaniel 1994).

Hispanics have often been described as having a "macho" familistic culture, in which high levels of family extension are paired with a strong but much more hierarchical relationship between men and women. Asians show a high level of family cohesion with an emphasis on extended-family coresidence (Burr and Mutchler 1988). Consistent with these findings, all three groups have been found to leave home more slowly than non-Hispanic Whites, with Hispanics disproportionately leaving home to marriage and Blacks disproportionately leaving home, unmarried; Asians are in between (Goldscheider and Goldscheider 1993).

Nearly all of the detailed, multivariate empirical analyses of Black family patterns of all types, however, stem from data covering the post-World War II period, and this is even more the case for Hispanics and Asians. The historical studies that have attempted analyses of the Black family of the past have normally been based on studies of a single locale in a limited time period, normally under slavery (e.g., Stevenson 1995; Kulikoff 1986; Malone 1992; Manfra and Dykstra 1985) and rarely, if ever, compare Blacks with Whites in the area (Gutman 1976). Those that use different time points use only two quite disconnected time points (e.g., Morgan, et al. 1993; Watkins et al. 1994). This strategy is particularly problematic for understanding changes in family patterns over the course of the 20th century, which has been marked by wide swings in marital and fertility behavior (Haines 1996; Bean, Mineau, and Anderton 1990; Coale 1967).[2]

Given the lack of historical analysis, there is considerable disagreement over the possible causes of these ethnic differences in contemporary American family processes, particularly with regard to Black-White differences. Research on the Black family has been subjected to wildly discrepant interpretations from the Moynihan report of the 1960s to the present, and not nearly enough research has been carried out to resolve these discrepancies (Wilson 1994). Much the same can be argued about the general level of research on Hispanic and other ethnic family patterns.

One central axis of disagreement focuses on the relative importance of culture and social class for Black family distinctiveness. Some argue that cultural patterns originating in the West African societies from which so many African Americans were taken are the source of Black-White differences (McDaniel 1994; Morgan et al. 1993). Others have focused on the special position of Blacks in American society, both on the long-term effects of discrimination against them (often referred to as the poverty and slavery explanation of Black-White differences) and on their consequent vulnerability to structural changes, such as the decline in job opportunities in the central cities where Blacks had moved (Wilson 1987; Massey and Denton 1993).

The controversy over Black-White differences in family patterns has clouded the analysis of other major ethnic subpopulations. But a similar set of research and theoretical traditions has emphasized the centrality of both cultural and structural factors in understanding other ethnic communities. The research tradition emphasizing cultural factors in ethnic patterns examines ethnicity primarily in the context of immigration and the "cultural" baggage that accompanied immigrant groups to America, important only during the process of ethnic acculturation and assimilation (Gordon 1964; Glazer and Moynihan 1970). Other scholars emphasize the importance of structures that reinforce continuity, focusing on the contexts that reinforce continuity or that enhance assimilation (Goldscheider 1986; Alba 1990).

Our framework for understanding race and ethnic variation and changes over time in the processes of leaving home involves both structural and cultural components. The data we have, however, do not lend themselves to the direct measurement of either dimension. All we can do is use the richness of the data on the nest-leaving leaving process, providing as it does information on the timing of leaving and returning home and the routes taken, together with the temporal sweep of the data, covering as it does most of the 20th century, to rule out some of the positions that have been taken in the controversies over differences in Black, White, Asian, and Hispanic families. Even when we focus on the contemporary period, ignoring the historical dimension,[3] these data provide new information on differences in the nest-leaving process and on its links to intergenerational and gender relationships among these groups. We will examine these first and then turn to an analysis of changes in leaving home, to see how well the recent past has represented the more distant past, and if not, what the changes can tell us.

ETHNIC DIFFERENCES IN THE NEST-LEAVING PROCESS

We examine differences in leaving and returning home for both dimensions that have shaped the American ethnic mosaic—race and immigrant origin. It is important to separate these two dimensions because among immigrants, the problems linked with leaving and returning home are often exacerbated by the possibility that "home" is in a different country: The first generation often arrives without its parents, and hence, as we will demonstrate, is very unlikely to return home. The separation is particularly important when we consider the leaving-and returning-home patterns of Hispanics, a high proportion of whom (45 percent) are not native-born.

LEAVING HOME AMONG ETHNIC GROUPS

Our first analysis of ethnic differences in the timing of leaving home suggests that only one group is distinctively different from the others—non-Hispanic Whites, controlling for the other major factors affecting the likelihood of leaving home (Figure 9.1).[4]   They leave home much more rapidly than do Blacks, Hispanics, or Asians, among whom there are only small and insignificant differences. On this dimension, then, each of these groups is more "familistic" than the majority population, with odds of leaving home about two-thirds those of non-Hispanic Whites.

These results suggest that minority status structures differences in leaving-home patterns, reinforcing the importance of the family in overcoming disadvantage and discrimination. When we look beyond the simple dimension of the timing of the parent-child residential separation, however, and consider the differences in the routes they take out of the home and the odds of returning home, we see much greater differences among groups. Each one achieves its slow overall rate of leaving home in a distinctive way, by avoiding certain routes but not others.

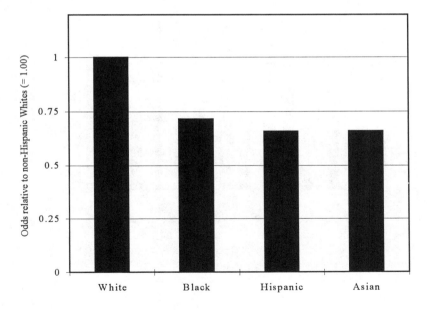

Figure 9.1. Ethnic Differences in Leaving Home
SOURCE: Calculated by the authors from the NSFH, controlling as well for nest-leaving cohort, sex, family structure and social class.

Blacks and Asians, but not Hispanics, leave home to marry more slowly—
only about half as fast—as non-Hispanic Whites (Figure 9.2). Blacks and
Hispanics, but not Asians, are less likely to leave home to attend school, join
the military, or cohabit, also by about half; Hispanics and Asians, but not
Blacks, are significantly less likely to leave home to be independent; and all
three groups leave home more slowly to take a job. Hence, when we think of
Hispanics as distinctively oriented toward marriage as a route out of the home,
it is only relative to other minority groups; they do not differ from non-Hispanic
Whites. Similarly, when people perceive many young Blacks leaving home to
be independent, this is primarily the case relative to the other minorities; they
are much less distinctive in this route when the comparison is with non-
Hispanic Whites. Asian distinctiveness in leaving home to go away to school is
also not distinctive vis à vis the majority, just relative to other minority groups.[5]

What makes the marriage route so distinctive for Hispanics, then, is not
that they take it so rapidly, because, at least relative to non-Hispanic Whites,
they do not, but that they take other routes so slowly. The same can be said for
Asians leaving for school and for Blacks leaving for independence. They stand

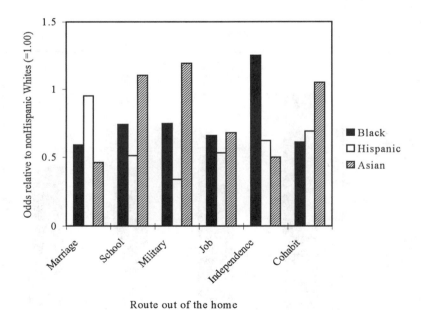

Route out of the home

Figure 9.2. Ethnic Differences in Leaving Home by Route Taken
SOURCE: Calculated by the authors from the NSFH, controlling as well for nest-leaving cohort, sex,
family structure and social class.

out, but not relative to the majority, although detailed studies of the separate groups often makes it seem that way. Rather, these are simply interesting and important exceptions to a general pattern of longer intergenerational coresidence among minorities than among non-Hispanic Whites, which extends even to leaving home for the military, to take a job, and to cohabit, all of which tend to be more rare at a given age in the nest-leaving process among members of these groups than for the majority.

RETURNING HOME AMONG ETHNIC GROUPS

As with so many of the other factors we have considered—social class, region, religion, gender—there are no significant differences among these groups in the overall likelihood of returning home, but there are differences when the separate routes are considered. This was the case among Blacks, Hispanics, and Asians relative to non-Hispanic Whites. Given the small size of the Asian group, and hence the small number who returned home, however, we were unable to test them for the separate routes. Hence, here we will focus on Blacks and Hispanics in comparison with non-Hispanic Whites.

Members of these two minority groups resemble the majority non-Hispanic White group for only the two routes out of the home that can be expected to lead to longer-term independence: (a) those involving new family formation—marriage and cohabitation or single parenthood—and (b) leaving to take a job (Figure 9.3). Blacks are somewhat more likely than Hispanics to return home in each of the two new family routes, but none of the differences is significant. They are both somewhat less likely to return home if they left to take a job, with little difference between Blacks and Hispanics.

For the other three routes out of the home, however, differences appear, although more between the majority and the two other groups than between the minority groups, themselves. Both Blacks and Hispanics are more likely to return home than are non-Hispanic Whites from the two semiautonomous routes out of the home, school and military service (although the difference between Blacks and non-Hispanic Whites is not statistically significant for those who left home to attend college). They are both *less* likely to return home, however, from independence.

IMMIGRANTS AND THE NEST-LEAVING PROCESS

For the analysis of leaving home, we were able to divide immigrants to the United States into two groups. About a sixth of the non-native-born are from more industrialized countries, most of whom (76 percent) came from the United Kingdom, Germany, and Canada, which for convenience we will refer

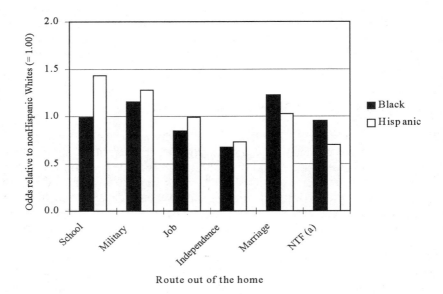

Route out of the home

a. Nontraditional family.

Figure 9.3. Ethnic Differences in Returning Home by Route Taken
SOURCE: From Table A.3 in the appendix.

to as "Western-origin immigrants." The rest are from less industrialized countries, primarily from Latin America (67 percent), whom we will refer to as "non-Western." The proportion of immigrants from more developed countries is small because only the oldest members of the oldest cohort could have been members of the 20th century's first wave of immigration. This division into Western and non-Western-origin countries tells us less about the characteristics of the immigrants themselves and more about what they have to go back to. Immigrants are usually highly selective of the more educated, and we control for educational level in our multivariate analysis.

What is striking in the nest-leaving process of immigrants of all origins is the dominance of taking a job as a reason for leaving home (Figure 9.4). Although overall, there are relatively small differences in the likelihood of leaving home between immigrants and the native-born (and particularly between the native-born and those from Western countries), this is the result of immigrants being relatively unlikely to leave home by most routes taken by the native-born, but much more likely to leave home to take a job. Among both,

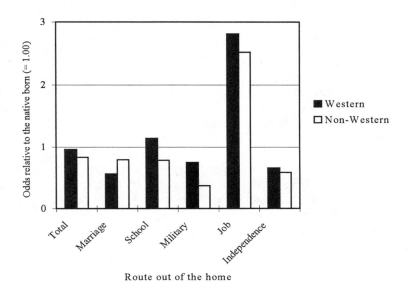

Route out of the home

Figure 9.4. Difference in Leaving Home by Immigrant Origin
SOURCE: Calculated by the authors from the NSFH, controlling nest-leaving cohort, sex, ethnicity, family structure and social class

those from Western and non-Western countries, the odds of leaving home to take a job are more than 2.5 times those of the native-born.

This pattern of differences by route is quite similar for the two immigrant groups, although this is less the case when we divide these groups into sons and daughters (Chapter 7). Neither indicated independence-related reasons very often. Those from non-Western origins were more likely to leave home to marry, likely reflecting both the more traditional families of their primarily Hispanic communities and the smaller size of the marriage market for immigrants from Western countries. In contrast, those with Western origins were more likely to leave home to attend school than those from non-Western origins, probably reflecting their greater educational preparation in their home countries. It is also likely that obtaining higher levels of education was the reason many came to the United States from these countries, and in particular to obtain specialized training useful when they return home. Often their level of education turned out to be as useful and, perhaps, better paid in the United States, so they remained. In any case, it is clear that they are unlikely to return to their parents. Immigrants are much less likely to return home than the native-born—less than half—and this does not vary much between groups or reasons for leaving home (data not presented).

CHANGES IN NEST-LEAVING

In this section, we focus on ethnic differences in the timing of the departure of young adults from the parental home and the routes they have taken in the transition to adulthood.   This focus allows us at least a partial view of ethnic changes in both intergenerational relationships (between parents and children) and in marriage, a central route out of the home.   We use our reconstructed historical data to cover most of the 20th century and to identify differences between Black Americans, Hispanics, and non-Hispanic White populations.   The analysis of these patterns provides a strong empirical basis for rejecting some of the explanations that have been offered to account for the current status of both Black and Hispanic family patterns.   First, however, we need to develop the questions, evidence, and arguments systematically.

We have already documented that the age at leaving home has changed over the 20th century, declining for most of the period with a partial reversal in the late 1970s and 1980s.   The routes taken out of the home have also changed with declines in the proportion leaving home in conjunction with getting married, obtaining a job, and serving in the military and with increases in the proportion leaving for higher education or just to be independent (Chapter 2). The question we address here is, have these broader changes characterized the families of Black and Hispanic Americans?   Have there been enduring differences between Blacks and Whites as the result of particular values derived from West African or Hispanic culture? Have differences in nest-leaving between Hispanics and non-Hispanic Whites faded over time, as has been the case on other dimensions of economic and social life (Massey and Denton 1993)?

More specifically, based on arguments about the importance of cultural differences or poverty for understanding Black-White differences, have Blacks left home at later ages than non-Hispanic Whites throughout the period? Given current differences in marital patterns (significantly lower rates of marriage among African Americans), have Black Americans been less likely than Whites to leave home in conjunction with marriage throughout the period? Finally, given the rapid relocation of American Blacks from southern rural areas to northern cities and the subsequent deindustrialization of those cities, have family differences between Blacks and Whites widened in recent decades?

Turning to Hispanics, current research suggests that they will be more likely than others to remain home until they marry. Based on general theories of ethnicity, however, particularly those that emphasize tendencies toward assimilation among ethnic populations, one would expect convergence over time in the transition to adulthood between Hispanics and non-Hispanic

Whites. Has this indeed been the case? The results might not be clear-cut, however, because a focus on changes over time represents a particular challenge in the historical reconstruction of Hispanic populations. This is the case because the construction "Hispanic" involves multiple ethnic origins, and the internal ethnic composition of the Hispanic population in the United States has changed over time (Bean and Tienda 1987; Goldscheider and Goldscheider 1994b). The ethnic origins of those usually categorized "Hispanic" include Mexicans, Puerto Ricans, Cubans, and Central Americans, among others. Despite this multiplicity, some evidence suggests that these diverse Hispanic populations have important family-based similarities, despite heterogeneous socioeconomic and cultural origins (Goldscheider and Goldscheider 1993).[6]

We address these questions controlling statistically for parental education, childhood family structure, and gender for all groups. We are able to use our nest-leaving cohorts to distinguish three historical periods: (1) the post-1966 period, which has been the subject of most systematic research and serves as our reference group; (2) the 1945 to 1965 period, when Black migration from the South was at its height but before the major stream of Hispanic immigrants arrived; and (3) the pre-1945 period, when most Black Americans still lived in the rural South.

RACE AND ETHNIC DIFFERENCES IN TIMING AND ROUTE

When we examine the nest-leaving patterns of these three cohorts, the overall pattern of historical change is less complex than we have documented for the total population (Chapter 2). The recent decline in the rate of leaving home (and hence, the increased age at leaving) does not appear; the extremely rapid nest-leaving of the 1966 to 1973 Vietnam cohort has been averaged in with the slower tempo of the two youngest cohorts. It seems unlikely, however, that more than three points are needed to capture differences among ethnic groups over time, and in fact, the pattern we see is quite complex.

Black Americans left home significantly more slowly than did Whites in the post-1965 period, consistent with research on recent cohorts (Figure 9.5).[7] This was clearly not the case in the pre-1944 period, however, when there were no differences between Blacks and non-Hispanic Whites. Both groups left home relatively slowly, about 70 percent as fast as the most recent cohort of non-Hispanic Whites. The dramatic increase in speed of leaving home experienced by non-Hispanic Whites in the two decades after World War II was nearly absent for Blacks, whose rate of leaving home increased slightly and then decreased, changing very little throughout the period.

Hispanics left home more slowly—that is, at a later age—than did non-Hispanic Whites throughout the period. Like non-Hispanic Whites (and unlike Blacks), Hispanics increased their speed of leaving home over time—that is, left at an early age. However, they followed a different pattern than Whites,

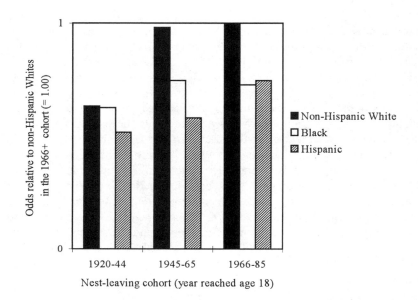

Figure 9.5. Changing Effects of Ethnicity on Leaving Home
SOURCE: From Table A.7 in the appendix.

with the major acceleration taking place after 1965; for Whites, this took place between the earlier two periods.

Hence, the pattern of differences between Blacks and non-Hispanic Whites is one of great divergence between the pre- and post-World War II cohorts, followed by a stable, continued large gap as we moved to the more recent period. Hispanics, in contrast, appear to be following the same trajectory as non-Hispanic Whites in the changes in their timing of leaving home, although with a lag. The great increase in rate of leaving home of non-Hispanic Whites in the post-World War II cohorts was matched by Hispanics two decades later, which was not the case among Blacks. Hispanic parents have recently begun to get a taste of the empty nest that non-Hispanic White parents had already grown accustomed to; whereas the pattern of continued parent-child coresidence among Blacks has, by remaining essentially unchanged, become increasingly distinctive.

We have seen, however, that ethnic differences in timing often obscure even larger differences in routes out of the home, because the various routes often respond to changes in the world outside the family quite differently. Decreases in marriage delays this route out of the home, as can difficulties in the job market. We have already seen that the great decline in marriage in the Black community has not been compensated for by increases in cohabitation (Figure 9.2, earlier) because Blacks, like Hispanics, are much less likely to take this route, which has only been important in its incidence in the last two decades, than are non-Hispanic Whites. Changes in the job market could also hit these groups differently, given the extent of racial occupational concentration (Lieberson 1980; Lieberson and Waters 1988; Wilson 1987). The importance of leaving home for school and the military has also changed over this period, perhaps in different ways for these groups. Does any of the information about changes in the routes taken out of the home help place these overall changes into some more concrete context?

There were substantial differences between Hispanics and non-Hispanic Whites in the trends evident for the routes taken out of the home and even greater differences between the trends of Blacks and non-Hispanic Whites. Some patterns appear to portray convergence, even if to a moving target; others present more complex and problematic interpretations. Leaving for marriage or to take a job are both among the most important routes out of the home over this time period and show some of the strongest differences by race/ethnicity. There are also important differences, however, in the trends for school and independence.

Leaving home to attend college has become a growing route out of the home, and this is basically true for each of these groups (Figure 9.6). For non-Hispanic Whites, all of the increase in this route out of the home took place between the pre-1945 and 1945 to 1965 periods, with no increase over the two subsequent decades. Blacks and Hispanics have been less likely than non-Hispanic Whites to take this route throughout the period.

Both groups, however, show at least slight signs of convergence toward the level of non-Hispanic Whites. There has been particularly strong growth among Hispanics on this important dimension, although part of this reflects the extraordinarily low levels of leaving home via this route among pre-World War II Hispanics. Growth has been much slower among Blacks, who show no leaps of the size that non-Hispanic Whites displayed after World War II, or the giant steps Hispanics have taken between each interval. At least part of their greater similarity with non-Hispanic Whites in the most recent period, moreover, is the result of the slight decline in this route shown by the majority group. Nevertheless, leaving home for school shows some convergence in the context of a growing route out of the home.

In contrast, there is clear evidence of convergence between Blacks and Whites in the likelihood of leaving home for the military (Table A.9 in the appendix). This likely reflects the formal integration of these ethnic groups in the armed services. However, this has become a small portion of those leaving home in the post-1965 period. Convergence has worked the other way among those leaving home to cohabit or live as single parents. This route out of the

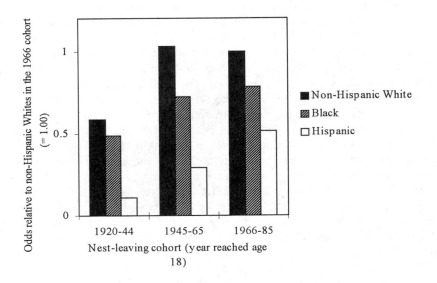

Figure 9.6. Changing Effects of Ethnicity on Leaving Home for School
SOURCE: Calculated from coefficients in Table A.7 in the appendix.

home was much less common for Whites than for the Blacks or Hispanics in the past, but Whites have surpassed both groups in the post-1965 period. However, this nest-leaving route remains relatively unimportant for all groups. Blacks also led Whites in the increase in the "independence route" in the past, but there appears to be no difference between them in the most recent period (Figure 9.7). When compared with Blacks or non-Hispanic Whites, Hispanics remain less likely to leave just to be independent.

Hence, to understand the great changes among these ethnic groups, particularly the large differences in the patterns of change over time between Blacks and non-Hispanic Whites, it is necessary to move beyond these smaller routes, which in any event show patterns of convergence. We need to examine changes in leaving home for marriage and to take a job. What has been happening with the routes most closely linked with the central roles of adulthood, and what does this tell us about how the past and the future connect?

Beginning with the differences between Blacks and non-Hispanic Whites, we see that for those who left home to get married, Blacks and non-Hispanic Whites were remarkably similar in the first cohort, as they were in their overall timing of leaving home (Figure 9.8). In subsequent cohorts, however, Blacks

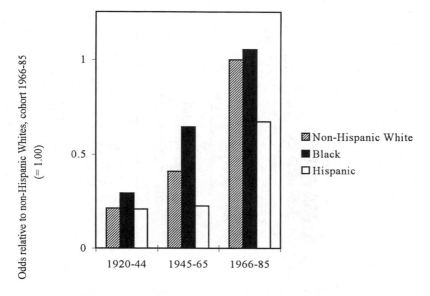

Nest-leaving cohort (year reached age 18)

Figure 9.7. Changing Effects of Ethnicity on Leaving Home for Independence
SOURCE: Calculated from coefficients in Table A.7 in the appendix.

and non-Hispanic Whites experienced very different trajectories. Only Whites experienced the marriage behavior associated with the baby boom, dramatically decreasing their age at marriage and hence, accelerating their likelihood of leaving home for marriage. This pattern of early nest-leaving associated with a young age at marriage was followed by a reversal to an intermediate level.

In contrast, Blacks decreased their rate of leaving home for marriage continuously throughout the period. At first, there was a small decrease, perhaps reflecting the disruptions of migration as potential partners delayed their plans to marry until getting settled, or perhaps never met at all. As we move from the immediate post-World War II period to the recent period, however, the decline in leaving home for marriage was much more substantial. As a result, a great gap appeared between Blacks and Whites during the 1945 to 1965 period in the probabilities of leaving home in conjunction with marriage, with the divergence in their trajectories. In the most recent period, their trajectories are more similar—both Blacks and non-Hispanic Whites became less likely to take this route (and in the case of Blacks, even further so)—but the gap has not closed at all.

The rate of leaving home for marriage for Hispanics remained essentially

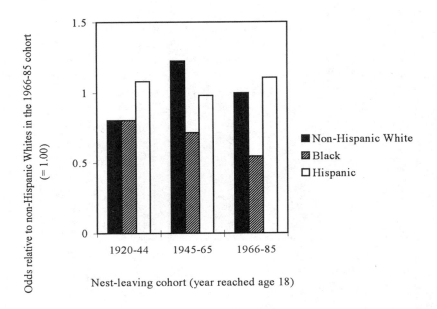

Figure 9.8. Changing Effects of Ethnicity in Leaving Home for Marriage
SOURCE: Calculated from coefficients in Table A.7 in the appendix.

unchanged during the period.   The Hispanic pattern therefore is clearly distinctive when compared both with non-Hispanic Whites and with Black Americans. Like Blacks but unlike non-Hispanic Whites, they show no sign of the postwar marriage boom. In the most recent time interval, Hispanics run counter to the trends observed for both of the other groups by not decreasing their likelihood of leaving home for marriage, and perhaps even increasing it.

Although the patterns are different, the story is very similar for leaving home associated with taking a job (Figure 9.9). During the first two time periods, Blacks and Whites had about the same likelihood of leaving home to take a job, but this is no longer the case. Although the pace of leaving home to take a job has slowed for both Whites and Blacks, the decline has been very large for Blacks in the most recent period. Few Black Americans in the 1980s and 1990s leave the parental home and establish a new home in conjunction with getting a first job or changing jobs.

Hispanics have gone against the trend, as they did for leaving home for marriage. They increased their relative use of this route, unlike the declines shown by the other two groups. This may represent a sort of convergence, or it may reflect the changing composition of the Hispanic population, which

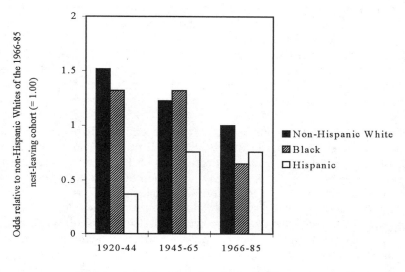

Figure 9.9. Changing Effects of Ethnicity on Leaving Home for a Job
SOURCE: Calculated from coefficients in Table A.7 in the appendix.

became increasing dominated by immigrants in the most recent period. Immigrants, as we observed earlier in Figure 9.3, are extraordinarily likely to report that they left home to find a job.

CONCLUDING OBSERVATIONS

Where do these empirical results leave our hypotheses about convergence and the persistence of cultural (or poverty) differences among ethnic groups? It is clear that most of the convergences among the groups that we examined were experienced by Hispanics, who became more similar to non-Hispanic Whites in leaving home for marriage and for employment. Only in leaving home for military service and cohabitation did Blacks reach parity with non-Hispanic Whites during the most recent period. However, these trends are of marginal importance. The convergence in leaving home for military service occurred just when it stopped being an important route out of the home and to a secure career; the convergence in cohabitation occurred because Whites, not Blacks, have increasingly used this route out of the home in recent decades.

It is also clear that there is little evidence of continuing differences between these groups over the period as a whole. Only the gap between Blacks and Whites in leaving home to go to school remained totally stable. The probability of leaving home to attend school is lower for Blacks than for Whites with no significant changes over time. Leaving home for higher education is the family process most closely linked with the reproduction of socioeconomic differences. Like Black's low migration rates to communities with greater opportunities (Clark 1992), going away to school also remains difficult in a deeply divided society.

In contrast, the other family processes show a major break between Blacks and non-Hispanic Whites in the post-World War II period. The relatively low levels of marriage became clearly distinctive among Black Americans during this period, suggesting a sharper increase in tension between the sexes among Blacks than among Whites. This pattern of nonmarriage has set the stage for the great differences in out-of-wedlock childbearing and the rearing of children in one-parent families. The divergence between Blacks and Whites in leaving home to find a job is likely to be directly connected with the increased differences in employment opportunities between these two groups. This pattern also suggests stronger intergenerational family ties in the Black community. From this point of view, White families may be sending their children away "too soon" (see Chapter 4) at least in the context of family values, educational investments, job opportunities, and intergenerational linkages.

Neither a long-term discrimination argument nor an Afrocentric approach appears to be an adequate explanation for the family distinctiveness of Black Americans, at least in terms of our focus on leaving the parental home. The evidence we present shows that most of the ethnic differences we observe in the timing of leaving home and the routes taken out of the home for the recent period do *not* characterize the earlier decades of the 20th century.

We now have the evidence available covering nearly the whole 1880 to 1990 period to take up the challenge to systematically investigate ethnic differences in depth and in detail in a broad range of family processes. The results we have presented suggest that there are empirical regularities that allow us to cut through the complexities in the minefield of ethnic differences in family processes. Such clarity can come only through a careful historical reconstruction of the past, for different ethnic groups, taking into account broad structural and cultural features. And this clarity depends on carefully delineating among family processes, probing both details and contexts. Oversimplified notions of Black patterns that have been derived from West African culture or Hispanic patterns that are embedded in the patriarchal forms of Hispanic family values need to be qualified and sharpened as we examine the details of historical changes and the complexities of family processes.

Our understanding of the ethnic differential in leaving home suggests that only when ethnic communities retain some aspects of language or live in residentially dense ethnic areas do their family patterns remain distinctive. In short, the structural basis of ethnicity that indicate community and shared values reinforces ethnic distinctiveness. When assimilation occurs, there are few supports to ethnic family continuities; ethnic groups lose their distinctive family traits, including their distinctive patterns of when young adults leave home and the context that pulls them from the parental home or pushes them out of the home. Hispanic populations have been subject to strong assimilatory pressures. Exposure to the culture in the United States and increasing use of English as a daily language appear to be important factors in their loss of distinctive family patterns. Nevertheless, the establishment of large Hispanic residential areas may have a counter-assimilatory tendency with regard to the specific family patterns that we are examining. Outside these larger residential enclaves, all Hispanics (and the ethnic diversity within the Hispanic population) are moving toward the White model. In contrast, the continuing racial divide between Blacks and Whites in America appears to be embedded in the society and culture and in the ways these groups relate to one another. A clear outcome of the racism and discrimination that continues in America is the distinctive family patterns of Blacks, particularly in ways that are disruptive to family life among the current generation. The retention of distinctive family processes in the transition to adulthood is likely to be limiting in the family formation and the economic activities of the next generation.

NOTES

1. When we refer to Blacks (or Black Americans), Hispanics, and White non-Hispanics we use capital first letters to signify that these are formal racial and ethnic constructions, not categories based on biology or nationality.

2. A partial exception is the census study by Ruggles (1994), who used reconstructed American census data from 1880 to 1980 to examine Black-White differences in single parenthood, children residing in households without their parents, and extended households.

3. Because most of the cases in the study are concentrated in the three youngest nest-leaving cohorts, their overall patterns primarily show relationships for these groups.

4. The analyses in this section include controls for nest-leaving cohort, gender, region, parental education and occupation, religion, and family structure.

5. Given the very low frequency of this route in the Pacific region where most Asians are concentrated, however, they might be more likely to take this route than are non-Hispanic Whites in this region.

6. A somewhat similar argument can be made for ethnic subpopulations within the category "Whites," despite its heterogeneity (Alba 1990).

7. The full results of our statistical analysis are presented in Table A.9 in the appendix, showing the relative odds of leaving home and of leaving home by a given route for our ethnic categories, nest-leaving cohorts, and other factors that influence the likelihood of leaving home.

CHAPTER 10

Religious Transformation and Family Values

R eligious institutions and religious creeds in America encourage familistic values. These values stress closeness to parents, the centrality of the marriage bond, the importance of parenthood and family-centered roles for women, and increasingly, men's family responsibilities, as well. Taken together, these religious values constitute a religious culture that reinforces family obligations and responsibilities. Religion and religious values are, therefore, likely to play an important role in our investigation of those family processes associated with the transition to adulthood and the decisions about the timing and route out of the parental home.

Some have argued that American society has become increasingly secular, which can be a problem for the family, given the importance of religion as a source of family-reinforcing values. The process of secularization encompasses formal and informal changes in the extent to which individuals distance themselves from religious culture and, in particular, from the literal interpretation of religious doctrine and from an intense identification with religious groups. Although most Americans consider themselves religious, some measures of religiosity show declines over time and indicate a reduction in the centrality of religion and its associated values that is almost revolutionary, particularly when critical decisions are made throughout the life course.[1]

One of the effects of the decline in religious centrality is the changed relationship of people to their families in general and to their parents and children, in particular. A weakening of ties to parents has combined with a decrease in the importance of marriage in adulthood and a greater emphasis on individual rather than family obligations. The greater independence of young adults in contemporary society has occurred both from religion and from the family values associated with religious commitments. The decline in religious values and the institutions that reinforce them are likely to strengthen the separation of residential independence from marriage in the transition to adulthood (see Goldscheider and Goldscheider, 1993). Those who are more intensely religious, who consider religion important in their lives, who are affiliated with religious communities that emphasize religious sources of family values are likely to emphasize marriage as a route out of the home, to avoid nonfamily routes and family routes that are not religiously sanctioned, such as cohabitation and unmarried parenthood. There is also some evidence of a conflict between religious and secular knowledge, from the Scopes trial to creationism, which might mean that the more religious are less likely to leave home for higher education. Such family-centeredness might also make the more religious more likely to return home in times of transition or crisis. There is reason to hypothesize that over time, the effect of religious commitment on the timing and routes taken out of the parental household has declined.

It is also the case, however, that the process of secularization has been highly uneven. The recent spread of religious fundamentalism in American society has led to increased polarization in religious outlook and constitutes a powerful indicator of the continuing importance of religious activities in secular American society (Darnell and Sherkat 1997). The general value placed on religion in the United States, the repeated expression of religious attitudes, and the proliferation of religious institutions and religious politics remain important reminders of the persistence of religion in the lives of many Americans, despite the general trends over time toward greater secularization.

Our investigation of religion and religiosity focuses attention on areas in which individuals and communities voluntarily connect themselves to communities that uphold and strengthen family values. Links to religious communities through formal religious group identification are expected to reinforce family-based norms. Family norms and lifestyles are maintained and transmitted through interaction among those who share similar religious affiliations and who have been exposed to religious values in schools and at home.

In this chapter, we first investigate the overall variation in the relationship between religion and the transition to adulthood in the 20th century. We shall clarify how much of this relationship is due to religious values per se or to other interrelated factors, such as the social class level of members of religious groups. We then examine change over time in the effect of religious affiliation on the leaving home process. Our three guiding questions are these: (1) How is religious affiliation linked to changes in the transition to adulthood? (2) How do religious commitments influence the family-related reasons for leaving home, specifically the growing importance of leaving home for independence rather than in conjunction with marriage? (3) What can we infer from changes over time about the impact of secularization in the historical transitions to adulthood that we have identified.

LINKS TO PREVIOUS RESEARCH ON FAMILY AND RELIGION

A rather elaborate research literature has documented strong links between family values and religious affiliation. Most studies show a significant relationship between religious commitments and familistic behavior. Differences by religion in the timing of marriage and in family size, as well as in average age at marriage, proportions marrying, and the incidence of divorce reflect variation in the extent and intensity of the family on adult lives (Thornton and Camburn 1989; Cherlin 1996; Lehrer and Chiswick 1993; Goldscheider and Goldscheider 1993). These family differences among religious groups are not simply the consequences of their educational, social class, or urban characteristics but are directly connected to the extent of religious commitments, the depth of religious values and the cohesion of religiously defined communities. The intensity of religious commitments (defined in a variety of ways as religiosity) has also been demonstrated to influence attitudes toward sex roles, adolescent sexual behavior and attitudes toward sexual activities (see studies cited above).

There is also a substantial literature on the changing relationship between religious affiliation and religiosity and fertility-related behavior, including contraceptive use and practices. This research literature is important in showing the declining impact of religious affiliation on the type of contraceptives used and on fertility behavior and attitudes among White Catholics and Protestants (Goldscheider and Mosher 1988, 1991; Mosher, Williams, and Johnson 1990). In the past, religious affiliation was one of the most important factors in accounting for differences in American's fertility behavior and expectations, more important than social class or community size. More recent fertility studies, however, have documented the virtual elimination of religious affiliation as a factor (Mosher, Williams, and Johnson 1990). Yet other studies have shown that religious values retain a powerful influence in the critical decisions young adults make about family formation and family values (Goldscheider and Mosher 1991; Thornton 1989). Differences on some dimensions of family-related behavior have diminished over time among religious groups, whereas other aspects of the family have not converged fully or at all by the 1990s.

Thus, conclusions from these various research studies have not pointed to identical trends over time in religious differences in family change. It is therefore difficult to generalize about the changing direction of religious variation in family-related behavior. Although religious affiliation and religiosity appear to have a continuing relationship to family processes, the relationship seems to have weakened in the last decades. More important, it has become clear that the decline of religious differentials in any one family-related process does not necessarily imply religious convergence in all family processes.

It is also the case that although there are often only small overall differences in family processes among the major religious groups, there appears to be growing variation within large religious categories. Religious denominations among "Protestants" reflect a range of values about familism. Similarly, Catholicism has evolved somewhat differently among different subcommunities, although we can distinguish only Hispanic and non-Hispanic Catholics. Our analysis of Hispanics emphasized their ethnic origins rather than their religious affiliation (Chapter 9). Thus, those who are affiliated with these two broad religious traditions are themselves a diverse category. There is also great diversity among the smaller religious groups, not all of which have been closely studied.

To clarify some of these complexities, particularly with regard to historical changes in the impact of religion on the transition to adulthood, we first examine overall patterns to identify differences by religious affiliation in the residential transition to adulthood. We are able to distinguish liberal and fundamentalist Protestants;[2] Catholics; Jews; members of the Church of Jesus Christ of Latter Day Saints (LDS), often called Mormons; and those of no religious affiliation. All others, who are primarily of non-Western religions, are grouped together as an "other" category. For the larger groups, we are able to examine change over time.

RELIGION AND LEAVING HOME: OVERALL PATTERNS

Overall, religious groups differ from each other in their leaving-home patterns, in timing and especially in the route taken out of the parental home (Figure 10.1). These differences are as great or greater than differences among racial or ethnic groups (compare Chapter 9) and are net of the social and demographic compositional differences among religious groups.

Catholics are most distinctive in their delayed timing of leaving home, with odds of leaving home only 82 percent of those of liberal Protestants. Jews also appear to leave home more slowly than do members of other religious groups. However, as we shall discuss in a subsequent section of this chapter, Jews have experienced the greatest change in nest-leaving over the time period we are examining, increasing their rate of leaving home to converge with Protestants and Catholics. Although this is also the case for Catholics, the extent of their convergence has been much less.

The only other group that is distinctive in rates of overall leaving includes those who claim no religious affiliation, who are more likely to leave home at a given age, with odds 12 percent greater of leaving home than liberal Protestants, the reference category. The other groups do not differ significantly

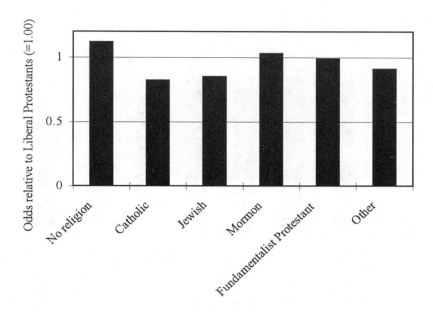

Figure 10.1. Religious Differences in Leaving Home
SOURCE: Calculated by the authors from the NSFH.

from the reference category, at least in their rate of leaving home, overall. Each group, however, has a distinctive pattern of routes out of the home.

Catholics leave home slowly by nearly every route (Figure 10.2). They are particularly unlikely to leave home to form nontraditional families via cohabitation or single parenthood, with odds barely two-thirds those of liberal Protestants. This seems consistent with a stronger moral stand, except that nearly the same pattern appears in their odds of leaving home to attend school or take a job (with odds of 75-80 percent of those of liberal Protestants), and their odds of leaving home to marry are little higher (85 percent those of the reference category). This suggests that what is important for Catholics is a strong attachment to the parental home. The exceptions tend to reinforce this interpretation, because the only two routes with "normal" rates of leaving home are independence (the favorite route of those running away from home) and the military, which stepchildren use to escape a difficult home situation. Each of these routes suggest that parental approval is not involved.

Other groups achieve their distinctive timing through a mixture of route choices. The rapid rate of nest-leaving among those with no religious affiliation in their childhood homes would have been even more rapid if they

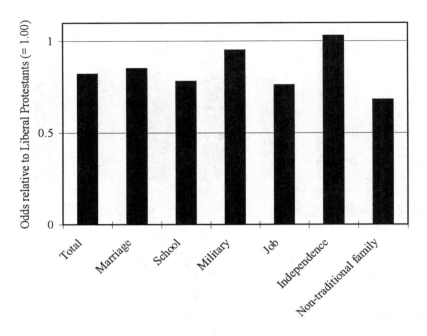

Figure 10.2. Routes out of the Home Among Catholics
SOURCE: Calculated by the authors from the NSFH.

had even average rates of leaving home to attend school; they are as unlikely to
take this route as Catholics (Figure 10.3). In contrast, they have 135 percent to
150 percent of the odds of liberal Protestants of leaving home for the various
other nonfamily routes—to take a job, enter the military, or be independent.
They also show a strong preference for the less sanctioned route to a new family
relative to marriage (with odds of 140 percent to leave home via cohabitation or
single parenthood and 94 percent for marriage, compared with liberal
Protestants). These results reinforce our link between family and religion,
because these children who grew up in homes with no religious affiliation show
a wide range of weak family outcomes. They break with their parental families
early, particularly to nonfamily situations. Furthermore, the family situations
they enter are particularly likely to be unstable and problematic. Finally, and
perhaps most painfully, they receive little relatively investment in their
economic futures, at least compared with liberal Protestants (and Jews).
Because this result controls for parental resources, it suggests that their parents
prefer to use their resources for purposes other than their children.

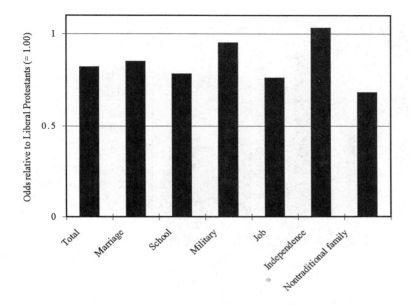

Figure 10.3. Routes Out of the Home Among Those With No Religious Affiliation
SOURCE: Calculated by the authors from the NSFH.

Mormons and those who are affiliated with fundamentalist Protestant denominations (e.g., Baptists) achieve their overall parity with liberal Protestants with somewhat similar combinations of routes (Figure 10.4). Each is much more likely to leave home to marry and much less likely to leave home to attend school (although the school difference is not significant for Mormons). Fundamentalist Protestants are otherwise not distinctive. Mormons, in contrast, are very likely to have a nonfamily living experience, particularly reporting that they left home to take on a job (a pattern that is particularly marked for young men, as we saw in Chapter 7). It seems likely that leaving to take a job reflects at least in part the policy of the LDS to send young adults on "missions," which often occur immediately after high school. Hence, their early nest-leaving appears to be consistent with a strong family-based set of values, reinforced by the Mormon Church, and represents neither a rejection of their family nor of their religious traditions.

Each of the groups with similar overall rates of leaving home is thus distinctive in the routes taken out of the home. Mormons differ from the two Protestant groups in their distinctive "job" pattern, whereas liberal Protestants differ from the other two by sending their children away to college but much

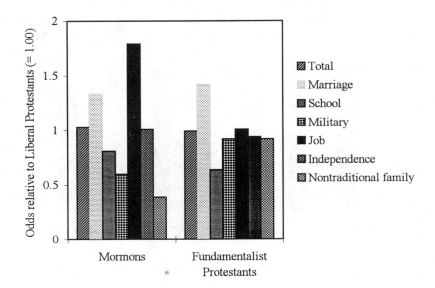

Figure 10.4.   Routes Out of the Home Among Mormons and Fundamentalist Protestants
SOURCE: Calculated by the authors from the NSFH.

less so to marriage. Hence, although the timing of the parent-child residential split is similar (and relatively early), suggesting relatively similar pressures to end the residential dimension of the parent-child relationship, they leave to quite differently structured lives. Catholics, in contrast, are distinctive primarily in leaving home slowly for nearly every route, but they largely resemble liberal Protestants in the configuration of routes they eventually take. Only those of no religious denomination in childhood are distinctive both in timing and in routes, suggesting both weak parent-child residential ties and weak family ties in adulthood.

These conclusions are reinforced by differences by religious affiliation in rates of returning home. As was the case for gender, differences in returning home are less sharp than those for leaving home (Chapter 7). There are also no differences in the overall rate of return, as was the case in the comparison of rates of leaving home between fundamentalist and liberal Protestants and Mormons, above. Hence, we have grouped these denominations somewhat differently, combining Mormons and fundamentalist Protestants, and also combining Jews, together with those of "other" and with no religious affiliations. The reference category remains the same (liberal Protestants).

Three patterns of difference stand out (Figure 10.5). Consistent with their high overall level of parent-child coresidence, Catholics who left home to attend college are significantly more likely to return home than the reference category (or than the other groups). They are less likely, however, to return home among those who left for marriage, consistent with the lower Catholic divorce rate that characterized most of the 20th century. They are also significantly less likely to return home than liberal Protestants if they left for independence. This result parallels one we documented for gender—that those who take a nonnormative route (in Catholic families, "normative" has to be interpreted in terms not of statistical frequency but of overall patterns, which reinforce staying home unless there is a very good reason) are unlikely to return home.

The combined group of fundamentalist Protestants and Mormons (which we call fundamentalist Christians) is distinctive only in its low rates of returning home among those who left for marriage. Given the high value of marriage in the constellation of routes out of the home among these groups, this difference suggests greater marital stability than among liberal Protestants. Also, this route is distinctive among the "other" group of Jews, those of no childhood religious affiliation, and those of other religions, but it is in the

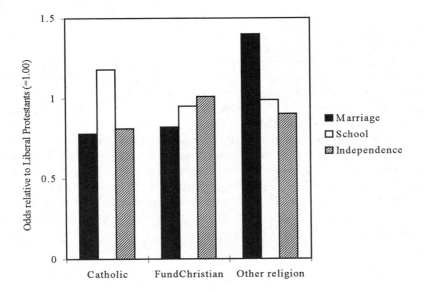

Figure 10.5. Religious Differences in Returning Home by Route Taken
SOURCE: Calculated by the authors from the NSFH.

opposite direction—much greater likelihood of a return. Given the historically low rates of divorce in the Jewish community (Cohen and Hyman 1986; Goldscheider 1989; Heilman 1995), this result is likely to be dominated by those of no religious affiliation, who have frequently been shown to have high rates of divorce (Lehrer and Chiswick 1996). Their parent-child ties are at least stronger than those they forge between adult men and women.

Our data do not allow us to identify and test empirically what accounts for these religious differences in leaving and returning home. Although the National Survey of Families and Households (NSFH) obtained a wide range of information on the current family values of respondents, these attitudinal measures relate to a time in their lives that for most is long after their nest-leaving experiences and could as easily be a product of them as their cause. As a result, we cannot investigate the direct relationship between childhood religious affiliation and family values over time.

Nevertheless, the evidence is consistent with the view that religious affiliation is linked with a set of values that influence young people's connections to their parental home and the choices they make about when to leave home and in what context. They are also consistent with the findings of a cohort-based study of the high school classes of 1980 and 1982. That study showed that a significant part of the religious differences in nest-leaving reflects these family values; when direct measures of family values were statistically controlled, few religious group differences remained (Goldscheider and Goldscheider 1993, Chap. 5). These findings strongly suggest that family values are the core set of factors that influence nest-leaving patterns among contemporary young adults.

We can infer only that similar family values have shaped religious differences in nest-leaving patterns in the historical past. What we can do, however, is to see whether the relationship between affiliation and values has changed. Have Catholics become less distinctive from mainstream Protestants, as the evolution of the Catholic Church in America has distanced more Catholics from official doctrine? Has the rise of fundamentalist Protestant sects been accompanied by a move toward the mainstream, or by increasing distinctiveness as the new members' enthusiasm is increased by intensified recruitment? Have the family transformations of the Jews reduced their "separateness" in America? The analysis of change over time should help us clarify the changing links between religious values and religious group membership.

CONVERGENCE AND DIVERGENCE: PROTESTANT-CATHOLIC
TRENDS AND PROTESTANT DENOMINATIONS

To understand how secularization and religious revival have changed the relationship between religion and the transition to adulthood, we distinguish those who reached age 18 before 1959 and since. When these comparisons are made systematically, two striking patterns emerge. One features substantial convergence between the two largest groups in American society—Catholics and mainstream Protestants. The other story is one of pretty impressive divergence among Protestant groups. The Jewish story is even more complex, so we will take it up in the next section.

There has been a clear convergence between Catholics and Protestants (at least among the liberal denominations) in the nest-leaving process. The pattern we described above, of overall slower leaving home by nearly every route for Catholics than for liberal Protestants was primarily a characteristic of the older cohorts (Figure 10.6); for the more recent cohorts, the Catholic and Protestant patterns, both in terms of timing of leaving home and the routes they have taken, have converged (becoming closer to 1.0). Few Protestant-Catholic differences in residential transition to adulthood remain for the cohorts reaching adulthood by the 1960s.

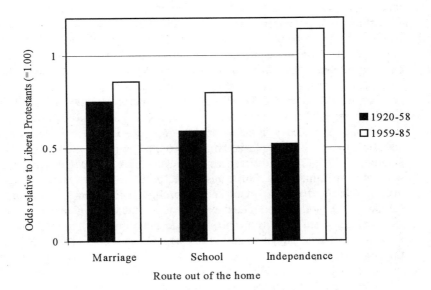

Figure 10.6. Convergence of Catholics and Liberal Protestants in Routes Taken
SOURCE: Calculate by the authors from the NSFH.

The gaps between these two groups decreased least in the most traditional route out of the home (marriage) and most for the newest (independence). As a result, Catholics still leave home for marriage more slowly than do liberal Protestants, and to school as well, just not as slowly as they had. The process of convergence may be completed in the future, or as has happened in Canada, new cleavages might develop between these two large Christian groups (Lebourdais and Juby 1997).

There was total convergence by 1960, however, in leaving home for independence. When this route out of the home was rare, it was much more rare for Catholics than for liberal Protestants. Clearly, Catholics experienced growth in this route even more rapidly than did others in American society, attaining odds of leaving home by this route 15 percent higher than the reference category (although the difference was not significant). These patterns of convergence in the Protestant and Catholic nest-leaving patterns parallel the findings noted earlier of convergence between Protestants and Catholics in their fertility behavior and attitudes. It appears that starting in the 1960s, and much more clearly thereafter, few family-related differences remained to differentiate Protestants from Catholics.

The second story is one of growing polarization in nest-leaving patterns among Protestants between their more liberal and their more fundamentalist denominations. Fundamentalist Christians (including Mormons, who strictly defined are not Christians, but given the greater similarity in their family-related behavior and attitudes to fundamentalist Protestants than to liberal Protestants, we have combined them with the former) have had distinctive patterns for as far back as our data are available. Nevertheless, these patterns have become even more distinctive among more recent cohorts. The break came a bit more recently than the Catholic-Protestant convergence, showing most clearly among the nest-leaving cohorts that came of age in 1965 or later.

Among the older, pre-1965 nest-leaving cohorts, fundamentalist Christians were significantly more likely than Protestants affiliated with liberal Protestant denominations to leave home in conjunction with marriage. They were also significantly less likely to leave home in conjunction with getting an education (Figure 10.7). These differences, however, have increased among recent cohorts. Fundamentalist Christians in the post-1966 nest-leaving cohorts are even less likely than their more liberal coreligionists to leave home for school (unlike the general trend noted earlier of an increase in leaving home for school). They are also even more likely to remain in the parental home until they marry. Thus, fundamentalist Protestants have become more distinctive in the contemporary period than they had been earlier. This pattern has resulted in greater polarization and heterogeneity among Protestants.

The growing heterogeneity among Protestants appears to characterize women even more than men (Chapter 7). The reduction of gender differences seems to characterize many religious groups. However, the growth of religious

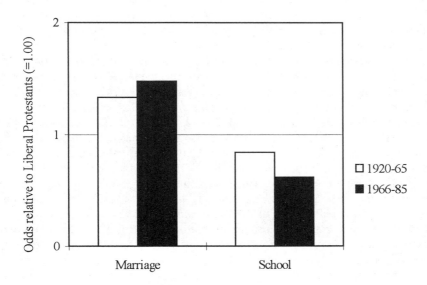

Figure 10.7. Divergence of Fundamentalist Christians and Liberal Protestants in Leaving Home for Marriage or School
SOURCE: Calculated by the authors from the NSFH.

fundamentalism may be reversing these processes, because these groups show very large gender differences.

ARE JEWS EXCEPTIONAL?

We would expect that Jews in contemporary American society would exhibit patterns characteristic of liberal Protestants, except for small insulated Jewish groups (e.g., Hasidic Jews).[3] Such is generally the case. However, a more detailed look at the changing patterns of nest-leaving among American Jews reveals the complexities of the transition to adulthood and provides some insight about general patterns characteristic of the historical evolution of changes in nest-leaving patterns in the United States.

Over the last century, Jews, like others in Western countries, have experienced a series of social demographic revolutions. In addition to the familiar transitions in mortality, fertility, and migration and in urbanization, education, and occupation, there have been important changes in the structure of Jewish families and the generational relationships among family members

(Goldscheider 1986; Goldscheider and Zuckerman 1985). The increasing periods of time that younger and older adults spend in nonfamily living arrangements are among the most striking new life course transitions that have emerged (see Goldscheider and Goldscheider 1997a).

The Jewish population in the United States has been characterized as highly familistic, with historically low proportions who never marry or dissolve their marriages (Farber, Mindel, and Lazerwitz 1981; Kobrin 1985; Goldscheider 1986). However, there is some evidence that Jews are losing their distinctiveness on these dimensions of family life (Lehrer and Chiswick 1996; Goldstein 1992). Much less is known about relationships between Jewish parents and their children—whether with regard to continuing coresidence into adulthood or other dimensions of familism. Older Jews are likely to endorse a "modern" norm of familism, which legitimates geographic and residential distance while reinforcing "keeping in touch"—sometimes called "intimacy at a distance" (Litwak and Silverstein 1990; Rosenmayr and Kochies 1963). Jewish parents also place greater importance on children's "autonomy," than do other parents, which might well translate into residential separation between the generations (Cherlin and Celebuski 1983).

What about the residential dimension of parent-child relationships during the younger generation's transition to adulthood? The research record, even for the recent period, is ambiguous. An analysis of the leaving-home patterns of young adults during the 1980s documented that young Jewish adults experience nonfamily living more than any other White group. They are also distinctive in having parents who are most likely to expect it for them, suggesting that this pattern is long-standing and reflects generational agreement (Goldscheider and Goldscheider 1993). However, an analysis of young adults leaving high school early in the 1970s showed that Jews were less likely to experience nonfamily living, at least outside of college dormitories, than otherwise comparable non-Jewish young adults (Goldscheider and DaVanzo 1989).

It is not at all clear whether these different research conclusions of the 1970s and 1980s represent changes over time in the living arrangements of young Jewish adults (a genuine difference between cohorts) or reflect differences in the samples studied and the analytic models used. Have the Jews in America always been distinctive in their leaving-home patterns? Or do the differing results between the cohorts of the 1970s and the 1980s indicate that rapid changes in living arrangements and in this dimension of familism are underway among young Jewish adults?

The NSFH data allow us to examine the probability of leaving home, comparing Jews and non-Jews entering young adulthood over much of the 20th century. Although the number of cases is small (around 200 persons self-identified as Jews), the data allow us to compare changes in living arrangements over time for the Jewish and non-Jewish White populations for the six decades 1925 to 1985. We focus on changes in the age at first leaving the parental home and on four routes out of the parental home—to marriage, to attend school, to independence, and to the military. These routes are examined for three broad nest-leaving cohorts: (1) the pre-World War II cohorts (before 1937), (2) the war and the baby boom (1938-1958), and (3) the more recent period (1959 to 1985).

The data reveal that although Jews have participated in the decline in age at leaving home, their decline has been even more rapid, converging with the white population in recent cohorts. This convergence is dramatic, because it ends an older pattern in which many young Jews remained in the parental home long into adulthood. We documented that among those coming of age during the Great Depression of the 1930s and before, a quarter remained home until age 24 (Chapter 2). Among Jews, the last quartile did not leave home until age 28 for these cohorts. Hence, the trend toward leaving home at earlier ages is quite striking among Jews so that by the most recent cohort, half of both Jews and the general White population left home before age 19.

This pattern of convergence shows clearly in Figure 10.8. It portrays the increasing rate of leaving home both for the non-Jewish White population and for the Jews. (The recent increase in age at leaving home does not appear, because the most recent cohort is too broad.) Non-Jewish young adults in the Depression cohorts and earlier left home only 63 percent as fast as those in the cohorts who came of age during World War II and the decade thereafter. The Vietnam and later cohorts continued this increase, but more slowly, leaving home on average 15 percent faster than did the middle cohort. Here, the much later age at leaving home of Jews appears for the first cohort in odds of nest-leaving that are only 40 percent those of non-Jews in the middle cohort, and the differences in the proportions of the two bars between the first two cohorts are not great. By the most recent cohort, however, Jews have converged and even exceed the non-Jewish White odds of leaving home. This is an extraordinary convergence, greater than that between Catholics and liberal Protestants, by far.

How much of this convergence is a reflection of differential ages at marriage or other differences between these two groups in routes out of the home? The convergence does not reflect changes in leaving home to marriage, because Jews have been much less likely than others to do so throughout this period (data not presented), and in fact, the early Jewish participation in the marriage/baby boom of the 1940s and 1950s (Della Pergola 1980), coupled with a pattern of leaving home at a later age, allowed marriage to remain an important route out of the parental home for a longer time among Jews than among others.

It also does not reflect greater Jewish participation in leaving home for independence. Leaving home for independence appears to have been a fairly common route out of the parental home for both groups of young adults during the Depression and earlier, primarily for males. Independence was not the point, and these young adults rarely established separate households, living

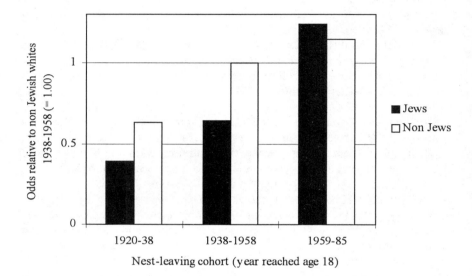

Figure 10.8. Jewish–non-Jewish Differences in Rates of Leaving Home by Nest-Leaving Cohort
SOURCE: Authors' calculations from the NSFH.

instead in the homes of their employers or in boarding/lodging houses (Hajnal 1982). For Jews, this pattern of leaving home may have been associated with their international migration to the United States and with a similar stage of independent living in boarding houses in America's urban areas (Glenn 1990).

The dramatic change in routes out of the home for Jews is not to residential independence before marriage but to attend school away from home. Leaving home for education is the first experience away from home for more than half the Jews who reached age 18 after 1958 (55 percent). This is the case for little more than a quarter of the general White population of young adults. Even when background factors are controlled, Jews are more than two-and-a-half times as likely to take this route out of the home, the youngest route of all. Thus, even as Jews became more similar to Whites in their overall timing of leaving home, they became more distinctive in terms of the routes out of the home. Hence, beneath the surface of convergence between Jews and others in leaving-home patterns there are sharp differences between them in the routes taken. These differences imply that intergenerational relationships are really very different between Jews and others, despite their similarities in the timing of leaving home (and their probabilities of returning home).

In particular, there is a major difference in the effects of parental education on nest-leaving patterns between Jews and non-Jews, differences that raise key questions about the role of family coresidence in the educational attainment and social mobility of children. In general, higher parental education is associated with leaving the parental home at a later age for most routes but at an earlier age to attend college away from home. Among the older cohorts of Jews, however, higher parental education had much less effect on their children's leaving home. The early cohorts of Jews were less likely than Whites in general to leave home to attend college. But this pattern did not mean that Jews were not getting educated. In fact, the late nest-leaving of the earlier cohorts of Jews was likely to reflect a strategy of financing higher education in the least expensive way, by supporting children to live at home and attend college.

This generational argument posits that Jews invested in the education of their children while being supportive of their continuing to live at home. It is consistent with the data showing that Jewish children of the early cohorts left home more slowly, particularly to attend college, than Whites in general. This occurred despite their parents' somewhat higher levels of education (25 percent of the Jewish parents had levels of education averaging more than high school compared with 14 percent of the parents of the general White population).

Nevertheless, when we consider the children of the earlier cohorts to approximate the parents of the youngest cohort, the data reveal that Jews were able to increase their level of college attainment faster than was the case for other Whites—63 percent of the most recent cohorts' parents averaged some college among Jews compared with only 35 percent among Whites. Remaining at home, in this case, led to increased investment in the next generation, providing the resources for the most recent generation of Jewish parents to send their children away to school in large numbers.

These results help clarify the puzzle in the literature, in which Jews were less likely to leave home for independence in the 1970s but more likely in the 1980s. This now appears to be empirically correct. The evidence portrays rapid changes between the 1960s to the 1980s, with Jews beginning far below other Whites in this behavior but increasing dramatically with time.

Our detailed analysis of leaving home in young adulthood has shown changes over time in both the timing and routes out of the home. Jews have become similar to the White population in the timing of leaving home but more distinctive in the routes selected. The emerging distinctive pattern among Jews has important implications for the relationships between parents and children. The investments made by Jewish parents in the education of the next generation link their children to them in ways that are different from what it had been in the past and distinctive from the general White pattern. Leaving home among Whites of the most recent generation has occurred at earlier ages than before and as often for "independence" as for education. The overwhelming reason young Jewish adults leave home at an early age is to go to college. This is a new form of "dependence" of one generation on another, one that may generate new family connections and support as parents facilitate the nest-leaving of their children, even when they continue to control the financial strings.

The increasing likelihood that Whites leave home for independence at a young age means greater emphasis on nonfamily living, individualism, and weaker family ties (and less financial commitment of parents to the education of their children beyond high school). In contrast, the Jewish patterns of early nest-leaving to attend college may result in new family-based ties and connections. Emerging patterns of family relationships between the younger and middle generations among Jews emphasize new forms of family connections that are not residentially based.

CONCLUDING OBSERVATIONS

Our analysis of the effects of religion on the timing of leaving home and the routes taken reveals a complex picture of change and variation. Several important findings highlight these complexities and point to important qualifications. They suggest ways to move beyond the description of religious differences to focus on significant analytic issues. Three findings are instructive:

Overall, contemporary variation by religious affiliation remains salient in the nest-leaving process, but these differences have significantly diminished among recent cohorts for large groups of the population. We interpret these changes as the consequences associated with secularization. The results imply the reduction in the centrality of religious values in the critical decisions that young adults and their parents are making in the transition to adulthood and in the relationships between the generations. As part of this secularization, there has been a major convergence in Protestant-Catholic differences in nest-leaving. Consistent with convergences in other family-related processes, the emergent similarities between these two religious groups reflect a growing homogenization of religious differences in America.

Nevertheless, several religious groups have remained distinctive and indeed appear to have become more distinctive in the recent period. These include Protestant fundamentalist denominations and the Mormon religious community. The strong family values and the cohesion of these more religiously committed communities link leaving home and the transition to adulthood with marriage. These more traditional family-centered groups display significantly lower rates of leaving home just to be independent from family.

A third important set of findings emerge from our detailed review of the changes in nest-leaving among American Jews. The major changes that have come to characterize this community suggest that the issues of nest-leaving cannot be viewed only in terms of the timing and age of leaving home. The importance of leaving home to go to a college has emerged for Jews in the contemporary period, and to lesser extent among other ethnic and religious groups. The evidence suggests that leaving home does not inevitably imply a break between the family of origin and the next generation. Indeed, leaving home may be facilitated by parents either by encouraging children to attend residential colleges or to reinforce parental independence. The early nest-leaving that characterizes Jews going to college or Mormons going on missions may reinforce generational ties and enhance family values. Thus, although leaving home often represents a significant break between generational dependence and autonomy, it may not in all cases. Only an analysis of context reveals when there is a break associated with leaving home and when there is a reinforcement of family and community ties.

Religious affiliation and religious culture continue to have important connections to family values and decisions that mark the transition to adulthood. These connections in contemporary American society are not identical to what they have been in the past. Religious systems and their family-related values often focus on segments of communities who are more committed to religion and more susceptible to their influence. Our analysis reveals, therefore, how secularization has altered the meaning of religions for the family and its values as well as how religious communities continue to have an impact on the decisions that young adults make in their transition to adulthood.

NOTES

1. On the issues of secularization, see Thornton and Fricke (1989), Greeley (1989), Stark and Brainbridge (1995). An extensive controversy has emerged over the ways in which religiosity is measured over time, the interpretation of research findings, and the adequacy of our empirical indicators. For the most recent debate over the use and measurement of church attendance from survey data see the symposium in the *American Sociological Review*, February 1998, and the articles in that issue by Caplow; Hout and Greeley; Woodbury; Hadaway, Marler, and Chaves; Smith; Presser and Stinson.

2. The category fundamentalist Protestants includes members of Baptist, Pentecostal, Nazarene, and Assembly of God denominations. The logic for coding this category is outlined in the appendix. We refer to Protestants who are not fundamentalists as "liberal" Protestants.

3. Hasidic Jews are a small proportion of the total Jewish population, and we have very little reliable information on their family patterns. Indirect and observational data

show that Hasidic and ultra-Orthodox Jews marry at a relatively early age, remain at home until they are married, and have large families. These patterns resemble in more extreme form the Mormon and fundamentalist Protestant patterns noted earlier. See, for example, Heilman (1992), Kranzler (1961), Mayer (1979), Shaffir (1986), Waxman (1983).

What Is New In Nest-Leaving In 20th Century America?

O ur analysis has examined the transition to adulthood in the United States over the last century through the prism of leaving and returning to the parental home. How new are the emerging patterns of leaving and returning home in the 1990s? What do these patterns of nest-leaving and returning suggest about the broader range of family issues that have come to characterize the United States as the 20th century draws to a close, so many of which focus on young adults? What do these detailed analyses of the timing of nest-leaving, the routes taken, and the return to the parental home teach us about changes in the relationships between the generations—parents and their children—and between men and women—fathers and mothers, sons and daughters—in the United States and perhaps in other industrialized countries as well? We thread these themes together in this chapter in the light of our detailed findings. We also speculate beyond what the evidence can reveal to suggest theoretical, methodological, and substantive challenges for future research.

WHAT'S NEW?

In their transition to adulthood, young adults in American society still leave the homes they grow up in to form homes of their own, as they have always done. Their age at leaving home, however, has fluctuated substantially, falling and then rising again. The "homes" they go to—the routes young adults take out of the home—have changed dramatically, and their likelihood of returning has almost doubled. Hence, although young adults at the end of the 20th century are living in their parental homes nearly as much as they did at the beginning of the century, these other changes imply that the meaning of this phenomenon is very different from what it was.

Many forces contributed to achieve this result. It is difficult to overestimate the impact of World War II on the nest-leaving process. Ages at leaving home were falling throughout the early part of the century and continued to do so for another three decades after that war began. Nevertheless, the cohort that came of age (18) in the 1938 to 1944 period experienced greater shifts in their timing of leaving home than did any other cohort, particularly relative to the Depression cohort that preceded them. The median age at leaving home dropped by 1.4 years between the Depression and the World War II cohorts, the steepest drop for any pair of cohorts. Even more dramatic was the decline in the proportions remaining home well into their 20s. In the Depression cohort, as many as 25 percent remained home past age 24; this had dropped to age 21 in the World War II cohort. The drop was much steeper for young men (not surprisingly), with the result that during this period and for a few thereafter, men left home at younger ages than women.

The war had an even stronger impact on young adults' nest-leaving pathways, and again, this was most obvious for young men. Nearly half the men in the World War II cohort left home to serve in the armed services, an increase from just 17 percent in the previous cohort (which itself is an overstatement, because many of these were late leavers who had stayed home until the war started). There was little return to "normalcy" when the war ended, however, because the age at leaving home continued to fall, if not so steeply. The high levels of mobilization linked with the cold war, Korea, and Vietnam meant that age 18 was the magic age for conscription for many men in the next several decades.

World War II also marked a watershed of sorts for young women, whose ages at leaving home fell almost as fast as young men's. How much this was the result of marrying young soldiers, how much it reflected young women's parallel desire to contribute to the war through war work, as British women did during World War I (Watson 1996), and how much it reflected the effect of growing up in families in which brothers leave home early is an interesting question for further research. Much of the effect must have been through marriage, however, because the war, rather than revolutionizing women's pathways out of the home as it did for young men, reinforced the older pattern of leaving home for marriage. The revolution in women's routes out of the home was postponed for two more decades, until the waning years of the baby boom.

The result was eventually the same for both young men and young women: The routes young adults currently are taking out of the home are sharply different from the routes that their grandparents took when they left home. Today they are far more likely to leave home to get an education. Higher education is much more important in this technologically complex end of the 20th century, although it is not always clear that continuing in school after high school requires leaving home. Young adults today are also far more likely to leave home to be more in control of their lives—that is, just for independence—and to form nontraditional families via single parenthood or cohabitation. These two new pathways began a spectacular increase in the 1960s, when many of the parents of the contemporary generation of young adults reached age 18. Earlier, only 10 to 15 percent left for independence and nontraditional family formation. These routes accounted for 30 percent among the cohorts of the 1970s and 40 percent among the 1980s cohorts.

These new pathways taken by young American adults reaching age 18 in the 1990s seem to be more fragile transitions to residential independence than in the past. World War II was also one of the cohorts that dramatically increased the likelihood of returning home, in part because so many left to join the armed services, and most of those who survived did return home. The continued increase in returning, however, is because nontraditional partnering, childbearing out of marriage, or living alone or with roommates tend to be vulnerable positions for young adults, given the resources most have available. Independence requires adequate financial resources or at least a job (or a partner) that can cover the costs of new living arrangements. Often, the resources available to young adults are marginal, and the jobs are not always very attractive, either in the short run or as a step to a longer-term career. Cohabitation is an even less firm commitment to a stable long-term relationship than contemporary marriage. So when the job becomes boring or the pay inadequate, when the resources dry up and independence or cohabitation isn't working out, the parental home looks attractive again as a way station to the next phase of adulthood. Returning home has increased in the recent period, not just because more are taking routes such as school that have always had a high probability of returning, but because the move away for independence has become steadily more reversible.

Children increasingly are returning home, at least when the locks on the door haven't been changed or the child's room hasn't been turned over permanently (e.g., to a boarder or perhaps to new exercise or computer equipment) or when the home itself has not been changed, such as by the addition of a stepparent. Often, this return is for a relatively short time, a cushion against the pains of failure and a time of refueling. This return home is increasingly a part of the contemporary dynamics of the transition to adulthood and is likely redefining the relationship between the generations. A return home after a substantial absence (and most have been away for at least a year or two) should realign the relationships between parents and children, because the children have already added experience and independence to their transition to adulthood. They are no longer the children who left but adults. Parents have had their own "independence" from their absent child and have developed new routines based on their emptier nest.

World War II, however important it was, was only one of the forces acting on the transition to adulthood. A common theme in our analysis is that the relationship between parents and their sons and daughters is not simply based on internal family dynamics that shift over the family life course. Much broader society-wide changes have influenced what parents and their children experienced and how their relationships with each other have been shaped.

Over the course of the 20th century, several major revolutions have occurred in the United States. If normally slower and less dramatic in the short run, they have cumulatively strongly influenced how the generations are linked to each other and thereby shaped the leaving and returning processes associated with the transition to adulthood.   We have identified and measured five historical transformations in the United States that seemed to us and to other social scientists to be directly relevant to the transition to adulthood. These include (1) increases in educational attainment, (2) changes in gender relationships, the changing nature of (3) ethnicity and (4) religion (both in terms of secularization and religious polarization), and (5) the revolution in family structure. Although many of their foundations reach back to the early years of the century and even before, most have had their sharpest impact in the years after World War II.

The immediate post-World War II cohorts were the first to see the fruits of the educational revolution. The two baby boom cohorts experienced the most rapid increase in parental education. Whatever privations their parents had known in their own young adulthoods, which were spent in the midst of depression and war, they were well positioned to take advantage of the opportunities of the postwar era to provide secure homes for their children.

More educated parents invest in the college education of their children and hence their children are more likely to leave home at young ages for college. They also protect their children from leaving home too soon for independence and from marrying early (although in the early years of the baby boom, this likely meant that they helped them return to school when they did marry very young).   Children growing up in poor households tend to leave home at an early age (and not for college) and to take fragile routes that reinforce the likelihood of later family and work instability. This was also the case for those whose families received public assistance (although these costs appear to have diminished considerably in the past two decades). Hence, increases in parental affluence and education smoothed their children's transitions to adulthood.

Looking beyond the revolution in parental resources, however, the lives of those who grew up in the late baby boom (1959-1965) were very different from those whose transition to adulthood was during the long years of the early baby boom (1945-1958). "Lifestyle" issues began to emerge, particularly related to issues of gender, but also in religion and family formation. The first sign of the gender revolution occurred in this period: Young women's leaving home for marriage declined most sharply between the early and later baby boom, making their routes out of the home more similar to young men's. There was plenty of room for this level to decline, however, because the entire period from World

War II through both stages of the baby boom was marked by great gender dissimilarity on this dimension. There was a long way to go then, even more than there is today. Part of the reduction in women's leaving home for marriage went into going away to college (although they still trailed men in this area) and part into greater independence. Much of the decline may have been concentrated in the Pacific region, because it was then that the Pacific region began its precipitous decline in the marriage route, diverging rapidly from the rest of the country.

The period between the early and late baby boom was also when the independence route first began its rapid rise, and again, it was the Pacific region that led in this new definition of the transition to residential independence. Catholics, too, were showing signs of losing their distinctiveness from liberal Protestants, years before Vatican II; the big convergence between these two groups occurred in the waning years of the baby boom. Thus, even in the late 1950s and early 1960s, the seeds of later change were rapidly germinating.

By the Vietnam nest-leaving cohort, the ethnic revolution had emerged, and there was further news on the religion front. While Hispanics were slowly converging with non-Hispanic whites in leaving home for marriage, jobs, and school throughout most of the century, Blacks were responding more dramatically to the social and economic dislocations of the late 1960s. The great decline in marriage as a route out of the home among Blacks first became prominent during this period, as did the decline in leaving home for jobs.

The trend toward religious convergence (and secularization) was also jolted by the emergence of sharp differences between the more liberal and fundamentalist Protestant denominations. The latter group has not fully participated in the decline in marriage as a route out of the home, particularly for women. Fundamentalist Protestants and Mormons have emerged as clearly distinctive religious communities, emphasizing the centrality of traditional family relationships. In contrast, in the same period, Jews went from a late to a very early pattern of leaving home. Rather than representing a break with the past, however, it appears to be merely a shift in the way Jews invest in the education of the next generation, leading to new forms of generational interdependence.

Change in family structure is the final revolution shaping nest-leaving in the 20th century. This revolution is the last in the sequence to make its mark. Given its current importance, we were surprised that the divorce revolution was not more closely linked with the historic changes in leaving and returning home. All of the 20th century reduction in the age at leaving home occurred before the divorce revolution.

In the next century, however, it should have a much greater impact. Changes in family structure, including both the departure of one parent and the acquisition of a stepparent, are already having profound effects on the contemporary nest-leaving process. Family instability reduces the likelihood that children will leave home to attend college or that they will return. Gaining a stepparent during adolescence or having stepsiblings accelerates all the routes out of the home, including leaving home for independence, entering the military, taking a job, and leaving for cohabitation and unmarried parenthood. Given the rapid acceleration in the proportions of young adults' parents who are separating and repartnering, these findings suggests that the parental investments that are critical for the successful launching of young adults into adulthood, particularly educational investments, may be in short supply in the next century.

Like the revolution in family structure, all of the other revolutions are continuing to have an impact, and the impacts are sometimes changing as the revolutions gain momentum. For most of the century, gender role changes were primarily affecting the routes taken out of the home, increasing the similarities between the sexes on this dimension. Thus, for example, among the most recent cohorts, leaving home to go to school is no longer gender specific. More recently, however, there has been divergence in nest-leaving between young men and women, as daughters have become increasingly more likely than sons to leave home (despite the rapid decrease for both sexes in marriage—the most gender-differentiated route). Daughters are also less likely than sons to return home, decreasing their rates of returning even as sons have increased theirs. This suggests that the world outside the home may have become more egalitarian than the family home environment, which is still more congenial to sons than to daughters.

These two dimensions—the relationships between parents and children within the family and the opportunities outside the home that shape children's lives after they are adults—are both reflected in the variations and changes in the nest-leaving process. It is helpful to distinguish the factors that influence the timing of leaving home and the likelihood of returning from those that affect the pathways children take out of the home. The first set, the overall timing of leaving home and the likelihood of returning, should reflect how well the relationships between the parents and their children allow them to live together reasonably amicably. The second set should reflect the structures that young people must fit into as adults. These structures draw men out to serve in the military and women to adult roles in which being wives and mothers takes primacy over careers and the preparation needed for them. They provide the children of the more affluent the opportunity to attend a residential college.

These two dimensions—routes, on the one hand, and the overall likelihood of leaving and returning, on the other—are not fully separable. Difficulties in the job market (or with relationships) might encourage longer parent-child coresidence than either prefer (although if the home situation is uncomfortable enough, most will leave quickly). One route—leaving home for independence—would seem to be more closely tied to the parent-child relationship than to the work and family structures men and women confront as adults. Overall, however, it is a useful distinction, which tells us much about what is happening in the American family and about the likely adult lives of the next generation.

PARENT-CHILD RELATIONSHIPS

Most reassuring for our understanding of factors conditioning parent-child relationships is our finding that, despite the intuitive and theoretical appeal of economic resources as a basis for understanding changes in leaving and returning home, they really do not seem to matter when we consider the parent-child dimension of the process.   There is almost no relationship between measures of parental resources and the timing of leaving home (once the effects on leaving home to attend college are eliminated) and none at all on the likelihood of returning home. When Hansel and Gretel were forced to leave home, it was not because their woodchopper father was poor. Being more or less affluent does not appear to shape parents' willingness to share their homes with their children.

The evidence suggests that two other dimensions we examined are relatively much more important factors. These are parental family structure— after all, it was Hansel's and Gretel's stepmother, who by forcing them out, exposed them to the wicked witch—and family values. We have already reviewed the sobering effects of family structure, which paint a picture of leaving home early, particularly too early (at age 15 or 16), and less possibility of returning, as well as decreased investment in education. Here, we want to pull together our findings on ethnicity, religion, and region. In the absence of direct measures, they are our strongest indicators of values about familism. Their pattern of effects suggests their link to the strength of parent-child relationships.

There are more findings linking familistic values with leaving home, although some also carry over to returning home. Overall, non-Hispanic White Americans, and particularly liberal Protestants and those with no childhood religious affiliation, leave home earliest. Among non-Hispanic Whites, both Catholics and Jews leave home more slowly (although this pattern has recently reversed for Jews), and Blacks, Hispanics, and Asians all leave home more slowly. Most of these differences also appear in the likelihood of leaving for independence, reinforcing our interpretation that these groups maintain a strong parent-child coresidential tie. With such data, it is not possible to say definitively that minority ethnic and religious groups have more supportive parent-child relationships. The lack of independence might signal excessive dependence rather than helpful interdependence. It seems likely, however, that these are ties that provide young adults overall with greater support than is the case among the majority groups, possibly because the latter have less need, given their more privileged status.

Variation among the regions of the United States also seems to reflect often long-standing differences in values, rather than changes in the economic situations of the different regions. Most appear to reflect values about the relationships between men and women, as we shall discuss below, but some also focus on the parent-child relationship. The most dramatic is the east-west gradient in the importance of "independence" as a reason people gave for leaving home. This suggests a definition of adulthood based less on the acquisition of concrete adult roles of work and family than on the sheer fact of separation from parents. More puzzling is the general pattern of delayed nest-leaving among those who grew up in the Mid-Atlantic and Midwest regions. This is clearly tied exactly to these adult roles; young adults from these regions leave home more slowly, not only overall but also to marriage and jobs, than do those in the regions of the country we have called the traditional core. Discovering what the factors are that keep young people home longer in these communities, however, requires further research.

ADULT LIVES OF WORK AND FAMILY

Class and gender are clearly the most powerful factors shaping the routes young adults take out of the parental home. As we noted above, children from more affluent families are much more likely to leave home to further their educations, and to take routes that delay their entry into unstable relationships (cohabitation and young marriage) and career paths. Sons and daughters, despite the massive changes wrought by the gender revolution, still take very different pathways out of the home, with daughters still much more likely to remain home until marriage and sons much more likely to experience "a room of their own" in young adulthood.

Gender differences in the likelihood of leaving home for marriage actually increased between what historians sometimes call "the first gender revolution" of the early part of the century, when women were given the constitutional right to vote, and "the second gender revolution" that began in the late 1960s and brought women closer to parity with men both in the likelihood of having a paid job and in being paid equally for equal work. Whether in reaction to the first revolution or, more likely, to the decades shaped by the Great Depression of the 1930s and by World War II, the two baby boom cohorts were the time of the greatest difference between men and women in leaving home for marriage. Another way to look at this pattern is that whereas World War II began men's massive move out of the home before marriage, women's decline followed 20 or so years later. This sequence parallels adult men's move out of the home for work (which happened primarily in the 19th century) and the comparable move for adult women, which was delayed until the mid-20th century.

Values about the centrality of marriage in adult lives (and particularly in adult women's lives) are also evident in our results for ethnicity, religion, and region, shaping the relationships between men and women much as they do the relationships between parents and children. Hispanic Americans are clearly distinct on this dimension from non-Hispanic whites, retaining many more of their children in the parental home until marriage, although this difference has been eroding. More recently, fundamentalist Protestants and Mormons have been resisting the decline in the marriage pathway, particularly for daughters, and as a result have become more distinct from other Christian groups. The regions at the traditional core of the country have also been resisting the move away from marriage as the pathway out of the home and have been resisting as well the growth in nontraditional family formation. That these results do not simply reflect differences in values, however, is underlined by the fact that the decline in the marriage route among Blacks is extremely recent and hence may be more the result of changed opportunities for men and for women than of rapid changes in values.

ARE AMERICAN NEST-LEAVING PATTERNS UNIQUE?

In this analysis, we have told an American story about leaving and returning home in the 20th century, uncovering the historical sources of contemporary nest-leaving patterns and revealing where there is continuity and distinctiveness in the most recent cohorts. Are the patterns that we have analyzed more broadly characteristic of European, Westernized, industrialized countries? In this final section, we briefly consider some comparative cross-national evidence to suggest some common features among countries and some unique American features.

All countries are unique in their specific histories and in their particular combination of economic and political contexts, their values and the pace of social change. Yet many share the processes of political, social, and economic transformations that have been critical for the transformation of the family. Many are therefore likely to share in the general trends over time in the relationship between the generations and between women and men. This is particularly the case in the most recent decades, as globalization and the revolution in communications have increasingly reduced the pockets of cultural uniqueness around the world and particularly among the most industrialized nations.

Nonfamily living, both in young adulthood (leaving home before marriage) and at other stages of the life course, is part of the package of recent family changes that have swept much of the industrialized world in the past quarter of a century. Indeed, the growth in nonfamily living and in childbearing and in raising children outside marriage have become so extensive that they have been called "the second demographic transition" (van de Kaa 1987). An emerging body of comparative literature is likely to be helpful in understanding the American case, just as the historical analysis has been helpful in understanding contemporary patterns.[1]

Two dominant themes characterize a set of recent European studies of nest-leaving in Germany, France, Italy, the Netherlands, and Spain (Cherlin, Scabini, and Rossi 1997a). First, it is clear that economic conditions are of importance in understanding the timing of leaving home and the paths taken. Independence among young adults requires a set of economic conditions: resources that parents can use to support the independent residence of their children and/or the ability of children to sustain their independence through having steady employment. Thus, the transition to adulthood everywhere is linked to the importance of increasing affluence and the role of the economic difficulties of the 1990s.

There are also family-related contexts that shape nest-leaving. The timing of marriage, and its relative importance among young adults, is clearly linked with leaving home. The family context of the parental home is also of importance in providing a supportive environment for children to remain at home for a longer period of time or welcoming children back home in difficult times. The emergence of alternatives to marriage, particularly cohabitation, nonfamily living arrangements, and unmarried parenthood, have been clearly linked to the timing and the routes taken out of the home.

Many circumstances differ among these countries. They differ dramatically on the level of commitment in male-female relationships, with considerably higher levels of cohabitation and of childbirth and child-raising outside of marital unions for France, Germany, and the Netherlands than for Italy and Spain. These countries also differ dramatically in employment policies. France, Germany, and Italy, like many other European countries with a strong social safety net, protect the jobs and wages of the currently employed and tolerate very high levels of unemployment. In 1997, the unemployment rates for these countries were 11.3 percent for Germany, 11.9 percent for Italy, and 12.8 percent for France ("Europe Isn't Working" 1997). These rates generally bear most heavily on the unskilled and those living in depressed areas but also particularly on the young. Unemployment is even more extreme in Spain, recently reaching the highest level in the European Union, 23 percent. The Netherlands, in contrast, like the United States and the United Kingdom, has cut benefits and encouraged employment growth, if often mostly of "lousy jobs" (Burtless 1990), with the result that its unemployment rate is barely half that of these other countries, 6.2 percent.

Obviously many other, more deeply seated differences among these countries need to be taken into account. They have different histories and cultures that they value highly. Nevertheless, some of the results of these studies of Western industrialized countries are suggestive for understanding the American patterns. The high-unemployment economies of Italy and Spain likely encourage young people to remain home until they can "get on the ladder" and acquire a secure job with the government or a large enterprise. The lower-unemployment economies of the Netherlands and the United States may provide jobs that, although unlikely to be "career" opportunities and thus not a basis for making long-term plans and commitments, are more likely to allow young people to move out of their parental homes into shared apartments with roommates and/or cohabiting partners.

There is one conspicuous and particularly important difference that makes the American case distinctive. The United States has by far the highest proportion of young adults who attend college and is also the only country where such a high proportion do so while living away from home. This has been associated with particularly American patterns of semiautonomous living arrangements among very young adults, similar to the military experience of generations past. But this residential college pattern is more common in America among both young women and men. It is likely to account for the overall higher rates of return home in the United States and the declining age of first leaving home. It is also likely to alter the relationships of parents to their sons and daughters and gender relationships both for parents and the children.

CONCLUDING OBSERVATIONS

This study has painted change in nest-leaving in the 20th century with detailed information but often with a very broad brush, shedding much new light but leaving many challenges to be addressed. We often do not have ideal measures for many of the relationships we study, although it is doubtful that better data will emerge in the near future. Perhaps the most important omission, however, relates to point of view.

Our study is done from the point of view of young adults leaving home. This is dictated by our interest in covering as much of the 20th century as possible. Nevertheless, this means that we are looking only at one side of the family transformations as they are experienced by the parents: The same behavior that takes young adults away from home brings their parents to the empty nest stage of their lives. Undoubtedly, the process looks different from the parents' point of view. Do they relate to the child's decisions differently when it is their first child to leave home—or their last? We know that having more siblings makes young adults leave home faster, but more could be done to examine the effects of birth order (although we still would not know "leaving order"). Do mothers differ from fathers, and do employed mothers differ from housewives? Although we have unusually rich data on parental background, it would have been very useful to have much more.

The transition to adulthood has been radically changed over the 20th century. Not everything has changed, but cumulatively, the changes that have occurred have transformed the ways in which parents and children, husband and wives, brothers and sisters relate to one another. It is difficult for those who take for granted the patterns evident at the end of the 20th century to imagine what it was like during the Depression, when substantial numbers (up to a quarter) had never left home as late as age 24, or the world of the early baby boom, in which many young men and women married while still in their teens. Nevertheless, these changes are part of the broader transformation of families as the 20th century comes to a close.

One way or another, children separate from their parents or their parents separate from them at some point in their lives. The timing when this happens in the life course of parents and of children and the reasons children leave home—that is, the paths they take out of the parental home—are central to the relationships between the generations, among siblings, and between young women and men. Sometimes the separation of young adults from the parental home is permanent as children form new families of their own, never to return home permanently. The new generation develops new relationships with their parents and their parents' with their children and grandchildren. Sometimes the children who have left their parents home return home at least for a short period of time to recover from a failed marriage or relationship or from an inadequate or dead end job. Sometimes, parents have abandoned their children by changing the environment of their family or the composition of their households, making a return home more difficult or at least making the current home significantly different from the home that the child left.

Clearly, the residential break between the generations in the transition to adulthood is not necessarily permanent. But even when children return home, they are different for the experiences they have had away from parents; their parents are often different as well for having experienced a period of time without their children. Whether children return home or not, they are likely to forge new relationships with their parents and their parents with them. This transition to adulthood, as all transitions, is often tense, requiring adjustments on all sides, as new persons enter the generational relationship and other persons depart. This dynamic of change in time and context, over the life course and between the generations are the building blocks forming the foundation of emerging communities and social change.

NOTES

1. Most of the English-language studies of leaving home have focused on North American and other English-speaking countries, including in addition to the United States, Australia (Young 1974, 1975, 1987), Canada (e.g., Mitchell, Wister, and Burch 1989, Peron, Lapierre-Adamcyk, and Morissette 1986), and the United Kingdom (see especially Kiernan 1986, 1989; Kerkhoff and Macrae 1992). Detailed and direct cross-national comparisons are weak and mostly descriptive (e.g., Kiernan 1989). There are

no research studies available for industrialized countries comparable with the analysis of young adult living arrangements in six Latin America countries (DeVos 1989). We have recent studies on France and Italy (Scabini and Cigoli 1997; Rossi 1997; Leridon and Toulemon 1995; Pinnelli and De Rose 1995), Spain (Cordon 1997), Germany (Nave-Herz 1997; Mayer and Schwarz 1989), and the Netherlands (vanHekken et al. 1997; Jong-Gierveld, Liefbroer, and Beekink 1992).

APPENDIX

Studying Nest-Leaving in 20th Century America

O ur study of leaving and returning home in the United States over much of this century was made possible by the data collected by the National Survey of Families and Households (NSFH). This survey has transformed the study of the nest-leaving process, as it has many other dimensions of family life, by providing information on leaving and returning home for people who came of age over a broad range of time periods and also about the characteristics of their families and their own histories of family formation, work, school, and military service. It is unlikely that we will ever obtain better data for studying changes in nest-leaving in the 20th century.

These data have made this study as rich and authoritative as it is; many other studies on this subject are possible. More could be done, even on the questions we address here, as we will indicate below. Nevertheless, like all data sets, the NSFH has limitations as well as strengths. In this appendix, we describe the data and discuss the measures we constructed from the questions asked. We outline the methods we used to study leaving and returning home and how these processes have changed, so that both their strengths and limitations are clear. We also present a set of reference tables that are the sources of many of the simple figures that appear throughout the text.

THE DATA: THE NATIONAL SURVEY OF FAMILY AND HOUSEHOLDS

The National Survey of Families and Households (NSFH) was carried out in 1987-1988. The NSFH was designed at the Center for Population and Ecology of the University of Wisconsin (for details see Sweet, Bumpass, and Call 1988a). Fieldwork for the survey was carried out by the Institute for

Survey Research at Temple University during 1987 and 1988. Based on a multistage areal sampling plan, interviews were face-to-face, with sensitive information obtained through a self-administered questionnaire filled out by the respondent at various points in the course of the interview. Complete interviews were conducted with 13,008 men and women. The main sample was 9,643 households. In addition, a double sampling was obtained of minorities, single-parent families, families with stepchildren, cohabiting couples, and recently married persons. The sample was representative of the population then living in the United States, aged 19 and older (or married). Information was obtained on a wide range of family-related behavior and attitudes.

The oversampling of members of minority groups, households containing single-parent families, stepfamilies, recently married couples, and cohabiting couples allowed for a sufficient number of cases to be analyzed for these segments of the population. This feature of the data was particularly important in our examination of nest-leaving patterns for Americans who were Black and Hispanic. To properly represent the population of the United States, all of the descriptive cross-tabulations are based on weighted data.

MEASURES

Our measures of nest-leaving processes (ages at leaving and returning home and routes taken out of the home) are based on a series of questions on that subject, which are discussed in detail in Chapters 2 and 3. We use ages at *first* leaving home and *first* returning home, because a high proportion (60 percent) never return. Our specification of routes taken out of the home generally distinguishes between those leaving for marriage, school, military service, a job, independence, or nontraditional family formation (single parenthood or cohabitation), although for some analyses, we have combined single parenthood with marriage and cohabitation with independence, based on the similarities in rates of returning home (low for the first pair and high for the second).

Our chief focus, however, is in *differences* in nest-leaving—differences over time, preeminently but also differences between men and women, between groups defined by religion, ethnicity and social class, between those who grew up in different sorts of families, and even between different regions of the country. Each of these dimensions presented its own challenges of definition and measurement. Table A.1 provides basic descriptive information for each of these variables, including means or proportions and standard deviations for continuous variables.

Nest-Leaving Cohort   By including adults of all ages and asking them questions about leaving and returning home in early adulthood, the survey allowed us to examine the nest-leaving patterns of young adults up to three-quarters of a century earlier, because the respondents were reporting on their own past histories. We used their current age to construct up to eight "nest-leaving cohorts" (defined by the year they reached age 18 and described in detail in Chapter 2).

We examined the quality of the data provided by the oldest respondents and found them essentially complete and believable, even up to age 95. This is likely to be the result of the survey's prior screening of respondents for difficulty in completing the interview and the fact that the data were collected in face-to-face interviews. There were few interviews of older persons, however (only 140 cases of persons older than 85). As a result, we include everyone aged 76 or older in a single group and use them to describe the leaving-home process for the pre-Depression period. We call this the "nest-leaving cohort" of the 1920s, although about a eighth of them actually reached age 18 prior to 1920.

Ethnicity Our primary measure of ethnic community membership divides the population into three groups: Blacks, Hispanics, and non-Hispanic Whites. For some analyses, we also examined the small number of Asians in the sample. We identified these groups based on answers to a combination of questions that allowed the respondents to self-identify themselves. Based on research showing that in the United States, the behaviors of persons of Hispanic origin who appear to be Black (and particularly their children) appear to reflect their race (as socially constructed) more than their Hispanic origin (Harrison and Bennett 1995:164-69; Massey and Denton 1993:112-14), we place those who respond that they are both Black and Hispanic in the Black category.

Origin Given the importance of immigration in 20th century U.S. history and the fact that many who immigrated to this country left home before arrival, we include a measure of non-U.S. birth, based simply on a question on where the respondent was born. For the analyses in Chapter 9, we divide this group into two, those who were born in more industrialized countries and those who were born in less industrialized countries. The basis of this distinction is discussed in that chapter.

Childhood Family Structure Because our focus is on changes in family living arrangements and the age at which change occurs (particularly leaving home), we paid particular attention to another source of information in the NSFH, the childhood residential history. These data provided annual information on whom the respondent lived with at every age up to age 19. In addition to providing information on childhood family structure, it also allowed us to cross-check respondents' responses about when they left home, at least for those who left before age 19. We had been particularly concerned that some early nest-leaving among the children of divorce was simply the result of shifting between parents. We found these two sets of information to be normally in agreement. Most (79 percent) who said they left home at a given age also reported some nonparental living arrangement in their residential history. Of the 270 cases of those who reported living in some parental situation the year after they left home, only 16 had "changed parents." Most of the rest had reported leaving home to attend school, suggesting that they, like many first-year college students and their parents, are somewhat confused about whom they really live with.

The annual parent history was used in most of our regression analyses to measure two varieties of childhood family structure: living in a stable two-parent family until leaving home or some other arrangement. For our analyses of the effects of family structure on leaving and returning home, we divided the possibilities into considerably more detail, considering both the timing of any disruption and the type. This allowed us to compare family structure versus family stability (because some respondents grew up with only one parent from birth), disruption early or late (making a break at adolescence, approximated as age 12), and single parent, remarried parent, and other family situations. Most of these variant family structures had similar effects on leaving and returning home, justifying our normal use of the single indicator, although several interesting variants are described in Chapter 6.

Parental education This is our major measure of social position of the respondent when growing up and the one that has the strongest effect on nest-leaving. We took the average of mother's education and father's education (using one, if the other was missing), specifying the variable continuously in some analyses and categorically in others. Given that people were often reporting on the educations of those who were long dead, however, a substantial portion of the sample (11 percent weighted, 12 percent unweighted) were missing information on the educational levels of *both* of their parents. The level increased with age, with about 45 percent of those in the oldest cohort missing information on parental education.

Fortunately, most of these cases (77 percent) had information on the usual occupations of one or both parents. We derived a set of imputation equations for parental education, based on the prestige scores for the mother's and father's occupations (filled in at the mean where missing with indicators of missing included as predictors) and included measures of ethnicity and region, as well. Because the relationships appear to have changed over time, we used a separate equation for each nest-leaving cohort. (For example, members of the older cohorts who grew up in the Pacific region had parents with higher than average educational levels, controlling for occupational prestige and ethnicity, but among the youngest cohorts, this had reversed.) These equations are available from the authors on request. The results of these equations (the coefficients and their standard errors) are used to impute parental education in our multiple-imputation procedure, described below.

Parental Occupational Prestige In addition to our measure of parental education, we also examined the effects of parental occupational prestige (Chapter 8). This measure is based on a constructed variable provided by the

NSFH that transforms information on usual occupation into prestige categories (see documentation of the NSFH). As with education, we use information for one parent when only that was available. When occupational information was available for both parents, however, we took a weighted average, counting the score for fathers twice as much as the score for mothers (based on the results of Nock and Rossi 1978).

Region   Our measure of regional variation was based on the regional categories created by the U.S. Bureau of the Census. For our major analyses, we combined several adjacent regions with similar patterns. (See additional details in Chapter 5.)

Religion in Childhood   We created a series of categories based on the respondent's reported religious denomination in childhood, using criteria described below. We applied this information, however, only to non-Hispanic Whites. Based on the research of many, including our own, it is clear that ethnic and religious background are interactive in the United States. Almost all Mormons and Jews are non-Hispanic Whites, particularly in the time period covered by our data. Furthermore, although both Hispanics and Blacks are religiously heterogeneous, research has shown (and we replicated it for these data) that there are much weaker differences by denomination among them than among non-Hispanic Whites (Goldscheider and Mosher 1991; Goldscheider and Goldscheider 1993). This suggests that racism and discrimination are powerful shapers of Black and Hispanic family patterns, leaving religious communities and doctrines less scope to shape behavior than is the case among non-Hispanic Whites.

For non-Hispanic Whites, we created seven groupings, expanding beyond the classic "Protestant-Catholic-Jew" (Herberg 1955). We added categories for "other" religions (primarily Moslem and Asian origin) and for "none." We also separated Mormons, a group as large as Jews in this survey and one that has grown rapidly in the 20th century.

Furthermore, we subdivided Protestants into their more liberal and fundamentalist branches, given the increasing polarization that has occurred among Protestant denominations. To make this last distinction, we took the 50+ Protestant denominations reported by the NSFH respondents and cross-tabulated them by the questions on religious fundamentalism. There were three such questions:

1.   I regard myself as a religious fundamentalist.
2.   The Bible is the answer to ... (COMPLETE)
3.   The Bible explains everything... (DITTO)

We divided denominations by whether the overall proportion agreeing or strongly agreeing with these questions on average was greater than half, which was the case for groups with a little more than a third of the total number of Protestants (37 percent). The majority of these are Baptists, with a substantial number of members of the Pentecostal, Nazarene, and Assembly of God, together with many other smaller groups. Those in denominations with lower proportions agreeing with the fundamentalism questions we call liberal Protestants. These are primarily Methodists, Lutherans, Presbyterians, Episcopalians, and those who answered simply Protestant.

There was very little ambiguity. The proportion of liberal Protestants who consider themselves fundamentalist was low, ranging between 12 percent (Episcopalians) and 23 percent (Congregationalists), with a somewhat higher level of agreement with the two questions on the value of the Bible (30-50 percent). The range on the basic fundamentalism measure for the larger groups of fundamentalists was between 34 percent (Baptists) and 64 percent (Assembly of God), with enthusiasm for the Bible's importance ranging between 75 percent and 85 percent. (The two other groups that consider the Bible their central religious text, Catholics and Jews, registered very low levels of agreement that they are fundamentalists, 18 percent of Catholics and 8 percent of Jews.)

METHODS

The information we present is based on two major types of analyses. We conducted a large number of descriptive cross-tabular analyses. We performed an even larger number of multivariate regression analyses. We present both sorts of results, with some of the latter in tables (both in the text and in this appendix) and in figures that appear to be results of simple cross-tabulations but in fact are net of a range of other effects.

Description Our most important goal has been to describe changes in nest-leaving patterns over the 20th century: changes in the age at which young adults leave home, in the routes they take out of the home, and their likelihood of returning home. Hence, we present a large number of descriptive tables and graphs, based on cross-tabulations of weighted data, such as the proportion returning home for each nest-leaving cohort. The graphs allow us to highlight particular effects. For the descriptive graphs, we ordinarily present percentages or proportions. For the multivariate results, however, we more commonly present the same "relative odds" that appear in the tables and text. These are somewhat problematic in graphical form, because the "no effect" point is 0 rather than 1. Hence, although a bar graph that shows differences in the likelihood of leaving home of two groups between relative odds of .8 and 1.2 can be interpreted as indicating that the latter category increases leaving more than the former, if both odds are below 1—for example, .7 and .9—the former has the "stronger" (and in this case, negative) effect.

Our graphs are also not always strictly comparable. Some run between 0 and 1, but others, depending on the effects, go as high as 4, indicating that some group has up to four times greater odds of leaving or returning home than the relevant reference category. Each graph is designed to highlight the finding being discussed so that we adjust the scale on the Y-axis to capture the appropriate contrast. Hence, a difference of .3 on one graph might look much larger than it does on another. All the axes are clearly marked.

Multivariate Analyses   We also have a series of clear analytic goals, including trying to account for the factors that have contributed to these changes. Furthermore, it is often the case that simple tabulations are misleading, because a presentation of ethnic differences in age at leaving home might reflect real differences between ethnic groups or it might reflect other factors that differ among Blacks, Hispanics, and non-Hispanic Whites, such as levels of income. Hence, we need to go beyond basic tabulations to some form of multivariate analysis. Furthermore, because not all in the NSFH have left home and among those who left, many might return home in the future (at least in the younger cohorts), we needed to use a method that takes this open-ended situation into account.

We constructed multivariate statistical models based on proportional hazards regression analysis (Lawless 1982) to study rates of leaving and returning home (distinguishing by route taken out of the home). The transition hazards or probabilities of leaving and returning are evaluated for all those 'surviving' in or away from the parental home, respectively, censoring those who have never left (or returned). A person's hazard, or probability, at time t of leaving home (or of returning home) for the first time is defined as the instantaneous probability of leaving/returning home at time t, given that the person has not yet left/returned home. Each person's hazard function is the product of a baseline hazard function common to all people in the regression and a factor that summarizes the person's descriptive covariates, which does not depend on age. Standard packages for fitting the proportional hazard model produce estimates of the natural logarithm of the relative risk, for binary covariates, or of the relative risk for a one-unit change, for continuous covariates. Thus, we show a relative risk of returning home for those who reached age 18 before 1930 of .65 compared with those reaching that age during the Vietnam era (1.00). This comparison means roughly that at any given age, the probability of the earlier cohort's returning home at any given time after leaving was about two-thirds that of those in the later cohort, other things equal. Many of the figures in the text are based on such results, noting that the relationship is net of the effects of the other factors in the model.

We performed many such regressions. The two fundamental regressions for leaving and returning home are presented in Tables A.2 and A.3, and form the basis for many of our textual figures. These are our best estimates for change over time, and thus form the core of the analyses in Chapters 2 and 3, which address the basic patterns of change in leaving and returning home. These regressions are based on a double set of multiple imputations, designed to minimize the effects of two measurement challenges we found in these data: (1) missing values for parental education (as we discussed above) and (2) uncertainty about ages of leaving home among those who left for marriage, school, and military service.

Our analysis of nest-leaving routes is based on the reasons respondents gave for leaving home. However, we were concerned about the validity of their responses. The presence of related information on the survey—dates of marriages and cohabitations, of college attendance, and of military service—allowed us to cross-check these data. It seemed likely that the dates in the life course histories, which were obtained in intervals of months, would be more accurately reported than the timing of leaving home, which was obtained in terms of age.

Overall, we found reasonable agreement between their activities and the reasons they gave for leaving home: Most who reported that they left home to get married at a given age reported marrying about that time. However, the fit was rarely perfect. Based on the marriage dates given in the NSFH, 37 percent of those who gave marriage as the reason for leaving home erred by a year or more in answering the question on their age at leaving home, although less than one-third of these were off by more than one year. The consistency between the reason given and the timing of the activity was closer for those who reported leaving for military service, with school-leaving in an intermediate position. These discrepancies introduce uncertainty regarding the actual age at leaving home. This uncertainty could bias coefficient estimates or increase standard errors in the analyses.

To address both the problem of reasons for leaving and that of the large number of cases missing parental education simultaneously, we generated five different "complete" data sets (the number recommended by Rubin 1987). We imputed ages at leaving home by replacing the ages for the cases with inconsistencies, independently for each such case, the five draws also being independent of each other. The replacements were drawn with equal probability from the stated age of leaving home and the alternative age that we computed. This scheme for drawing the imputations is the largest-variance probability distribution supported by the interval between the stated age and our alternative age and is conservative in that sense. It is important to note that this method of correction has no effect on the measured timing of leaving home that was *not* in conjunction with one of these life course events. There was no basis for correcting the information in the case of leaving home for independence, because of conflict with parents or many of the other reasons given for leaving home. It was also not possible to correct ages at leaving home for those leaving for a job, because the job histories were not sufficiently detailed to provide a reasonable match. Respondents could have been transferred within a firm (requiring a move) or could have left to look for a job but not obtained it for some time. For each constructed data set, we also imputed parental education for missing cases based on the cohort-specific means and variances we calculated through the method described above.

We evaluated the differences in the results obtained between the procedure based on multiple imputation and the much less computationally intensive method without "correcting" ages at leaving home (or including cases missing parental education). It clearly increased precision, making a few borderline effects significant. However, there was no change in the overall conclusions that would be drawn. Hence, we have included here many results that were not subjected to the additional check of multiple imputation.

For analyses that expanded beyond these basic regressions of Chapters 2 and 3, we present only the "new" information. Some analyses include more detailed specifications of our fundamental predictors—for example, expanding our measures of community to include religion or region of the country or expanding our measures of family background to provide details on type and timing of family structure, sex of siblings, or more refined measures of socioeconomic background, such as public assistance. We present these results either in the text, when appropriate, or in the tables that follow, but do not duplicate the results of Tables A.2 and A.3, because they do not differ materially. These results are fully tested for statistical significance.

We also present results of parallel regressions, in which case some of the differences have not been fully tested and must be treated as preliminary. This is a particularly important issue for analyses of change over time. The basic patterns are clearly well established, statistically. We also wanted to show that some of the relationships of interest had changed over time. In the case of ethnicity (the Hispanic convergence and the Black divergence with non-Hispanic Whites), we did such tests. In other cases, however (e.g., changes among regions, among those who received public assistance in childhood, or among religious groups), our results are based on separate runs for each nest-leaving cohort, which are too voluminous to present. In some cases, as well, we present results based on separate runs for men and women (Chapter 7) and for separate ages at nest-leaving (Chapter 4). These differences present a strong case based on their size and consistency and are likely to be statistically significant. This decision is based on our judgment, however, and not on conventional statistical tests.

TABLE A.1. Descriptive Statistics for the Analysis of Leaving and Returning Home

Variable Names	Definitions	Mean
Year reached age 18		
1920-29	1920s	0.048
1930-37	Depression	0.071
1938-44	World War II	0.087
1945-58	Early baby boom	0.173
1959-65	Later baby boom	0.114
1966-72	Vietnam (reference)	0.160
1973-79	Baby bust	0.163
1980-85	20-somethings	0.182
Age left home	Age left home for the first time for 4 months or more	
15-16	Left at age 15 or 16	0.062
17-18	Left at age 17 or 18	0.441
19-20	Left at age 19 or 20	0.271
21-22	Left at age 21 or 22	0.121
23-25	Left at age 23, 24, or 25	0.064
> 25	Left after age 25	0.041
Route taken		
School	Reason for leaving: to attend school	0.203
Military	Reason for leaving: to enter military service	0.085
Job	Reason for leaving: to take a job	0.116
Independence	Reason for leaving: personal/parental related	0.179
Marriage	Reason for leaving: to marry, join spouse	0.383
Cohabitation	Reason for leaving: live with boy/girl friend, child	0.034
Female	Respondent sex: female	0.523
Black	Respondent race: Black	0.110
Hispanic	Respondent origin: Hispanic; race: non-Black	0.068
Asian	Respondent origin: Asian; race: non-Black	0.012
Non-Western origin	Born in Africa, Asia, or Latin America	0.050
Western origin	Born in Europe or Oceanea or in Canada	0.013
Childhood family structure		
Stable 2-parent	2 parents throughout childhood	0.749
Stable 1-parent	1 parent throughout childhood	0.013
Stable 1-parent	2 parent, then 1parent, no other chg	0.113
Stepparent by 12	Stepparent by age 12, no further chg	0.049
Stepparent after 12	Stepparent after age 12, no further change	0.023
Other by 12	Other patterns, stable after age 12	0.019
Other after 12	Other patterns, unstable after age 12	0.034
Stepsibs	Any step- or half-siblings	0.119

Variable Names	*Definitions*	*Mean*
N sibs	Number of siblings	3.279
N brothers	Number of brothers	1.584
N sisters	Number of sisters	1.537
Parental ed	Mean of parents' educations	10.522
		(3.6)
Grammar	Neither parent attended high school	0.276
Some HS	Neither graduated from HS, at least 1 attended	0.214
HS graduate	Neither parent attended college, at least 1 grad HS	0.254
HS+	At least one parent attended college	0.256
Parental ed missing	Proportion imputed	0.114
Parental occ	Weighted mean of parents' occupations (father weight = 2/3)	31.791
Public assistance	Received public assistance in childhood	0.085
Pacific	Pacific census region	0.094
Mountain	Mountain census region	0.056
Traditional core	E-S Central, E-N Central, W-S Central, W-N Central,	0.578
Mid-Atlantic/Midwest	Middle-Atlantic and Midwest census region	0.209
New England	New England census region	0.053
Childhood Religion (Whites only)		
Catholic	Roman Catholic or Orthodox	0.233
Jewish	Jewish	0.026
No religion	None specified	0.038
Other religion	Islam and Asian-origin religions	0.013
Mormon	Church of Jesus Christ of Latter Day Saints	0.026
Fundamentalist Prot.	Prot. denom. that takes Bible literally	0.173
Liberal Protestant	Other Prot. denomination	0.311
N		12,205

Source: National Survey of Families and Households, 1987/88 (Sweet, Bumpass and Call 1988a).

TABLE A.2. Basic Models of Leaving Home, Total and by Route Left

	Total	Mar/child	School	Military	Job	Ind/Cohab
Leave cohort						
1920-1929	0.542 *	0.696 *	0.593 *	0.146 *	1.435 *	0.200 *
1930-1937	0.586 *	0.782 *	0.444 *	0.534 *	1.581 *	0.524 *
1938-1944	0.734 *	0.732 *	0.584 *	2.347 *	1.564 *	0.249 *
1945-58	0.890 *	1.050	0.756 *	1.893 *	1.357 *	0.367 *
1959-65	0.909 *	0.943	0.986	1.185	1.200 ^	0.626 *
1966-72	1.000	1.000	1.000	1.000	1.000	1.000
1973-79	0.935 *	0.818 *	0.807 *	0.529 *	0.999	1.451 *
1980-85	0.820 *	0.722 *	0.654 *	0.355 *	0.907	1.441 *
Female	1.069 *	2.575 *	0.994	0.034 *	0.634 *	1.202 *
Black	0.795 *	0.685 *	0.754 *	0.682 *	0.872 ^	1.104
Hispanic	0.735 *	1.062	0.466 *	0.360 *	0.639 *	0.729 *
Non-U.S. born	0.728 *	0.573 *	0.907	0.427 *	1.904 *	0.561 *
Parental education						
Grammar	1.000	1.252 *	0.406 *	0.845 ^	1.478 *	1.005
Some HS	0.953 ^	1.149 *	0.781 *	1.004	1.294 *	1.054
HS	1.000	1.000	1.000	1.000	1.000	1.000
HS+	1.196 *	0.789 *	2.273 *	0.733 *	1.073	0.886 *
Not 2-bio family	1.045 *	0.993	0.675 *	1.171 *	0.969	1.534 *

SOURCE: Calculated by the authors from the NSFH.

* Significantly different from 1.0, P < .05.

^ Significantly different from 1.0, .05 < P < .10.

TABLE A.3. Basic Models of Returning Home, Total and by Route Left

	Total	Mar/child	School	Military	Job	Ind/Cohab
Leave cohort						
1910-29	0.649 *	0.508 *	0.863	0.820	0.680 ^	0.435 *
1930-37	0.717 *	0.583 *	1.016	0.731	0.756 ^	0.238 *
1938-44	0.777 *	0.675 *	0.911	1.057	0.727 ^	0.337 *
1945-58	0.831 *	0.849	0.820 ^	1.069	0.686 ^	0.689 *
1959-65	0.824 *	0.805 ^	0.813 *	1.044	0.761	0.806
1966-72	1.000	1.000	1.000	1.000	1.000	1.000
1973-79	1.039	1.185 *	1.044	0.831	0.997	0.951
1980-86	1.236 *	1.139	1.280 *	1.037	1.129	1.094
Female	1.054	1.438 *	1.141 *	0.719	0.790 *	1.040
Black	0.927 ^	1.221 *	0.988	1.151	0.845	0.710 *
Hispanic	1.001	1.026	1.429 ^	1.281	0.995	0.772
Non-U.S. born	0.562 *	0.474 *	0.619 *	0.975	0.503 *	0.631 ^
Parental education						
Grammar	0.985	0.960	0.953	0.981	1.104	0.990
Some HS	1.084	1.037	1.026	1.076	1.204	1.126
HS	1.000	1.000	1.000	1.000	1.000	1.000
HS+	1.002	1.055	0.995	1.135	0.922	1.009
Not 2-bio family	0.761 *	0.760 *	0.918	0.705 *	0.698 *	0.722 *
Age left home	0.931 *	0.916 *	0.988	1.035	0.911 *	0.918
Route taken						
Mar/child	0.491 *	na	na	na	na	na
School	1.000	na	na	na	na	na *
Military	1.449 *	na	na	na	na	na
Job	1.154 *	na	na	na	na	na
Ind/cohab	0.991	na	na	na	na	na

SOURCE: Calculated by the authors from the NSFH.
* Significantly different from 1.0, P < .05.
^ Significantly different from 1.0, .05 < P <.10.

TABLE A.4. Comparing Factors Affecting Leaving Home By Age (odds ratios)

	Overall				Independence				Marriage			
	Total	15-16	23-25	26-45	Total	15-16	23-25	26-45	Total	15-16	23-25	26-45
Year reached 18												
1920-38	0.60 *	0.99	0.52 *	1.05	0.30 *	0.56 ^	0.08 *	0.31 *	0.76 *	0.54 *	0.728 *	1.347 ^
1938-44	0.78 *	1.16	0.68 *	0.76	0.35 *	0.51 ^	0.26 *	0.71	0.77 *	0.82	0.949	0.943
1945-58	0.93 *	1.19	0.75 *	0.92	0.51 *	0.93	0.43 *	0.78	1.08 *	0.93	1.061	0.999
1959-72	ref	ref	ref	ref	ref	ref	ref	ref	ref	ref	ref	ref
1973-85	0.91 *	1.29 *	0.97	1.11	1.44 *	1.69 *	1.29	1.86 ^	0.78 *	0.83	0.971	1.138
Female	1.07 *	1.46 *	1.03	0.90	1.32 *	0.73 *	1.28	1.40	0.94 *	14.09 *	1.341 *	0.901
Parental education	1.02 *	0.94 *	1.02	1.04 *	1.01	0.92 *	1.00	1.07	0.97 *	0.90 *	0.997	1.029
Parental occupation	1.00 *	1.00	1.01 *	1.00	1.00 *	1.01	1.01	1.00	1.00 *	0.99	1.006 ^	1.006
Number of siblings	1.02 *	1.05 *	1.03 *	1.04 *	1.00 *	1.04	1.04	1.08 *	1.00 *	1.04 ^	1.034 ^	0.998
Family structure												
Stable 1-parent	0.90	1.35	0.72	0.60	0.98	0.46	0.55	1.12	1.01	2.24 *	0.93	0.738
Change to 1-parent	1.00	1.11	0.88	0.81	1.32 *	1.36	1.31	1.54	0.96	0.88	0.826	0.56 *
Stepparent by 12	1.20 *	1.81 *	0.92	0.82	1.48 *	1.70 *	0.90	0.33	1.27 *	1.87 *	0.99	0.71
Stepparent after 12	1.22 *	2.06 *	1.70	0.42	1.80 *	2.47 *	1.92	0.00	1.18	2.01 *	1.419	0.752
Other by 12	0.96	1.09	1.40	0.91	1.32 *	0.39	1.24	2.64 ^	0.94	1.46	1.883 *	0.275 ^
Other after 12	0.89 *	1.27	0.12	0.74	1.44 *	1.79 *	1.52	0.62	0.73 *	0.91	1.259	0.648
Stepsiblings	1.22 *	1.56 *	1.03	1.61 *	1.48 *	2.37 *	1.11	1.44	1.12 ^	1.15	0.802	1.377
Black	0.80 *	0.71 *	0.85	1.16	1.21 *	1.15	1.36	1.60 ^	0.64 *	0.54 *	0.6 *	0.704 ^
Hispanic	0.66 *	0.66 *	0.79 ^	1.57 *	0.58 *	0.81	0.86	1.18	0.78 *	0.51 *	0.835	1.438 ^

SOURCE: Calculated by the authors from the NSFH.

*Significantly different from 1.0, P<.05.

^ Significantly different from 1.0, .05 < P <.10.

TABLE A.5. Route Differences in the Effect of Region on the Odds of Leaving and Returning Home

				Route Out of the Home			
Region	Total	Marriage	School	Military	Job	Indep	Cohab
				Leaving Home[a]			
Pacific	0.96	0.85 *	0.65 *	1.31 *	0.97	1.35 *	2.37 *
Mountain	1.07	0.95	1.02	1.71 *	0.73 ^	1.22	1.65 ^
Traditional core	1.00	1.00	1.00	1.00	1.00	1.00	1.00
Mid-Atlantic/Midwest	0.81 *	0.80 *	0.78 *	1.14	0.59 *	0.94	1.24
New England	0.96	0.74 *	1.07	1.58 *	0.70 *	0.90	2.59 *
				Returning Home[b]			
Pacific	1.09	0.98	1.15	1.01	1.27	0.98	1.37
Mountain	0.97	0.95	1.01	0.94	1.48 *	0.85	0.88
Traditional core	1.00	1.00	1.00	1.00	1.00	1.00	1.00
Mid-Atlantic/Midwest	1.06	0.90	1.21 *	1.27 *	1.24 ^	0.89	0.94
New England	1.01	0.93	0.98	1.44 *	1.45 ^	0.92	0.74

SOURCE: Calculated by the authors from the NSFH.

a. Controlling as well for nest-leaving cohort, sex, ethnicity, and family structure and social class.

b. Controlling for variables above, age left, and route taken.

* Significantly different from 1.0, P < .05.

^ Significantly different from 1.0, .05 < P < .10.

TABLE A.6. Models of Leaving and Returning Home (transformed logit coefficients)

	Overall	School	Military	Job	Indep	Marry	Cohab	Return
Family structure[a]								
Stable 1-parent	0.901	0.488 *	1.111	0.705	0.983	1.007	0.866	0.859
Change to 1-parent	0.996	0.721 *	0.953	0.950	1.324 *	0.956	1.672 *	0.888 *
Stepparent by 12	1.204 *	0.781 *	1.201	1.251 ^	1.480 *	1.269 *	1.406 *	0.720 *
Stepparent after 12	1.220 *	0.668 *	1.428 ^	1.203	1.800 *	1.177	2.757 *	0.712 *
Other by 12	0.965	0.698 *	0.772	1.107	1.324 *	0.944	1.192	0.393 *
Other after 12	0.886 *	0.533 *	0.845	0.842	1.436 *	0.733 *	1.775 *	0.607 *
Stepsiblings	1.223 *	0.834 *	1.340 *	1.289 *	1.477 *	1.122 ^	1.571 *	1.048

SOURCE: Calculated by the authors from the NSFH.

a. Controlling as well for measures of nest-leaving cohort, sex, ethnicity, and family social class.

* Significantly different from 1.0, P < .05.

^ Significantly different from 1.0, .05 < P < .10.

TABLE A.7. Changing Effects of Ethnicity on the Odds of Leaving Home, Total and by Route

Factors	Total	Marriage	Cohab	School	Military	Job	Indep
< 1944	0.631 *	0.804 *	0.000 *	0.585 *	1.589 *	1.513 *	0.210 *
1945-65	0.976	1.225 *	0.069 *	1.030	2.641 *	1.225 *	0.408 *
1966+(ref)							
Black	0.725 *	0.547 *	0.514 *	0.786 *	0.931	0.652 *	1.055
BLK <1944	1.365 *	1.829 *	na	1.063	0.846	1.336 *	1.328
BLK 45-65	1.047	1.066	5.028 *	0.894	0.613 *	1.649 *	1.501 *
Hispanic	0.744 *	1.106	0.860	0.515 *	0.301 *	0.758 ^	0.673 *
HSP <1944	1.100	1.215	na	0.361	2.241	0.320 *	1.449
HSP 45-65	0.794 *	0.724 ^	1.976	0.552 ^	1.100	0.818	0.815
Female	1.075 *	2.675 *	2.056 *	1.007	0.035 *	0.650 *	1.077 ^
NOT2BIO	1.059 *	0.994	1.958 *	0.626 *	1.115 ^	1.075	1.557 *
n sibs	1.012 *	1.018 *	1.034	0.952 *	0.977 ^	1.073 *	1.035 *
Pared < HS	1.016	1.215 *	1.064	0.621 *	0.984	1.261 *	0.954
Pared > HS	1.195 *	0.790 *	0.799	2.232 *	0.722 *	1.034	0.900
NON U.S.	0.733 *	0.571 *	0.504 *	0.907	0.455 *	1.826 *	0.619 *

SOURCE: Calculated by the authors from the NSFH.

* Significantly different from 1.0, P < .05.

^ Significantly different from 1.0, .05 < P < .10.

REFERENCES

Alba, Richard. 1990. *Ethnic Identity: The Transformation of White America.* New Haven, Ct: Yale University Press.

Aquilino, W. S. 1990. "The Likelihood of Parent-Child Coresidence: Effects of Family Structure and Parental Characteristics." *Journal of Marriage and the Family* 52:405-19.

———. 1991. "Family Structure and Home-leaving: A Further Specification of the Relationship." *Journal of Marriage and the Family* 53:999-1010.

Arnett, Jeffrey. 1997. "Young People's Conception of the Transition to Adulthood." *Youth and Society* 29:3-23.

Astone, Nan and Sara McLanahan. 1991. "Family Structure, Parental Practices, and High School Completion." *American Sociological Review* 56:309-20.

Avery, Roger, Frances Goldscheider, and Alden Speare. 1992. "Feathered Nest/Gilded Cage: The Effects of Parental Resources on Young Adults' Leaving Home." *Demography* 29:375-88.

Bean, Frank and Marta Tienda. 1987. *The Hispanic Population of the United States.* New York: Russell Sage.

Bean, Lee, G. Mineau, and D. Anderton. 1990. *Fertility Change on the American Frontier.* Berkeley: University of California Press.

Becker, Gary. 1991. *A Treatise on the Family.* Enlarged ed. Cambridge, MA: Harvard University Press.

Bellah, R. N., R. Madsen, W. M. Sullivan, A. Swidler, and S. M. Tipton. 1985. *Habits of the Heart: Individualism and Commitment in American Life.* Berkeley: University of California Press.

Bianchi, Suzanne. 1987. "Living at Home: Young Adults' Living Arrangements in the 1980s." Paper presented at the annual meeting of the American Sociological Association, August, Chicago.

Blossfeld H. and G. Rohwer. 1995. "West-Germany." In *The New Role of Women: Family Formation in Modern Societies*, edited by H. Blossfeld. Boulder, CO: Westview.

Boulanger, P-M, A. Lambert, P. Deboosere, R. Lesthaeghe, and J. Surkyn. 1997. *Menages et Familles.* Recensement Général de la population et des logements au 1er mars 1991, No. 4. Brussles: Ministère des Affaires Économique.

Boyd, Monica and Edward Pryor. 1989. "The Cluttered Nest: The Living Arrangements of Young Canadian Adults." *Canadian Journal of Sociology* 15:462-79.

Brenton, Myron. 1978. *The Runaways: Children, Husbands, Wives and Parents.* Boston: Little Brown.

Buck, N. and J. Scott. 1993. "She's Leaving Home But Why? An Analysis of Young People Leaving the Parental Home." *Journal of Marriage and the Family* 55:863-74.

Bulcroft, Richard, D. Carmody, and K. Bulcroft. 1996. "Patterns of Parental Independence Giving to Adolescents: Variations by Race, Age, and Gender of Child." *Journal of Marriage and the Family* 58:866-83.

Bumpass, Larry L., James A. Sweet, and Andrew Cherlin. 1991. "The Role of Cohabitation in Declining Rates of Marriage." *Journal of Marriage and the Family* 53:913-25.

Burr, Jeffrey and Jan Mutchler. 1993. "Ethnic Living Arrangements: Cultural Convergence or Cultural Manifestation?" *Social Forces* 72:169-79.

Burtless, Gary. 1990. *A Future of Lousy Jobs?* Washington, DC: Brookings Institution.

Caplow, Theodore. 1998. "The Case of the Phantom Episcopalians." *American Sociological Review* 63:112-113.

Castleton, Ann and Frances Goldscheider. 1989. "Are Mormon Families Different? Household Structure and Family Patterns." In *Ethnicity and the New Family Economy: Living Arrangements and Intergenerational Financial Flows*, edited by F. Goldscheider and C. Goldscheider. Boulder, CO: Westview.

Chase-Lansdale, Lindsay and R. Gordon. 1996. "Economic Hardship and the Development of 5- and 6-year-olds: Neighborhood and Regional Perspectives." *Child Development* 67:3338-67.

Cherlin, Andrew J. 1992. *Marriage, Divorce and Remarriage.* Rev. Ed. Cambridge, MA: Harvard University Press.

———. 1996. *Public and Private Families: An Introduction.* New York: McGraw-Hill.

Cherlin, Andrew and Carin Celebuski. 1983. "Are Jewish Families Different? Some Evidence from the General Social Survey." *Journal of Marriage and the Family* 45:903-10.

Cherlin, Andrew, K. Kiernan, and P .L. Chase-Lansdale. 1995. "Parental Divorce in Childhood and Demographic Outcomes in Young Adulthood." *Demography* 32:299-318.

Cherlin, Andrew, Eugenia Scabini, and Giovanna Rossi, eds. 1997a. "Delayed Home Leaving in Europe and the United States." [special issue]. *Journal of Family Issues* 18.

Cherlin, Andrew, Eugenia Scabini, and Giovanna Rossi, eds. 1997b. "Still in the Nest." *Journal of Family Issues* 18:572-75.

Christian, Pat. 1989. "Non-Family Households and Housing among Young Adults." In *Ethnicity and the New Family Economy*, edited by Frances Goldscheider and Calvin Goldscheider. Boulder, CO: Westview.

Christie, Alastair. 1997. "Refuges for Young Runaways." *Youth and Policy* 58:17-28.

Clark, Rebecca. 1990. "Does Welfare Affect Migration?" Population Studies Center Discussion Paper Series, PSC-DPS-UI-1. Washington, D.C.: The Urban Institute.

Coale, Ansley. 1967. "Factors Associated with the Development of Low Fertility: An Historic Summary." Pp. 205-09 in *World Population Conference. 1965.* Vol. II. New York: United Nations.

Cohen, Steven M. and Paula Hyman. 1986. *The Jewish Family: Myths and Reality.* Edited. New York: Holmes & Meier.

Cordón, Juan. 1997. "Youth Residential Independence and Autonomy: A Comparative Study." *Journal of Family Issues* 18:576-607.

Danziger, Sheldon and Peter Gottschalk. 1995. *America Unequal.* New York: Russell Sage.

Darnell, Alfred and Darem Sherkat. 1997. "The Impact of Protestant Fundamentalism on Educational Attainment." *American Sociological Review* 62:306-15.

DaVanzo, Julie and Frances Goldscheider. 1990. "Coming Home Again: Returns to the Nest in Young Adulthood." *Population Studies* 44:241-55.

DeVos, S. 1989. "Leaving the Parental Home in Six Latin American Countries." *Journal of Marriage and the Family* 51:615-26.

Ellwood, D. and M. Bane. 1985. "The Impact of AFDC on Family Structure and Living Arrangements," In *Research in Labor Economics*, Vol. 7, edited by Roland G. Ehrenberg. Greenwich, CT: JAI.

Estess, Patricia S. 1994. "When Kids Don't Leave: How to Cope with our Stay-at-Home- Offspring," *Modern Maturity*, (November-December).

"Europe Isn't Working." 1997. *The Economist*, 343 (April 5), p. 16.

Farber, Bernard, Charles Mindel, and Bernard Lazerwitz. 1981. "The Jewish American Family." Pp. 350-385 in *Ethnic Families in America: Patterns and Variations*, 2d ed., edited by Charles Mindel, R. Habenstein, and R. Wright. New York: Elsevier North Holland.

Farley, Reynolds. 1995. *State of the Union: America in the 1990s.* New York: Russell Sage.

Farley, Reynolds and Walter Allen. 1987. *The Color Line and the Quality of Life in America.* New York: Russell Sage.

Farrow, J., R. Deisher, J. Kulig and M. Kipke. 1993. "Health and Health Needs of Homeless and Runaway Youth." *Journal of Adolescent Health* 13:717-26.

Frey, William and A. Speare. 1988. *Regional and Metropolitan Growth and Decline in the United States.* New York: Russell Sage.

Glazer, Nathan and D. Moynihan. 1970. *Beyond the Melting Pot.* Cambridge: MIT Press.

Glenn, Susan. 1990. *Daughters of the Shtetl: Life and Labor in the Immigrant Generation.* Ithaca, NY: Cornell University Press.

Glick, Paul. 1947. "The Family Cycle." *American Sociological Review* 12:164-74.

Glick, Paul and C. Lin. 1985. "More Young Adults Are Living with Parents: Who Are They?" *Journal of Marriage and the Family* 48:107-12.

Glick, Paul and R. Parke. 1965. "New Approaches to Studying the Life Cycle of the Family." *Demography* 2:187-202.

Goldin, Claudia. 1990. *Understanding the Gender Gap: An Economic History of American Women.* New York: Oxford University Press.

Goldscheider, Calvin. 1986. *Jewish Continuity and Change: Emerging Patterns in America.* Bloomington: Indiana University Press.

Goldscheider, Calvin and Frances Goldscheider. 1987. "Moving Out and Marriage: What Do Young Adults Expect?" *American Sociological Review* 52:278-85.

Goldscheider, Calvin and W. Mosher. 1988. "Religious Affiliation and Contraceptive Usage: Changing American Patterns, 1955-82." *Studies in Family Planning* 19:48-57.

Goldscheider, Calvin and W. Mosher. 1991 "Patterns of Contraceptive Use in the United States: The Importance of Religious Factors." *Studies in Family Planning* 23:288-90.

Goldscheider, Calvin and Alan Zuckerman. 1984. *The Transformation of the Jews.* Chicago: University of Chicago Press.

Goldscheider, Frances. 1997. "Recent Changes in U.S. Young Adult Living Arrangements in Comparative Perspective." *Journal of Family Issues* 18:708-24.

Goldscheider, Frances, Ann Biddlecom, and Patricia St. Clair. 1994. "A Comparison of Living Arrangements Data in the National Survey of Families and Households and the U.S. Censuses, 1940-1980." RAND Working Draft 94-12. Santa Monica, CA: RAND

Goldscheider, Frances and Julie DaVanzo. 1985. "Living Arrangements and the Transition to Adulthood." *Demography* 22:545-63.

————. 1986. "Semiautonomy and Leaving Home in Early Adulthood." *Social Forces* 65:187-201.

————. 1989. "Pathways to Independent Living in Early Adulthood." *Demography* 26:597-614.

Goldscheider, Frances and Calvin Goldscheider. 1991. "The Intergenerational Flow of Income: Family Structure and the Status of Black Americans." *Journal of Marriage and the Family* 53:499-508.

————. 1993. *Leaving Home Before Marriage: Ethnicity, Familism, and Generational Relationships.* Madison: University of Wisconsin Press.

————. 1994a. "Family Structure, Leaving Home, and Investments in Young Adulthood." *Cahiers Quebecois de Demographie* [Special Issue on Childhood], 23,1:75-100.

————. 1994b. "Leaving and Returning Home in 20th Century America." *Population Reference Bureau Bulletin.* Vol. 48, No.4.

————. 1997a. "Generational Relationships and the Jews: Patterns of Leaving Home, 1930-1985." In *Papers in Jewish Demography, 1993.* Proceedings of the Eleventh World Congress of Jewish Studies, Jerusalem.

————. 1997b. "The Trajectory of the Black Family: Ethnic Differences in Leaving Home over the Twentieth Century." *Journal of the History of the Family* 2:295-306.

————. 1998. "The Effects of Childhood Family Structure on Leaving and Returning Home." *Journal of Marriage and the Family* 60:745-56.

Goldscheider, Frances, Calvin Goldscheider, James Hodges, and Patricia St. Clair. 1994. "Living Arrangements Changes in Young Adulthood: Evidence for the Twentieth Century." Paper presented at the RAND Conference on the Family and Public Policy, Santa Monica, CA.

Goldscheider, Frances and Celine LeBourdais. 1986. "The Decline in Age at Leaving Home, 1920-1979." *Sociology and Social Research* 72:143-45.

Goldscheider, Frances, Arland Thornton, and Linda Young-DeMarco. 1993. "A Portrait of the Nest-Leaving Process in Early Adulthood." *Demography* 30:683-99.

Goldscheider, Frances and Linda Waite. 1991. *New Families, No Families? Transformation of the American Home.* Berkeley: University of California Press.

Goldstein, Sidney. 1992. "Profile of American Jewry: Insights from the 1990 National Jewish Population Survey," Pp. 77-173. *American Jewish Year Book, 1992.* Philadelphia: Jewish Publication Society of America.

Gordon, Milton. 1964. *Assimilation in American Life.* New York: Oxford University Press.

Greeley, Andrew. 1989. "Protestant and Catholic: Is the Analogical Imagination Extinct." *American Sociological Review* 54:485-502.

Gross, Jane. 1991. "More Young Single Men Hang onto Apron Strings: Recession and Pampering Keep Sons at Home." *New York Times*, 140, June 16, pp. 1, 18.

Gutman, Herbert. 1976. *The Black Family in Slavery and Freedom, 1750-1925.* New York: Pantheon.

Haaga, John. 1988. "The Revival of Breastfeeding in the U.S., 1963-81." Santa Monica, Ca.: RAND.

Hadaway, C. Kirk, Penny Marler, and Mark Chaves. 1998. "Overreporting Church Attendance in America: Evidence that Demands the Same Verdict." *American Sociological Review* 63:122-30.

Haines, Michael. 1996. "Long-Term Marriage Patterns in the United States from Colonial Times to the Present." *History of the Family* 1:15-40.

Hajnal, John. 1982. "Household Formation Patterns in Comparative Perspective." *Population and Development Review* 8:449-94.

Harrison, R. and C. Bennett. 1995. "Racial and Ethnic Diversity." In *State of the Union: America in the 1990s*, Vol. 2, edited by Reynolds Farley. New York: Russell Sage.

Haurin, D., P. Hendershott, and D. Kim. 1993. "The Impact of Real Rents and Wages on Household Formation." *Review of Economics and Statistics* 75:284-93.

Heer, David, Robert Hodge, and Marcus Felson. 1985. "The Cluttered Nest: Evidence That Young Adults Are More Likely to Live at Home Now Than in the Recent Past." *Sociology and Social Research* 69:436-41.

Heilman, Samuel. 1992. *Defenders of the Faith: Inside Ultra Orthodox Judaism.* New York: Schocken.

————. 1995. *Portrait of American Jews: The Last Half of the 20th Century.* Seattle: University of Washington Press.

Herberg, Will. 1955. Protestant-Catholic-Jew. New York: Doubleday.

Herrnstein, Richard and Charles Murray. 1994. *The Bell Curve.* New York: Free Press.

Hochschild, Arlie. 1989. *The Second Shift: Working Parents and the Revolution at Home.* New York: Viking.

Hogan, Dennis. 1981. *Transitions and Social Change.* New York: Academic Press.

Hout, Michael and Andrew Greeley. 1998. "What Church Officials' Reports Don't Show: Another Look at Church Attendance Data." *American Sociological Review* 63:113-19.

Jayakody, Rukmalie. 1996. "Returns to the Parental Home after a Marital Disruption," Paper presented at the annual meetings of the Population Association of America, March, Washington, DC.

Jaynes, Gerald and Robin Williams, eds. 1989. *A Common Destiny: Blacks and American Society.* Washington, DC: National Academy Press.

Johnson, William R. and J. Skinner. 1986. "Labor Supply and Marital Separation." *American Economic Review* 76:455-69.

Jong-Gierveld, J., A. C. Liefbroer, and E. Beekink. 1991. "The Effect of Parental Resources on Patterns of Leaving Home among Young Adults in the Netherlands." *European Sociological Review* 7:55-71.*The*

Kent, R. 1992. "Household Formation by the Young in the United States." *Applied Economics* 24:1129-37.

Kerkhoff, A. and J. Macrae. 1992. "Leaving the Parental Home in Great Britain: A Comparative Perspective." *Sociological Quarterly* 33:281-301.

Kiernan, Kathleen. 1986. "Leaving Home: Living Arrangements of Young People in Six West-European Countries." *European Journal of Population* 2:177-84.

————. 1989. "The Departure of Children," In *The Later Phases of the Family Cycle: Demographic Aspects*, edited by E. Grebenik, C. Hohn, and R. Mackensen. Oxford, UK: Clarendon.

Koball, Heather. 1995. "Men's Marriage Timing across Cohorts and Race: The Impact of the Early Adult Years." Unpublished master's thesis, Department of Sociology, Brown University.

Kobrin, Frances. 1976. "The Primary Individual and the Family: Changes in Living Arrangements in the United States since 1940." *Journal of Marriage and the Family* 38:233-39.

————. 1985. "Family Patterns among the Yiddish Mother-Tongue Subpopulation: U.S. 1970." Pp. 172-83 in *The Evolving Jewish Family, edited by* S. Cohen and P. Hyman. NY: Holmes & Meier.

Kramarow, Ellen. 1995. "Living Alone among the Elderly in the United States: Historical Perspectives on Household Change." *Demography* 32:335-52.

Kranzler. George. 1961. *Williamsburg: A Jewish Community in Transition.* New York: Feldheim.

Kulikoff, A. 1986. *Tobacco and Slaves: The Development of Southern Cultures in the Chesapeake, 1680-1800.* Chapel Hill: University of North Carolina Press.

Lawless, J. F. 1982. *Statistical Models and Methods for Lifetime Data.* New York: John Wiley.

LeBourdais, C. and H. Juby. 1997. "When the Laggard Becomes the Leader." Paper presented at the annual meetings of the Population Association of America, March, Washington, D.C.

Lehrer, Evelyn and Carmel Chiswick. 1993. "Religion as a Determinant of Marital Stability." *Demography* 30:385-404.

Leibowitz, Arleen, Marvin Eisen and Winston Chow. 1986. "An Economic Model of Teenage Pregnancy Decision-Making." *Demography* 23:67-77.

Leridon, H. and L. Toulemon. 1995. "France." In *The New Role of Women: Family Formation in Modern Societies*, edited by H. Blossfield. Boulder, CO: Westview.

Lesthaeghe, Ron. 1988. "Cultural Dynamics and Economic Theories of Fertility Change." *Population and Development Review* 14:1-44.

————. 1995. "The Second Demographic Transition: An Interpretation." Pp. 17-62 in *Gender and Family Change in Industrialized Countries*, edited by K. O. Mason and A. M. Jensen. Oxford: Clarendon Press.

Lesthaeghe, Ron and D. Meekers. 1986. "Value Changes and the Dimensions of Familism in the European Community." *European Journal of Population* 2:225-68.

Lesthaeghe, Ron and G. Moors. 1995. "Living Arrangements, Socio-Economic Position and Values among Young Adults." In *Europe's Population in the 1990s*, edited by D. Coleman. Oxford: Oxford University Press.

Lesthaeghe, Ron and J. Surkyn. 1988. "Cultural Dynamics and Economic Theories of Fertility Change." *Population and Development Review* 14:1-45.

Levy, Frank. 1987. *Dollars and Dreams: The Changing American Income Distribution.* New York: Russell Sage.

Lieberson, Stanley. 1980. *A Piece of the Pie: Blacks and White Immigrants Since 1880.* Berkeley: University of California Press.

Lieberson, Stanley and Mary Waters. 1988. *From Many Strands: Ethnic and Racial Groups in Contemporary America.* New York: Russell Sage.

Lindberg, Laura D. 1996. "Trends in the Relationship between Breastfeeding and Postpartum Employment in the United States." *Social Biology* 43:191-202.

Litwak, Eugene and M. Silverstein. 1990. "Helping Networks among the Jewish Elderly Poor." *Contemporary Jewry* 11:3-50.

Malone, A. P. 1992. *Sweet Chariot: Slave Family and Household Structure in Nineteenth-Century Louisiana.* Chapel Hill: University of North Carolina Press.

Manfra, J. A., and R. P. Dykstra. 1985. "Serial Marriage and the Origins of the Black Stepfamily: The Rowanty Evidence." *Journal of American History* 72:18-44.

Massey, Douglas and Nancy Denton. 1993. *American Apartheid: Segregation and the Making of the Underclass.* Cambridge, MA: Harvard University Press.

Mayer, Egon. 1979. *From Suburb to Shtetl: The Jews of Boro Park.* Philadelphia: Temple University Press.

Mayer, K. and K. Schwarz. 1989. "The Process of Leaving the Parental Home: Some German Data." In *The Later Phases of the Family Cycle: Demographic Aspects,* edited by E. Grebenik, C. Hohn, and R. Mackensen. Oxford, UK: Clarendon.

McDaniel, Antonio. 1994. "Historical Racial Differences in Living Arrangements of Children." *Journal of Family History* 19:57-77.

McLanahan, S. and L. Bumpass. 1988. "Intergenerational Consequences of Family Disruption." *American Journal of Sociology* 94:130-52.

McLanahan, S. and G. Sandefur. 1994. *Growing Up with a Single Parent.* Cambridge: Harvard University Press.

McPhillips, Jody. 1994. "Lack of Jobs Keeps Them at Home." *Providence Journal-Bulletin,* April, 8, pp. A1, A11.

Michael, R. and N. Tuma. 1985. "Entry into Marriage and Parenthood by Young Men and Women." *Demography* 22:515-44.

Michael, Robert, V. Fuchs, and S. Scott. 1980. "Changes in the Propensity to Live Alone: 1950-1976." *Demography* 17:39-56.

Mitchell, Barbara, Andrew Wister, and Thomas Burch. 1989. "The Family Environment and Leaving the Parental Home." *Journal of Marriage and the Family* 51:605-13.

Modell, John. 1989. *Into One's Own: From Youth to Adulthood in the United States, 1920-1975.* Berkeley: University of California Press.

Modell, John, Frank Furstenberg, and Theodore Hershberg. 1976. "Social Change and Transitions to Adulthood in Historical Perspective." *Journal of Family History* 1:7-32.

Morgan, S. Philip, Diane N. Lye, and Gretchen A. Condran. 1989. "Sons, Daughters, and the Risk of Marital Disruption." *American Journal of Sociology.* 94:110-129.

Morgan, Philip, Antonio McDaniel, Andrew Miller, and Samuel Preston. 1993. "Racial Differences in Household and Family Formation at the Turn of the Century." *American Journal of Sociology* 98:798-828.

Mosher, William, L. Williams and D. Johnson. 1992. "Religion and Fertility in the United States: New Patterns. *Demography* 29:199-214.

Nave-Herz, Rosemarie. 1997. "Still in the Nest: The Family and Young Adults in Germany." *Journal of Family Issues* 18:671-89.

Newcomer, Mabel. 1959. *A Century of Higher Education for American Women.* New York: Harper &Co.

Nock, Steven and Peter Rossi. 1978. "Ascription versus Achievement in the Attribution of Family Social Status." *American Journal of Sociology* 84:565-90.

Patterson, Orlando. 1991. *Freedom in the Making of Western Culture.* New York: Basic Books.

Payne, M. 1995. "Understanding 'Going Missing': Issues for Social Work and Social Services." *British Journal of Social Work* 25:333-48.

Perin, Ivan. 1995. "Returning to Roost in the Empty Nest." *Baltimore Sun*, January 29, p. 22.

Peron, Y., E. Lapierre-Adamcyk, and D. Morissette. 1986. "Depart des Enfants et Contraction des Familles d'apres les Recensements Canadiens de 1971 et de 1981." *European Journal of Population/Revue Europeenne de Demographie* 2:155-75.

Pinnelli, A. and A. D. Rose. 1995. "Italy." In *The New Role of Women: Family Formation in Modern Societies.*, edited by H. Blossfeld. Boulder, CO: Westview.

Pitkin, John and George Masnick. 1988. "The Relationship Between Heads and Nonheads in the Household Population." In *Family Demography: Methods and their Applications*, edited by John Bongaarts at al. London:Oxford University Press.

Presser, Harriet B. 1972. "The Timing of First Birth, Female Roles and Black Fertility." *Milbank Memorial Fund Quarterly* 49:329-59.

Presser, Stanley and L. Stinson. 1998. "Data Collection Mode and Social Desirability Bias in Self-Reported Religious Attendance." *American Sociological Review* 63:137-45.

Qiang, L. 1993. *On the Threshold of Residential Independence.* Unpublished Ph.D. dissertation, Department of History, Brown University.

Ravenera, Zenaida, F. Rajulton and T. Burch. 1995. "A Cohort Analysis of Home-Leaving in Canada, 1910-1975." *Journal of Comparative Family Studies* 26:179-93.

Riche, M. F. 1990. "Boomerang Age." *American Demographics* 12:25-27, 30, 52-53.

Rindfuss, R. 1991. "The Young Adult Years: Diversity, Structural Change, and Fertility." *Demography* 28:493-512.

Rindfuss, R., S. P. Morgan and G. Swicegood. 1988. *First Births in America: Changes in the Timing of Parenthood.* University of California Press.

Rindfuss, R. and A. VandenHeuvel. 1990. "Cohabitation: A Precursor to Marriage or an Alternative to Being Single?" *Population and Development Review* 16:703-26.

Rosenmayr, L. and E. Kockeis. 1963. "Propositions for a Sociological Theory of Aging and the Family." *International Social Science Journal.* 15.

Rossi, G. 1997. "The Nestlings: Why Young Adults Stay at Home Longer: The Italian Case." *Journal of Family Issues* 18:627-44.

Rubin, David B. 1987. *Multiple Imputation for Nonresponse in Surveys.* New York: John Wiley.

Ruggles, Steven. 1994. "The Origins of African-American Family Structure." *American Sociological Review* 59:136-51.

Ruggles, Steven. 1996. "Living Arrangements of the Elderly in the United States." In *Aging and Intergenerational Relations: Historical and Cross-Cultural Perspectives*, edited T. K. Hareven. Berlin, Germany: de Gruyter.

Saluter, A. 1994. *Marital Status and Living Arrangements: March 1993.* US Bureau of the Census, Current Population Reports, Series P-20-478. Washington, DC: U.S. GPO.

———. 1996. *Marital Status and Living Arrangements: March 1994.* U.S. Bureau of the Census, Current Population Reports, Series P-20-484. Washington, DC: U.S. GPO.

Scabini, E. and V. Cigoli. 1997. "Young Adult Families: An Evolutionary Slowdown or a Breakdown in the Generational Transition?" *Journal of Family Issues* 18:608-26.

Schnaiberg, A. and S. Goldenberg. 1989. "From Empty Nest to Crowded Nest: The Dynamics of Incompletely Launched Young Adults." *Social Problems* 36:251-69.

Schwartz, Kurt. 1988. "Household Trends in Europe After World War II." In *Modeling Household Formation and Dissolution*, edited by in N. Keilman, et al. London: Oxford University Press.

Shaffir, William. 1986. "Persistence and Change in the Hasidic Family." Pp. 187-99 in *The Jewish Family: Myths and Reality*, edited by Steve M. Cohen and Paula Hyman. New York: Holmes & Meier.

Short, K. S. and T. Garner. 1990. *Living Arrangements of Young Adults Living Independently: Evidence from the Luxembourg Income Study.* U.S. Bureau of the Census, Current Population Reports, Series P-23. Special Studies no. 169. Washington DC: U.S. GPO.

Smith, Tom. 1998. "A Review of Church Attendance Measures." *American Sociological Review* 63:131-36.

Speare, A. and F. Goldscheider. 1983. "A Dynamic Analysis of Household Change and Residential Mobility." *Proceedings of the American Statistical Association.*

Spitze, Glenna D. 1978. "Role Experiences of Young Women: A Longitudinal Test of the Role Hiatus Hypothesis." *Journal of Marriage and the Family* 40:471-80.

Stark, Rodney and William Bainbridge. 1995. *The Future of Religion: Secularization, Revival, and Cult Formation.* Berkeley: University of California Press.

Steinmetz, Suzanne. 1987. "Family Violence." In *Handbook of Marriage and the Family*, edited by Marvin Sussman and Suzanne Steinmetz. New York: Plenum.

Stevenson, Brenda. 1995. "Black Family Structure in Colonial and Antebellum Virginia: Amending the Revisionist Perspective." Pp. 27-56 in *The Decline in Marriage among African Americans*, edited by M. Belinda Tucker and C. Mitchell-Kernan. New York: Russell Sage.

Suitor, Jill and Karl Pillemer. 1987. "The Presence of Adult Children: A Source of Stress for Elderly Couples' Marriages?" *Journal of Marriage and the Family* 49:717-25.

Sweet, James, L. Bumpass, and V. Call. 1988. "The Design and Content of the National Survey of Families and Households." NSFH Working Paper No. 1, Madison: University of Wisconsin.

Sweet, James and L. Bumpass. 1988. "Cohabitation and Marriage in the 1980s." *Demography* 25:497-508.

———. 1989. "Changing Attitudes Towards Family Issues in the United States." *Journal of Marriage and the Family* 51: 873-93.

Thornton, Arland. 1989. "Changing Attitudes towards Family Issues in the United States." *Journal of Marriage and the Family* 51:873-93.

———. 1991. "Influence of Parents' Marital History on Children." *American Journal of Sociology* 96:868-94.

Thornton, Arland and D. Camburn. 1989. "Religious Participation and Adolescent Sexual Behavior and Attitudes." *Journal of Marriage and the Family* 51:641-53.

Thornton, Arland and T. Fricke. 1989. "Social Change and the Family." In *Demography as an Interdiscipline*, edited by J. M. Stycos. New Brunswick, N.J.: Transaction Books.

Tucker, M. Belinda and C. Mitchell-Kernan. 1995. "Trends in African American Family Formation: A Theoretical and Statistical Overview." Pp. 3-26 in *The Decline in Marriage among African Americans*, edited by in M. Belinda Tucker and C. Mitchell-Kernan. New York: Russell Sage.

U.S. Bureau of the Census. 1992. *Marital Status and Living Arrangements: March 1991.* Current Population Reports, Series P-20-461,. Washington, DC: US GPO.

van de Kaa, D. J. 1987. "Europe's Second Demographic Transition." *Population Bulletin* 42:1-57.

VanHekken Suus, L. DeMey and H. Schulze. 1997. "Youth Inside and Outside the Parental Home: The Case of the Netherlands." *Journal of Family Issues* 18:690-707.

Waite, Linda., F. Goldscheider, and C. Witsberger. 1986. "Nonfamily Living and the Erosion of Traditional Family Orientations among Young Adults." *American Sociological Review* 51:541-54.

Ward, Russell and Glenna Spitze. 1996. "Will the Children Ever Leave? Parent-Child Coresidence History and Plans." *Journal of Family Issues* 17:514-39.

Watkins, Susan, et al. 1994. *After Ellis Island: Newcomers and Natives in the 1910 Census.* New York: Russell Sage.

Watson, Janet. 1996. *Active Service: Gender, Class, and British Representation of the Great War.* Unpublished Ph.D. dissertation, Department of History, Stanford University.

Waxman, Chaim. 1983. *America's Jews in Transition.* Philadelphia: Temple University Press.

White, Lynn. 1992. "The Effect of Parental Divorce and Remarriage on Parental Support for Adult Children." *Journal of Family Issues* 13:234-50.

———. 1994. "Coresidence and Leaving Home: Young Adults and their Parents." *Annual Review of Sociology* 20:81-102.

White, Lynn and Alan Booth. 1985. "The Quality and Stability of Remarriages: The Role of Stepchildren." *American Sociological Review* 50:689-98.

White, Lynn and David Brinkerhoff. 1981. "Children's Work in the Family." *Journal of Marriage and the Family* 43:789-98.

White, Lynn and N. Lacy. 1997. "The Effects of at Home Leaving and Pathways from Home on Educational Attainment." *Journal of Marriage and the Family* 59:182-95.

White, Michael. 1987. *American Neighborhoods and Residential Differentiation.* New York: Russell Sage.

Whittington, L. and H. E. Peters. 1996. "Economic Incentives for Financial and Residential Independence." *Demography* 33:82-97.

Williams, Linda and Basil Zimmer. 1990. "The Changing Influence of Religion on U.S. Fertility." *Demography* 27:475-81.

Wilson, William Julius. 1987. *The Truly Disadvantaged: The Inner City, the Underclass and Public Policy,* Chicago: University of Chicago Press.

———. 1994. "Studying Inner-City Dislocations." *American Sociological Review* 56:1-14.

Woodbury, Robert. 1998. "When Surveys Lie and People Tell the Truth: How Surveys Oversample Church Attenders." *American Sociological Review* 63:119-22.

Woodward, C. Vann. 1966. *The Strange Career of Jim Crow.* 2d rev. ed. New York: Oxford University Press.

Young, Christabel. 1974. "Ages, Reasons, and Sex Differences for Children Leaving Home." *Journal of Marriage and the Family* 36:769-78.

———. 1975. "Factors Associated with the Timing and Duration of the Leaving-Home Stage of the Family Life Cycle." *Population Studies* 29:61-73.

———. 1984. "The Effect of Children Returning Home on the Precision of the Timing of the Leaving Home Stage of the Family Life Cycle." Seminar on the Demography of the Later Phases of the Family Life Cycle, Berlin.

————. 1987. *Young People Leaving Home in Australia: The Trend toward Independence*. Department of Demography, Australian National University, Canberra: Australian National University Press.

Zhao, J., F. Rajulton, and Z. Ravanera. 1993. "Family Structure and Parental Characteristics Analysis of Home-Leaving of Children Reported by Parents: General Social Survey, Canada." Discussion Paper no. 03-2, Population Studies Centre, University of Western Ontario.

INDEX

ABOUT THE AUTHORS

Frances Goldscheider is University Professor and Professor of Sociology at Brown University. She has been the Director of the Population Studies and Training Center and the Chair of the Sociology Department there and the Editor of *Demography*, the official publication of the Population Association of America. She serves on the editorial boards of major sociology journals, including the *Journal of Marriage and the Family* and *Social Forces*. Her book *New Families, No Families? The Transformation of the American Home* (with Linda Waite) was awarded the Duncan Prize of the Sociology of Population Section of the American Sociological Association. She is a leading expert on the demography of families and households in the United States and has published numerous articles on family structure and nest-leaving. Her current research focuses on comparing family patterns in Sweden and the United States.

Calvin Goldscheider is Professor of Sociology and DOROT Professor of Judaic Studies at Brown University. He was Professor of Sociology and Demography at the Hebrew University of Jerusalem, Israel, and Chairman of their Department of Demography. His major research publications have focused on the sociology and demography of ethnic populations, historically and comparatively, with a particular emphasis on family and immigration. He has published extensively in these fields in the leading sociology and demography journals. His major books include *Population, Modernization and Social Structure*; *The Population of Israel*; *The Transformation of the Jews*; *Jewish Continuity and Change: Emerging Patterns in America*; and most recently, *Israel's Changing Society: Population, Ethnicity and Development*. He has edited a series of books on population and development issues, including most recently, *Population, Ethnicity and Nation-Building* and *Population and Social Change in Israel*.

Both authors have been Research Associates at RAND in their Labor and Population Center in Santa Monica, California, and are Faculty Associates of the Population Studies and Training Center at Brown. Together they have written *Leaving Home before Marriage: Ethnicity, Familism and Generational Relationships* and *The Ethnic Factor in Family Structure and Mobility* and edited a volume on *Ethnicity and the New Family Economy*.

257